Women, Judging and the Judiciary

Women, Judging and the Judiciary examines debates about gender representation in the judiciary and the importance of judicial diversity. It offers a fresh look at the role of the (woman) judge and the process of judging and provides a new analysis of the assumptions which underpin and constrain debates about why we might want a more diverse judiciary, and how we might get one.

Through a theoretical engagement with the concepts of diversity and difference in adjudication, *Women, Judging and the Judiciary* contends that prevailing images of the judge work to exclude those who do not fit the judicial norm. Such has been the fate of the woman judge. However, by getting a clearer sense of what our judges really do and how they do it, the woman judge and judicial diversity more broadly no longer threaten but enrich the judiciary and judicial decision-making. So viewed, the standard opponent to measures to increase judicial diversity – appointment on merit – becomes its greatest ally: a judiciary is stronger and the justice it dispenses better the greater the diversity of its members, so if we want the best judiciary we can get, we should want one which is fully diverse.

Women, Judging and the Judiciary will be of interest to legal academics, lawyers and policy makers working in the fields of judicial diversity, gender and adjudication and, more broadly, to anyone interested in who our judges are and what they do.

Erika Rackley is a Senior Lecturer in the Law School, Durham University, UK. She is co-author, with Kirsty Horsey, of *Tort Law* (Oxford: Oxford University Press, 2nd edn, 2011) and co-editor, with Rosemary Hunter and Clare McGlynn, of *Feminist Judgments: From Theory to Practice* (Oxford: Hart, 2010) and, with Janice Richardson, *Feminist Perspectives on Tort Law* (Abingdon: Routledge, 2012).

Women, Judging and the Judiciary

From difference to diversity

Erika Rackley

Routledge
Taylor & Francis Group

a GlassHouse book

First published 2013
by Routledge
2 Park Square, Milton Park, Abingdon, Oxon OX14 4RN

Simultaneously published in the USA and Canada
by Routledge
711 Third Avenue, New York, NY 10017

A GlassHouse Book

Routledge is an imprint of the Taylor & Francis Group, an informa business

British Library Cataloguing in Publication Data
A catalogue record for this book is available from the British Library

Library of Congress Cataloging in Publication Data
A catalog record for this book has been requested

ISBN: 978-0-415-54861-8 (hbk)
ISBN: 978-0-415-63001-6 (pbk)

Typeset in Baskerville
by RefineCatch Limited, Bungay, Suffolk

For E. H. B. and L. J. R.

Contents

Acknowledgements

This book started as my doctoral thesis and has ended up as something quite different. Along the way it has benefited from conversations with many friends and colleagues. Particular thanks go to Joanne Conaghan and Clare McGlynn. I am indebted to them in ways that can only be imperfectly expressed here. They have gone far beyond the call of duty and friendship on more occasions than was reasonable to expect and are a constant source of encouragement and inspiration. I'm glad to have them in my corner. I am also extremely grateful for the support of Baroness Hale and for her agreeing to write the foreword for this book. Special thanks are also due to Neil Cobb whose conversations in LGS seminars and in the Head of Steam after work inform and entertain in equal measure. A number of other colleagues also took the time to comment on draft chapters or to provide me with the statistical information included in Chapters 1 and 2 – to them, and the many others with whom I have spoken about diversity, women judges and mermaids, thank you.

During the writing of this book I have been fortunate to be able to present my work at a number of conferences and workshops including the International Seminar on Women in the Legal Professions in Buenos Aires; the Workshop on Gender and Judging at the International Institute of the Sociology of Law in Oñati; and at the Centre for Feminist Legal Studies at the University of British Columbia, which welcomed me as visiting scholar in the spring of 2010. The book is better for the insightful comments from those who attended these occasions. I am also grateful to the Arts and Humanities Research Council who sponsored a period of research leave during which I worked on an early draft of the book (REF: 152733/138415), to Colin Perrin for his advice when drafting the proposal for this book and to Melanie Fortmann-Brown for her patience as deadlines passed.

The writing of this book would not have been possible without the constant encouragement of my close friends and family. I am grateful for their love and support, and most of all for their knowing when to stop asking about the book. Final thanks go to Charlie for his generosity, insight and sense of perspective.

The manuscript for the book was submitted to the publishers before the publication in March 2012 of the (disappointing) Final Report of the House of

Lords Select Committee on the Constitution Inquiry into Judicial Appointments and Alan Paterson and Chris Paterson's excellent *Guarding the Guardians?* report. Although I am grateful to have been able to incorporate a few brief references to these reports, they deserve greater consideration than I have been able to give them here. The book contains substantially revised versions of my earlier published work including: 'Representations of the (woman) judge: Hercules, the little mermaid and the vain and naked Emperor', *Legal Studies*, 22(4), 2002, 602–624; 'Difference in the House of Lords', *Social & Legal Studies*, 15(2), 2006, 163–185; 'Judicial diversity, the woman judge and fairy tale endings', *Legal Studies*, 27(1), 2007, 74–94; 'What a Difference Difference Makes: Gendered Harms and Judicial Diversity', *International Journal of the Legal Profession*, 15(1–2), 2008, 37–56; 'In Conversation with Lord Justice Etherton', *Public Law*, Oct 2010, 655–662.

Foreword

Once we accept that who the judge is matters, then it matters who our judges are.
(Erika Rackley, 2013)[1]

It is well known that the United Kingdom, and in particular England and Wales, lags behind most comparable Western democracies in the composition of its judiciary. We remain overwhelmingly white and male, the more so the higher one climbs the judicial ladder. While there has been some progress towards greater diversity in the lower ranks ('below the salt', as some of them feel), progress in the higher ranks has been remarkably slow. I am the lone woman in the Supreme Court of the United Kingdom, whereas a third of the US Supreme Court Justices are women and in Canada and Australia they are over 40 per cent. The confidence of Lord Chief Justices in the 1990s that all those bright young women joining the legal profession would soon 'trickle up' to the top was misplaced.

Those Lord Chief Justices clearly thought that it would be a good thing to have more women judges. This is now a truth almost universally acknowledged. But if it is such a good thing, why has it not yet happened? It could be, of course, that while those in a position to do something about it say that something must be done, they do not really mean it. We are lucky enough to have an extraordinarily able, hard-working and independent judiciary, so why should we mind if they are mostly white and male, and at the higher levels mostly privately and Oxbridge educated? Isn't everyone's 'default' picture of a judge a mature man with a commanding presence?

There are, as Erika Rackley explains, three sets of reasons why we should mind: legitimacy, equity and difference. Legitimacy is about the confidence of the public, and Parliament and the Government, that the judiciary is there to serve the whole population and not just a section of it. Equity is about recognising the abilities of all those able young women who have been coming into the law in numbers equal

1 See page 164 of this book.

to or greater than men for decades now. Difference is about making a difference to the way cases are actually decided, especially at the higher levels.

As Rackley shows, it is easy to agree with reasons one and two but do nothing much about it. All things being equal, it would be a good idea, both for the image of the judiciary and for women generally, to have more women judges. But of course that must not lead to appointing people just because they are women. Diversity must not be pursued at the expense of merit. It is more important to have the best man for the job. So diversity and merit are set in opposition to one another.

Some of us think that this is a false dichotomy. It is grounded in a narrow (and some may think peculiarly alpha male) concept of merit – in which everyone can be graded in order from top to bottom according to some supposedly objective criteria of judging ability. Given the variety and complexity of the qualities necessary to be a judge, it would be surprising if this were so. Given the influence which the serving judiciary still have upon the appointments system, it is not at all surprising that judges continue to be appointed mostly in their own image. As the Chief Justice of Canada has put it, 'merit is in the eye of the beholder'.

Rackley therefore turns her attention to reason three: making a difference. It is not that there is a unique or essentially different female 'voice' with which all women judges sing. This is demonstrably not true. It is in the very nature of judging. Judging is not just the mechanical application of clear rules to known facts. Judges have to make choices – when law runs out, when law is not clear, when law gives them a choice. Anyone, male or female, black or white, brings their own experience and values to making those choices. These 'inarticulate premises' have been acknowledged since the phrase was first used by Justice Holmes of the US Supreme Court more than 100 years ago. 'The reason why England needs a more diverse bench is because there needs to be greater diversity in the "inarticulate premises"'.[2] Women who have led women's lives have just as much to contribute as have men who have led men's lives. At appellate levels, judging is a collective activity and the law is enriched by a diversity of experiences contributing to the collective decision. Diverse experience of life makes for better judging not worse: 'the promise of a diverse judiciary is not the promise of a multiplicity of approaches and values each fighting for recognition, but of a judiciary enriched by its openness to viewpoints previously marginalised and decision-making which is better for being better-informed'.

Viewed in this light, diversity is an important component of merit, not in opposition to it. Rackley makes an attractive case, but frankly acknowledges that it is unlikely to cut much ice with, for example, Lord Irvine, whose evidence to the

---

2 See R. Stephens, 'Reform in haste and repent at leisure: Iolanthe, the Lord High Executioner and Brave New World', *Legal Studies*, 24, 2004, 33.

House of Lords Constitution Committee was that 'to assert that diversity is a component of merit is sleight of hand, and not a very skilful one at that'.[3]

But there are other voices. Lord Bingham, undoubtedly the greatest judge of the early 21st century, pointed out that 'the term [merit] is not self-defining'. It 'directs attention to proven professional achievement as a necessary condition, but also enables account to be taken of wider considerations, including the virtue of gender and ethnic diversity'.[4]

What a shame that Lord Bingham is no longer with us to lend his weight to the argument!

Brenda Hale
April 2012

3 Lord Irvine, Oral Evidence to the House of Lords Select Committee on the Constitution Inquiry into the Judicial Appointments Process, 6 July 2011, Q28.
4 'The Law Lords: who has served', in L. Blom-Cooper, B. Dickson and G. Drewry (eds), *The Judicial House of Lords 1876–2009*, Oxford: Oxford University Press, 2009, p. 126.

Introduction

Kenneth Clarke, Lord Chancellor and Secretary of State for Justice:
I can't remember how many women are in the Supreme Court.
Lord Pannick: One.
Kenneth Clarke: One, is it? It remains a priority.[1]

Judicial diversity has indeed been a priority for some time now. Few would now deny, openly at least, the value of a diverse judiciary. Debates as to why we want judicial diversity, and suggestions as to how we might secure it, have become a more or less permanent fixture on the legal and political landscapes. And, with these arguments having been made and won, it was easy to assume that diversity would follow. Yet it hasn't. We find ourselves little closer to a more representative Bench; judicial diversity is in danger of becoming a priority without priority. In the face of such slow progress we appear to have nothing new to say. We are in danger of losing an audience who has heard it all before, who have brought into the rhetoric that, although progress is 'too slow', diversity will come.[2] So, while agreement on the importance of a diverse judiciary is a start, it is clear that more needs to be said and done to make it a reality.

This book is an attempt to re-energise and re-focus debates about judicial diversity. It offers a fresh look at the role of the (woman) judge and the process of judging, and re-examines the assumptions which underpin and constrain debates about why we might want a more diverse judiciary and how we might get one.

---

1 House of Lords Select Committee on the Constitution, Annual Meeting with the Lord Chancellor, 19 January 2011, Q27 (unrevised transcript).
2 See, eg, Advisory Panel on Judicial Diversity, *The Report of the Advisory Panel on Judicial Diversity 2010*, London: Ministry of Justice, 2010 (Neuberger Report); Judicial Diversity Taskforce, *Improving Judicial Diversity Progress towards delivery of the 'Report of the Advisory Panel on Judicial Diversity 2010'*, London: Ministry of Justice, May 2011 (McNally Report); Judicial Appointments Commission, *Annual Report 2010/11 Building the Best Judiciary for a Diverse Society*, London: Judicial Appointments Commission, 2011; Kenneth Clarke, Oral evidence to the House of Lords Select Committee on the Constitution Inquiry into the Judicial Appointments Process, 18 January 2012, Q378.

It makes an argument for judicial diversity, grounded in the substantive difference women judges make to the quality of judicial decision-making, and demonstrates how the inclusion of varied perspectives and experiences on the Bench makes for a better judiciary, for better decision-making. This provides a counter to criticism that attempts to diversify the composition of the Bench threaten the quality of the justice dispensed. That it is the result of 'political correctness gone mad',[3] or akin to treating the judiciary as some kind of 'social experiment'.[4] It shows how the pursuit of diversity is not stymied by the primacy of appointment on merit: a judiciary is stronger and the justice it dispenses better the more diverse its members. In other words, if we want the best judiciary we can get, we should also want one which is diverse.

Before continuing, some initial explanations and clarifications are necessary. First, although this book is about judicial diversity, as is clear from its title, its focus is on the position of *women* in the judiciary. This is not intended to privilege sex over, or to deny the importance of, other identity characteristics.[5] On any view, a truly diverse judiciary requires the presence of an array of identity characteristics, backgrounds, and experiences. And so, although I focus on the place and role of women judges, this neither involves nor implies any denial of the problems – perhaps more significant problems – facing other under-represented groups and the book should be read with this in mind. Nor is it to suggest that the category woman is not differentiated by class, age, religion and so on. That said, while recognising that the reasons for the under-representation of different identity groups vary, many of the arguments I make for the importance of having more women judges of all identities and of the value of a diverse judiciary are of broader application and, I believe, could be extended, with the necessary alterations, to other groups and other diversity characteristics. I simply do not do so here.

Second, the book focuses primarily on the senior judiciary in England and Wales – the High Court, Court of Appeal and (UK) Supreme Court.[6] This is not to suggest that diversity is not important across the judiciary as a whole. However, it is clear that there are greater problems with increasing diversity at its highest levels. Moreover, despite efforts to facilitate greater progression within the judiciary, promotion from the Circuit bench to the High Court remains rare. As a result,

3   Shami Chakrabarti, 'The Judiciary: Why Diversity and Merit Matter' in *Judicial Appointments: Balancing Independence, Accountability and Legitimacy*, London: Judicial Appointments Commission, 2010, p. 67, 69.

4   Lord Irvine, Oral evidence to the Home Affairs Select Committee, The Work of the Lord Chancellor's Department, 13 October 1997 [69].

5   These include, but are not limited to, the protected characteristics listed in the Equality Act 2010 – age, disability, gender reassignment, marriage and civil partnership, pregnancy and maternity, race, religion and belief, gender and sexual orientation (s 4) – as well as class, professional and educational background.

6   The UK Supreme Court is the highest court in England and Wales, as well as for Northern Ireland and Scotland. Scotland and Northern Ireland have a separate court system and judiciary below this which do not form part of my discussion in this book. That said, it is likely that the theoretical arguments for judicial diversity made here will have application beyond the book's main jurisdictional focus.

while efforts to increase diversity across the lower judiciary have met with some success, this is unlikely to trickle-up to the senior judiciary in the near future. Looking at diversity across the judiciary as a whole can therefore give a distorted picture both of the progress so far and the chances of improvement in the future. More funda-mentally, we might think that the upper echelons of the judiciary is where diversity matters the most, not only in terms of public confidence and democratic legitimacy but also – and importantly for the purposes of this book – because it is where women judges might have the bigger impact on the law and judicial decision-making.

Finally, a note on terminology is appropriate here. The distinction between sex (as a biological category) and gender (as a social process) is well established, although not without controversy.[7] On this basis, we might distinguish women (and men) judges as categories addressed to their gender, from female (and male) judges as categories addressed to their sex. The argument made in this book concerns the impact of *gender* on judicial decision-making, that is the difference *the experience* of being a woman, or indeed being a man, makes to how women and men judge. While this argument assumes that women and men have different gendered experiences of society and the world none of this is to suggest that *all* women, or *all* men, share certain innate characteristics or have the same experi-ences: gender, while an important feature of one's identity and personality, is not all-defining. Throughout this book I use women and female, and male and men, interchangeably – often opposing women judges with male judges. I do so not because I am unaware of, or seeking to open up and engage with, distinctions between sex and gender, but for a far more mundane and pragmatic reason: to avoid linguistic awkwardness.[8]

---

7 See generally, Cynthia Fuchs Epstein, *Deceptive Distinctions*, New Haven: Yale University Press, 1988; Judith Butler, *Gender Trouble: Feminism and the Subversion of Identity*, New York: Routledge, 1990; Judith Lorber, *Paradoxes of Gender*, New Haven: Yale University Press, 1994; Mimi Marinucci, *Feminism is Queer*, London: Zed Books, 2010, pp. 67–82.

8 It might also be argued that referring to *women* judges is 'vaguely offensive', that the *prefix* draws atten-tion to the fact women judges are unusual (Marinucci, *Feminism is Queer*, p. 73), paradoxically rein-forcing the assumption of the judge as male (see, eg, Regina Graycar, 'The Gender of Judgments: An Introduction' in Margaret Thornton (ed), *Public and Private – Feminist Legal Debates*, Oxford: Oxford University Press, 1995, p. 262, 264–265). However, given the historical and intuitive symmetry between men and judges the term 'judge' is not gender-neutral as this argument suggests. It is impor-tant therefore to make explicit and direct references to *women* judges not only to avoid ambiguity, but also to expose hidden gendered assumptions highlighting relevant and significant differences between men and women in the role, albeit while still working toward a time when such a prefix is superfluous. To this end, this book is, like Clare McGlynn's *The Woman Lawyer – Making the Difference*, unashamedly about *women* judges. Like McGlynn, I believe that 'if we never say "woman judge", we will almost always think of a man . . . If we do not consider the fact that women are disadvantaged, because we fear drawing attention to the fact that women are different from men, we will not be able to start to tackle the cause of such disadvantage' (Clare McGlynn, *The Woman Lawyer – Making the Difference*, London: Butterworths, 1998, p. 4). However, this is not to deny that male lawyers and judges who fail to conform to the 'masculine' norm are also disadvantaged and as such become 'other' (see, eg, Richard Collier, '"Nutty Professors", "Men in Suits" and "New Entrepreneurs": Corporality, Subjectivity and Change in the Law School and Legal Practice', *Social & Legal Studies*, 7, 2008, 27).

Outline of the book

Discussions about judicial diversity typically coalesce around two issues: first, why we have not got a diverse judiciary and how might we get one? And second, why should we want greater diversity among judges? What are we seeking to gain from judicial diversity? This book is no exception. It falls broadly into two parts, mapping (with one brief exception at the end of Chapter 1) onto each of these issues in turn.

The first three chapters set the scene for the argument that follows in the rest of the book. Chapter 1 details the position of women judges in England and Wales and worldwide. It provides a statistical profile and overview of the judiciary, tracking the progress of women over the last two decades. It goes on to consider traditional arguments for judiciary diversity. It suggests that although there is a consensus that a diverse judiciary is a good thing, consideration is not always given to *why* this is the case. This matters because even though the common arguments for judiciary diversity, grounded in democratic legitimacy, equality of opportunity, and (to a lesser extent) the value of varied perspectives, all point in the same direction – the value of a diverse judiciary – they suggest different routes to how we might get there. This is developed in Chapters 2 and 3, which address what are typically seen as the two principal causes for the present lack of diversity: the make-up of the legal profession as a whole, particularly in its upper echelons, and the process by which judges are selected. Chapter 2 considers the structural and cultural barriers preventing women lawyers from progressing to the upper levels of the legal profession. It argues that the legal profession is able to dictate the pace of change and that, so long as this continues to be the case, those charged with diversifying the Bench have little room for manoeuvre. This argument is expanded in Chapter 3, which examines recent changes and proposals for reform to the judicial appointments process. It is suggested that the ability to effect substantial change has been limited by the demographics and agenda of the legal profession, as well as the failure of the Ministry of Justice and Judicial Appointments Commission to consider positive and proactive steps specifically targeted at bringing about serious changes to the make-up of the judiciary.

The remaining three chapters make the case for judicial diversity. Central to this are arguments about judicial difference, and in particular the difference of women judges. Traditionally, women judges have had a prickly relationship with claims of difference. An explanation for this is provided in Chapter 4, which suggests that the experience of the woman judge is typified by isolation and exclusion with the possibility of acceptance only at the price of the very attributes that set her apart. One lesson to be taken from this is that there is an image of the judge, what I term the 'default judge', which women simply do not fit, and which causes us to treat women judges with suspicion or hostility.

In Chapter 5, we see that this mistrust is in part true: women judges *are* different. However, where we have gone wrong is in our understanding of the judge and what judges do. Once we get a clearer sense of what judging requires and how judges decide cases, we can see that judges do more than just apply predetermined rules, that there are times when judges – especially at senior levels – are called upon to make decisions where the existing rules provide no clear answer. In such cases the judge must turn to her own sense of justice, her own understanding of what the law should be. Insofar as this is informed, at least in part, by the judge's own background, values and experiences, these will be questions on which judges will differ. The question then is what difference *gender* makes to a judge's decision-making. Without doubt, this is tricky terrain. Arguments for judicial diversity grounded in an assumption or expectation of women judges' 'difference' have fallen out of favour in recent years. Attempts to find and articulate a common perspective, or 'different voice', shared by all (or at least most) women judges have been widely derided as essentially and evidentially flawed. However, the argument made here – that women judges make a substantive difference to the quality of judicial decision-making – does not stand and fall on an ability to identify a single, unified women's voice. Rather all we need to establish is that gender is *one* factor which influences how judges judge. Indeed, to suggest otherwise is to argue that, of all the factors that might shape a judge's views on such occasions, gender is *never* one of them. This is not only deeply implausible but runs counter to what women judges themselves are telling us.

And so, in Chapter 6, it is argued that, far from being a cause for concern, women judges' difference is an inevitable and welcome feature of a diverse judiciary. By getting a clearer sense of what our judges really do and how they do it, we can see that women judges, and judicial diversity more broadly, do not threaten but rather enrich the judiciary and judicial decision-making, that more women on the Bench would enhance the quality of the justice dispensed. Difference then becomes a means to ensuring greater diversity. In looking for, and celebrating, judicial difference, we find a better argument as to why diversity of judges and in judging is important, one that allows us to see that 'diversity is necessary to enhance the possibility of good judgment'.[9] Not only that, we have an argument that stands up to the standard opponent to measures to increase judicial diversity: the necessity of appointment on merit. The pursuit of diversity and appointment on merit go hand in hand with the common aim of ensuring that our judiciary is the best it can be.

---

9 Jennifer Nedelsky, 'Judgment, Diversity and Relational Autonomy' in Ronald Beiner and Jennifer Nedelsky (eds), *Judgment, Imagination and Politics*, Maryland: Rowman and Littlefield, 2001, 103, p. 118.

Chapter I

Positioning the woman judge

> The youngsters believe that we come from a narrow background – it's all
> nonsense – they get it from that man Griffith.
>
> (Lord Denning)[1]

Despite general acceptance of judicial diversity as an almost unqualified 'good
thing', the common perception of the judge as a 'white man, probably educated at
public school and Oxbridge' remains largely accurate.[2] As will become clear over
the course of the next three chapters, debates abound as to why we have not got a
diverse judiciary, whether we might want one, and how and when we might get
one. But just how un-diverse is the judiciary in England and Wales, and how does
the position of women, in particular, compare to men in judiciaries worldwide?
And if, as appears to be the case, the judiciary *is* 'pale and male', and is likely to be
for some time yet, should we be concerned? Why is diversity something we want
to see in our judiciary?

A pen portrait of the judiciary of England and Wales

According to Judicial Office statistics, as of January 2012, there are 3,792 judges
in the judiciary in England and Wales, just over 824 of whom are women.[3] In the

---

1 In John Griffith, 'That Man Griffith', *London Review of Books*, 12(20), 25 October 1990, 15–16.
2 This description is taken from the Judiciary of England and Wales website ('Diversity – gender, age
  and ethnicity'. Online. Available: http://www.judiciary.gov.uk/about-the-judiciary/judges-
  magistrates-and-tribunal-judges/judges-career-paths/diversity-gender-age-ethnicity   (accessed
  12 February 2012)).
3 This figure excludes magistrates and tribunal judges. All statistics relating to the judiciary in
  England and Wales are taken from the Judiciary of England and Wales website ('Diversity statistics
  and general overview'. Online. Available: http://www.judiciary.gov.uk/publications-and-
  reports/statistics/diversity-stats-and-gen-overview (accessed 12 February 2012)) and the Lord
  Chancellor's Department website (on file with author) unless otherwise stated. The inadequacy of

senior judiciary, that is the High Court and above, there are just 21 women judges, representing 11.7 per cent of the Bench at this level. As can be seen from Table 1.1, the figures are stark. Lady Hale, the UK's first and last woman Lord of Appeal in Ordinary, is the only woman on the Supreme Court bench. She has sat alone alongside her male colleagues since 2004, during which time nine further appointments have been made.[4] When it comes to administrative and leadership positions within the senior judiciary, women fare even worse. Only one woman has ever held one of these positions – Lady Justice Butler-Sloss who was the first woman appointed to the Court of Appeal in 1988 and who was President of the Family Division between 1999–2005. Since her retirement none of the senior judges – that is the Lord Chief Justice, Master of the Rolls, President of the Supreme Court (the Senior Law Lord as was), Deputy President or any of the Heads of Division – has been a woman.[5] The fact that there has not yet been a second woman judge in either the Supreme Court or as a Head of Division (and that we are still waiting

Table 1.1 Members of the senior judiciary in England and Wales by gender in 2012

	Men	Women	% Women
Justices of the Supreme Court/Lords of Appeal in Ordinary	11	1	8.3
Heads of Division	5	0	0
Lord Justices of Appeal	33	4	10.8
High Court Judges	109	16	12.8

Source: Judiciary of England and Wales website.

current official statistical data on the judiciary is widely acknowledged (see, eg, Advisory Panel on Judicial Diversity, *The Report of the Advisory Panel on Judicial Diversity 2010*, London: Ministry of Justice, 2010 [48–52], Recommendation 6 (Neuberger Report); House of Lords Select Committee on the Constitution, 'Judicial Appointments', 25th Report of Session 2010–2012, March 2012, [106–108] (Judicial Appointments Report)). Publicly available figures are incomplete, out-of-date and often inaccurate. Efforts have been made in this chapter to rationalise these figures where possible in order to present an accurate snapshot of the judiciary in England and Wales in the spring of 2012.

4 This fits a common pattern in many common law jurisdictions, identified by Kate Malleson, whereby there is a significant gap between the appointments of the first and second woman to the upper ranks of the judiciary. In England and Wales, for example, Lady Justice Butler-Sloss, the first woman appointed to the Court of Appeal, sat alone for 11 years, while in the US it took 15 years for another woman to be appointed to the Federal Bench following Florence Allen's appointment in 1934. In Australia, there was a 20 year gap between the first and second appointments to a state Supreme Court ('Prospects for Parity: the Position of Women in the Judiciary of England and Wales' in Ulrike Schultz and Gisela Shaw (eds), *Women in the World's Legal Professions*, Oxford: Hart Publishing, 2003, p. 175, 177).

5 It has been suggested that Lady Justice Hallett, currently Vice President of the Queen's Bench, is next in line for the position of Lord Chief Justice (Joshua Rozenberg, 'Lady Justice Hallett could become the first woman Lord Chief Justice', *Law Society Gazette*, 12 May 2011).

for a woman Lord Chief Justice) underlines Albie Sachs's view that the very 'lists of female "firsts" . . . are reminders of continuing male domination rather than signs of female advancement'.[6] In a similar vein, it is worth noting that, although there are now four women in the Court of Appeal, this is an increase of just one in six years. In fact, just one more woman sits in the Supreme Court, Court of Appeal or as a Head of Division combined, than was the case almost a decade ago.[7] Between 1 October 2000 and 1 October 2011, only one of the 17 appointments (5.9 per cent) from the Court of Appeal to the position of Lord Chief Justice, Head of Division or the Supreme Court has been a woman.

There has been slightly more progress in the High Court where there are now 16 women judges (around 13 per cent). Perhaps unsurprisingly, women are better represented in the Family Division where they make up around 33 per cent, compared to 12 per cent of the Queen's Bench Division and just 5.9 per cent of the Chancery Division. This is important. There are almost twice as many Chancery judges than Family judges in the current Court of Appeal, despite the Divisions being of similar size, suggesting that judges stand a greater chance of promotion from the Chancery Division.[8] What this means is that, although the presence of women judges has increased in the pool as a whole, their chances of being appointed to the Court of Appeal have not improved at the same rate.

Of course, it is important not to treat the judiciary of England and Wales as a wholly homogeneous entity. There are clear differences in its demographic profile between the various levels of the judiciary. As one might expect, the position of women is better lower down the judicial ranks. Just under 30 per cent of all circuit and district judges are women, although this decreases slightly to 26 per cent once part-time positions are excluded. However, within this there is significant regional variation. For example, just four women serve as circuit or district (county court) judges in Wales, alongside 53 men.[9] Women also tend to be better represented in the part-time judiciary. In 2010, around 16.5 per cent of recorders and 32.9 per cent of deputy district judges in the county courts were women.[10]

6 Albie Sachs and Joan Hoff Wilson, *Sexism and the Law: A Study of Male Beliefs and Judicial Bias*, Oxford: Martin Robertson, 1978, p. 178.
7 In 2002, there were three women in the senior judiciary: one as President of the Family Division and two in the Court of Appeal.
8 Although this is not necessarily the case for women lawyers. Lady Justice Arden is the first and so far only woman to be appointed to the Court of Appeal from the Chancery Division of the High Court.
9 Catherine Evans, "'Pale, male" courts in Wales "need more women judges"', *BBC News Online*, 27 May 2011.
10 There are some judicial posts, most notably Deputy High Court Judges, for which diversity statistics are not available purportedly for data protection reasons. Women are better represented on the tribunal Bench, making up 37% of tribunal members (judges and non-legal) (Robert Carnwath (Senior President of Tribunals), written evidence to the HL Select Committee on the Constitution Inquiry into Judicial Appointments Process, October 2011). 51.1% of magistrates in England and Wales are female.

Clearly these statistics can only tell us so much. As Kate Malleson has noted, the rise in the number of women entering the judiciary coincided with a significant period of growth in the judiciary as a whole. Between 1970–2000 the judiciary grew tenfold to just over 3,000.[11] This means that, at least in relation to some posts, although there has been an increase in the number of women appointed, the statistical impact of them joining the Bench has been modest. For example, although the number of women Recorders almost tripled in the 10 year period between 1998–2008 (from 69 to 201), the proportional representation of women at this level merely doubled from 8 per cent to 16.3 per cent. Nevertheless, while it is clear that the representation of women particularly in the senior judiciary remains low, there *has* been progress. The number, and proportional representation, of women in the Court of Appeal, High Court and circuit bench has more than tripled since the late 1980s. Overall, while changes to judicial posts make a direct comparison difficult, the number of women in the judiciary as a whole has risen from 4.6 per cent in 1989 to 21.7 per cent in 2012, decreasing to 3 per cent and 18.9 per cent respectively among the full-time judiciary.[12]

While there has been some increase in the number of women judges, as we can see from Table 1.3, judges from a black or minority ethnic background (BME) fare even worse.[13] BME judges comprise just 2.8 per cent of the senior judiciary and 4.1 per cent of the judiciary as a whole.[14] Mrs Justice Dobbs's hope that her appointment to the High Court in 2004 'would be the first of many' has not yet been realised.[15] She is one of just four BME judges in the High Court, and was the only visible BME judge until Mr Justice Singh's appointment in October 2011. She continues to be the only female BME judge in the senior judiciary. There are no BME judges of either sex in the Court of Appeal or Supreme Court. On current figures, Baroness Scotland's prediction in 2009 that we will have to wait another 10–20 years for a black Supreme Court Justice seems about right.[16] As with

---

11 Malleson, 'Prospects for Parity', p. 176.
12 1989 figures taken from Susan McRae, *The Report of the Hansard Society on Women at the Top*, London: The Hansard Society, 1990, p. 44.
13 In this book, I use the acronym BME, rather than BAME, for consistency with the Judicial Office. A direct comparison between the representation of women and members from BME groups may be misleading. Office for National Statistics figures, published in 2011, put the 'non white British' population at around 12.1%. Thus, while BME groups are clearly underrepresented in the judiciary, the statistical disparity is somewhat less than that of women who, in 2007, made up 50.8% of the UK population, outnumbering men at all ages over 31.
14 Caution must be exercised when using this data. Candidates are asked to provide the information on a voluntary basis. It is likely that there are inconsistencies in the self-reported data. For example, some judges who fall within the BME category may not identify as such, while others may refuse to state their ethnicity. There is a high level of unknown ethnicity, particularly among the senior judiciary (19.5%).
15 BBC News Online, 'High Court gets first black judge', 2 September 2004.
16 In Frances Gibb, 'How can ethnic minorities reach the top of the profession?', *The Times*, 23 April 2009.

Table 1.2 Women members of the salaried judiciary and recorders in England and Wales, 1976–2012

	1976	1989	1998	2004	2008	2012
Justices of the Supreme Court/Lords of Appeal in Ordinary	0	0	0	1 (8.3%)	1 (8.3%)	1 (8.3%)
Heads of Division	0	0	0	1 (20%)	0	0
Lord Justices of Appeal	0	1 (4%)	1 (3%)	2 (5.4%)	3 (8.1%)	4 (10.8%)
High Court Judges	2	1 (1%)	7 (7%)	8 (7.5%)	11 (10%)	16 (12.8%)
Circuit Judges	5	17 (4%)	30 (5%)	58 (9.5%)	87 (13.3%)	107 (16.5%)
Judge Advocates	–	–	–	–	0	1 (12.5%)
District Judges (County Court)	–	7 (4%)	38 (11%)	82 (18.9%)	98 (22.4%)	113 (25.5%)
District Judges (Magistrates' Court)	2 (3.9%)	8 (13%)	14 (15%)	20 (19.2%)	31 (22.8%)	38 (27.7%)
Masters, Registrars, Cost Judges, District Judges (PRFD)	1 (4.5%)	–	–	–	11 (22.9%)	14 (29.2%)
Recorders	7 (1.9%)	38 (5%)	69 (8%)	184 (13.3%)	194 (14.9%)	201 (16.5%)

Sources: Sachs and Wilson, Sexism and the Law, p. 175 (1976 figures); McGlynn, The Woman Lawyer, p. 173 (1989, 1998 figures); Judiciary of England and Wales website (2004, 2008, 2012 figures).

Table 1.3 BME members of the salaried judiciary and recorders in England and Wales, 1994–2012

	1994	1997	2004	2008	2012
Justices of the Supreme Court/Lords of Appeal in Ordinary	0	0	0	0	0
Heads of Division	0	0	0	0	0
Lord Justices of Appeal	0	0	0	0	0
High Court Judges	0	0	0	3 (2.7%)	4 (4.5%)
Circuit Judges	4	6 (1.1%)	4 (0.7%)	20 (3.1%)	15 (2.5%)
Judge Advocates	–	–	–	0	0
District Judges (County Court)	1	3 (0.9%)	11 (2.5%)	20 (4.6%)	21 (5.1%)
District Judges (Magistrates' Court)	–	–	3 (2.9%)	3 (2.2%)	4 (3.9%)
Masters, Registrars, Cost Judges, District Judges (PRFD)	–	–	–	1 (2.1%)	1 (2.9%)
Recorders	11	14 (1.5%)	45 (3.2%)	61 (4.7%)	21 (5.1%)

Sources: McGlynn, The Woman Lawyer, p. 174 (1994, 1997 figures); Judiciary of England and Wales website (2004, 2008, 2012 figures).

Note: Mrs Justice Dobbs was the first judge from a BME background to be appointed to the High Court in October 2004.

women judges, there are more BME judges in the lower courts and part-time judiciary. The number of BME Recorders, for example, has leapt from eight in 1992 and 14 in 1998 to 61 in 2012 (representing 6.5 per cent of the whole), and just over 10 per cent of tribunal judicial office-holders and 8 per cent of magistrates are from a BME group.

However, here too, these increases have not been accompanied by comparable increases in proportional representation. Although there are now over three times as many BME circuit judges their proportional representation has risen by just one per cent. Interestingly, even though the number of male BME judges is more than double that of women, women tend to be *better* represented among BME judges. While the number of male judges (of all backgrounds) exceeds that of women judges by 4.5:1, among BME judges this decreases to around 3.8:1. In 2010, 5.9 per cent of women circuit judges had a BME background, compared to 2.1 per cent of male circuit judges.[17] This was also the case in 2001 where, although

17 Data on the ethnicity of judges has been collected since 1991. During this time there have been inconsistencies in the way the data has been published. For example, while the diversity statistics published in 2011 are broken down according to ethnic group, they do not (unlike the data published between 2001–2010) distinguish between female and male judges, preventing important comparisons across diversity characteristics.

BME judges represented just 1.1 per cent of the circuit bench (six judges), of the 44 female circuit judges two (4.5 per cent) had a BME background.

The judiciary also lacks diversity in terms of the professional background of the judges. Despite representing just 10 per cent of the legal profession, barristers make up 62.4 per cent of the judiciary, and 98.8 per cent of the senior judiciary.[18] Moreover, as Table 1.4 shows, this domination is growing. In 2000, 13.5 per cent of the circuit bench were previously solicitors,[19] compared to 12.5 per cent in 2011. Similarly, the number of solicitors becoming recorders has dramatically decreased in recent years. In 2000, 11.2 per cent of recorders were solicitors compared to just 5.2 per cent in 2011. This will have a knock on effect on the representation of solicitors in the High Court (currently 0.9 per cent) as appointees are typically recorders prior to appointment. Again, solicitors are better represented among women judges. In 2010, just under 14 per cent of women circuit judges were former solicitors, compared to 11.4 per cent of men. And, the percentage representation of solicitors among women recorders is almost double that of men.

This is where official statistics on judicial diversity end. The 'Diversity Statistics', posted on the Judiciary of England and Wales website, focus exclusively on sex, ethnicity and professional background as the key indicators of diversity. This is

Table 1.4 Members of the salaried judiciary and recorders in England and Wales by profession, 2000–2011

	2000 Barrister	2000 % Non-Barrister	2011 Barrister	2011 % Non-Barrister
Justices of the Supreme Court/ Lords of Appeal in Ordinary	12	0	11	9.1
Heads of Division	5	0	5	0
Lord Justices of Appeal	35	0	37	0
High Court Judges	100	1	107	0.9
Circuit Judges	486	13.4	582	12.5
Judge Advocates	–	–	7	12.5
District Judges (County Court)	20	95	48	89.2
District Judges (Magistrates' Court)	–	–	48	65.0
Masters, Registrars, Cost Judges, District Judges (PRFD)	–	–	27	43.5
Recorders	805	11.2	1,158	5.2

Source: Judiciary of England and Wales website.

18 To date, just four solicitors have been appointed to the High Court.
19 Law Society, *Broadening the Bench: Law Society proposals for reforming the way judges are appointed*, London: Law Society, October 2000, p. 5.

problematic. In particular, as Leslie Moran has argued in the context of discussion about the visibility of sexual orientation in debates about judicial diversity, the absence of such data in relation to certain characteristics is often given as a reason for not recognising, and therefore not addressing, their absence on the Bench.[20] In other words, statistical invisibility promotes and reinforces the real-life invisibility of, or at least strategically hidden, identity characteristics on the Bench.[21] Moreover, the lack of transparency and inconsistencies, as well as 'gaps' in the data currently collected and published make it difficult to track the progress of diversity or to draw comparisons across categories. In July 2011, the Judicial Appointments Commission (JAC) announced that it was to start (voluntary) monitoring of sexual orientation and (religious) beliefs of candidates alongside sex, ethnicity, professional background and disability.[22] It is hoped that the Judicial Office will soon follow suit.

Nevertheless, while the senior judiciary remain somewhat inscrutable, it is possible to glean further information about various identity characteristics – age, sexual orientation, class, educational background and so on – from other sources including the JAC and Judicial Office websites. Thus, for example, while it is impossible to know how many gay and lesbian judges there actually are, we do know that there are two openly gay men in the senior judiciary – one in the Court of Appeal and one in the High Court – and one on the circuit bench.[23] We also know that the average age in the Supreme Court is 66.5 and that the youngest member (Lord Reed) is a relatively sprightly 55. In relation to the schooling of the judges, suggested by John Griffith a 'good indicator' of social and economic class background, very little has changed since Griffith's groundbreaking study in 1977. In 1940, around 80 per cent of the senior judiciary had been privately educated, in 1956 this figure stood at around 76 per cent and, between 1970–1975, 68 per cent of appointees to the High Court had attended public schools.[24] In 2005, a

---

20 Leslie J Moran, 'Judicial Diversity and the Challenge of Sexuality: Some Preliminary Findings', *Sydney Law Review*, 28, 2006, 565.

21 Of course, there are understandable reasons why judges may wish to keep certain aspects of their identity hidden. In relation to sexual orientation, for example, it was only in 1991 that the practice of only appointing men who were married to the Bench, introduced by Lord Hailsham, was ended. (See further, Adrian Fulford, 'Diversity Speech', Middle Temple Hall, London, 20 January 2009). Research in 2010 suggested that gay and lesbian lawyers continue to believe that being LGBT, being 'out at work' or a member of a LGBT network would have a negative impact on their application for judicial appointment (Leslie J Moran and Daniel K Winterfeldt, *Barriers to Applications for Judicial Appointment Research: Lesbian, Gay, Bisexual, and Transgender Experiences*, London: InterLaw Diversity Forum, 2011, pp. 48–49).

22 Talking to Frances Gibb at *The Times*, Christopher Stevens, Chair of the JAC, acknowledged that 'we can't claim to be inclusive of all under-represented groups unless we have some kind of score-keeping of the groups . . . whether black, gay, solicitors or women' (Frances Gibb, 'Citizens need to be confident that judges reflect the full diversity of modern Britain', *The Times*, 7 July 2011).

23 Afua Hirsch, 'Judicial culture still deters gay and lesbian lawyers, say researchers', *The Guardian*, 4 July 2010.

24 JAG Griffith, *The Politics of the Judiciary*, London: Fontana Press, 1977, pp. 26–27.

Sutton Trust survey found that three-quarters of the senior judiciary in 1989 *and* 2004 had attended fee-paying schools (compared to a national average of 7 per cent).[25] A later survey, published in 2009, found that the percentage of judges across the judiciary as a whole who had been privately educated had decreased by just 4 per cent to 70 per cent between 1989–2007.[26] In relation to university education, a survey of the senior judiciary between 1876–1972 found that 70 per cent had attended either Oxford or Cambridge.[27] In 1989, this stood at 87 per cent, decreasing to 80 per cent in 2004.[28] In 2012, all but one of the Supreme Court justices attended Oxford or Cambridge (91.6 per cent) compared to 80 per cent in 1987.[29]

25 Sutton Trust, *Briefing Note: The Educational Backgrounds of the UK's Top Solicitors, Barristers and Judges*, London: Sutton Trust, June 2005, p. 7.

26 Sutton Trust, *The Educational Backgrounds of Leading Lawyers, Journalists, Vice Chancellors, Politicians, Medics and Chief Executives: The Sutton Trust Submission to the Milburn Commission on Access to the Professions*, London: Sutton Trust, March 2009, p. 5. This is unlikely to change in the foreseeable future. The Panel on Fair Access to the Professions, chaired by Alan Milburn in 2009, singled out the legal profession as one of the most 'socially exclusive professions' (Panel on Fair Access to the Professions, *Unleashing Aspiration: The Final Report of the Panel on Fair Access to the Professions*, London: Cabinet Office, July 2009, p. 24). In 2009, 68% of barristers had attended independent schools (Sutton Trust, 'Submission to the Milburn Commission', p. 5). A later survey published in 2010, indicated that the proportion of magic circle partners who attended public school had risen by 12% between 1988 and 2004 (Andrew Pugh, 'Proportion of lawyers educated at public school far outstrips national average', *The Lawyer*, 15 November 2010).

27 JAG Griffith, *The Politics of the Judiciary*, London: Fontana Press, 1977, pp. 25–26.

28 Sutton Trust, 'Briefing Note', p. 7 (1989 and 2004 figures); Sutton Trust, 'Submission to the Milburn Commission', p. 5 (2007 figures).

29 JAG Griffith, *The Politics of the Judiciary*, 5th edn, London: Fontana Press, 1997, pp. 25–26. Penny Darbyshire argues that the narrow educational background of the senior judiciary should be neither a source of surprise nor criticism, suggesting that it would be more 'a matter of concern if senior judges were *not* highly educated and exceptionally intelligent' (Penny Darbyshire, *Sitting in Judgment: The Working Lives of Judges*, Oxford: Hart Publishing, 2011, p. 46). She points to a similar trend among senior judges in the US, Canada and across Europe. However, this predisposition toward a particular type and place of education has significant consequences for judicial diversity. Darbyshire's analysis does not allow for the fact that, given the lower socio-economic profile of BME groups generally, members of these groups are less likely to be found in the pool of privately-educated and elite university graduates. Despite their strong profile among law students generally, the proportion of BME students is highest at newer universities. This puts them at a disadvantage later in their careers. In fact, Tahir Abbas argues 'it is ethnic minorities possessing the personal and educational characteristics of their white-English selected-school educated counterparts who are most likely to succeed' (*Diversity in the Senior Judiciary: A Literature Review of Research on Ethnic Inequalities*, London: The Commission for Judicial Appointments, 2005, p. 5). That said, it should be noted that the predilection toward the Universities of Oxford and Cambridge does not appear to apply to appointments further down the judicial hierarchy. Research by Cheryl Thomas and Hazel Genn in 2006 found that the majority of applicants for deputy district judge positions had degrees from outside the top 12 institutions (*Appointment of Deputy District Judges 2003–2005*, London: The Commission for Judicial Appointments, 2006, p. 48) and only just over a third of circuit judges interviewed by Penny Darbyshire had attended 'Oxbridge' (Darbyshire, *Sitting in Judgment*, p. 46).

Thus, however much Lord Denning might have thought otherwise, there is little doubt that, especially in its upper echelons, the judiciary is drawn from a very narrow and limited pool. Although there are more women and BME judges than there have been previously, a senior judge is *still* more likely than not to be a white straight man, who has been privately educated and studied at Oxford or Cambridge before progressing on to the Bar. And, so long as this is the case, the common perception of the judiciary as pale and male is hard to rebut. Some 45 years since Mrs Justice Lane's trailblazing appointment to the High Court bench, the reality of a diverse judiciary remains some way off. In fact, in 2007, the Equal Opportunities Commission suggested that as many as 78 women were 'missing' from the upper echelons of the judiciary.[30] The most recent *Sex and Power* report suggests that is likely to take a further 45 years for these women to be 'found', that is before there is gender parity among senior judges.[31]

And yet, this all comes at a time of considerable political and judicial rhetoric and apparent goodwill for a more diverse judiciary. Diversity, we are told, is on its way:

> The journey to diversity is a long one. Progress is slow. It should be quicker. It will come. It will come. And I am here with you today to proclaim that I have a passionate belief that our community will be enriched when the judiciary properly reflects its broad diversity. The tide is for diversity. The tide is inexorable, and the tide always wins.[32]

This creates the impression that, although increasing judicial diversity takes time, we are getting there. However, what we can see when we look at the diversity statistics over a period of time is that this rhetoric of progress falls somewhat short. It misrepresents and obscures the reality which is that progress toward greater judicial diversity is painfully slow, and in danger of stagnating, or even in some cases going in reverse, the earlier gains are beginning to be lost. To be clear, in the decade between 2001 and 2011:

- The overall number of women in the Court of Appeal has increased by two, and the number of senior women judges (that is, in the Supreme Court and as a Head of Division) has remained the same: one.
- No-one from a BME group of either sex has been appointed to the Supreme Court, the Court of Appeal or as a Head of Division, and just two judges from a visible BME background have been appointed to the High Court.

---

30 Equal Opportunities Commission, *Sex and Power: Who Runs Britain? 2007*, London: Equal Opportunities Commission, 2007, p. 1.
31 Equality and Human Rights Commission, *Sex and Power: 2011*, London: Equality and Human Rights Commission, 2011, p. 3.
32 Lord Judge, 'Encouraging Diversity in the Judiciary', Minority Lawyers Conference, London, 25 April 2009.

- No solicitor has been appointed directly to the High Court.[33]
- The pool from which the senior judiciary is primarily drawn has in many respects become *less* diverse.

Further down the judicial hierarchy, although women have made some gains, these are far outweighed by those of men. For example, even though the number of women in the High Court has risen by eight, this is, in fact, two *fewer than* the increase in the number of men; similarly, while the number of women circuit judges has risen by 63, an additional 117 men now sit in on the circuit bench than in 2001. In other words, although there are more women judges, there are also (even) more men which means that, even though the number of women judges has increased, this has not been matched in their overall visibility and influence.

True diversity, particularly in the senior judiciary, is as far – if not further – away than ever. Women, although not only women, appear to be swimming against the tide, held back by an undercurrent flowing in the opposite direction. But what about other jurisdictions? Have efforts to increase the representation of women fared any better elsewhere?

A comparative perspective

Concern about the absence of women judges is not unique to the judiciary of England and Wales. Increasing diversity is 'one of the greatest challenges' facing judiciaries across many jurisdictions today.[34] Of course, in many instances, direct comparisons are not possible. Differences in legal traditions and in the organisa-tion and structure of the legal profession as well as disparities in terminology mean that for the most part we may well not be comparing like with like.[35] The purpose of the following snapshot of the position of women in some of the world's judici-aries can therefore only be, and is intended as, illustrative, rather than definitive. Nonetheless, the figures are revealing. Three common themes emerge. First, with the exception of Eastern Europe, judges in national courts are still predominantly male.[36] Second, again with some exceptions, women tend to be better represented

---

33 The last direct appointment of a solicitor to the High Court was Lawrence Collins (later Lord Collins) in 2000.
34 Kate Malleson, 'Introduction' in Kate Malleson and Peter H Russell (eds), *Appointing Judges in an Age of Judicial Power: Critical Perspectives from Around the World*, Toronto: University of Toronto, 2006, p. 3, 7. See further Ulrike Schultz and Gisela Shaw (eds), *Women in the World's Legal Professions*, Oxford: Hart Publishing, 2003; Ulrike Schultz and Gisela Shaw (eds), *Gender and Judging*, Oxford: Hart Publishing, forthcoming.
35 Ulrike Schultz and Gisela Shaw, 'Introduction: Women in the World's Legal Profession: Overview and Synthesis' in Ulrike Schultz and Gisela Shaw (eds), *Women in the World's Legal Professions*, Oxford: Hart Publishing, 2003, p. xxv, xxviii–xxxi.
36 Department of Economic and Social Affairs (DESA), *The World's Women 2010: Trends and Statistics*, New York: United Nations, 2010, p. 120.

in the judiciary as a whole, than in the highest national courts. Finally, there is a growing concern in a number of jurisdictions that the progress made by women over the last decade or so is beginning to stall or even reverse.

The representation of women in national courts varies considerably. A United Nations survey in 2010 of women's representation in national courts across Europe found that, of the 22 countries surveyed, women were better represented in judiciaries in Eastern Europe, where an average of 64 per cent of the judiciary are women (with Slovenia coming out on top with 75 per cent) compared to an average of 33 per cent in Western Europe.[37] Similarly, women account for around 60 per cent of the regular court judiciary and two-thirds of *arbitrazh* court judges in Russia,[38] and make up over half of the judiciary in Israel.[39] In North America, 41.6 per cent of the Canadian judiciary,[40] and around 30 per cent of the US federal court and district (or trial) judiciary, are women.[41] Women make up 32 per cent of the judiciary in Australia,[42] and 26 per cent of the judiciary in New Zealand.[43] In Northern Ireland, 43 per cent of the judiciary are women (including lay magistrates) with women making up 42 per cent of tribunal judges and just under 25 per cent of county court judges.[44] 21 per cent of judges on the Scottish Sheriff Courts are women.[45] At the other end of the spectrum, in Syria women make up just 14 per cent of the judiciary,[46] and just 8.3 per cent of the Indian High

---

37 DESA, *Trends and Statistics*, p. 121 (2003–2009 figures). The Netherlands is an exception to this. In 2010, women made up 52% of the judiciary (The Netherlands Council for the Judiciary Information Service figures, on file with author).

38 Alexi Trochev, 'Judicial Selection in Russia: Towards Accountability and Centralisation' in Kate Malleson and Peter H Russell (eds), *Appointing Judges in an Age of Judicial Power: Critical Perspectives from Around the World*, Toronto: University of Toronto, 2006, p. 375, 378 (2006 figures).

39 Greer Fay Cashman, 'Beinisch attends her final swearing-in ceremony', *The Jerusalem Post*, 3 January 2012.

40 Office for the Commissioner for Federal Judicial Affairs Canada, 'Number of Judges on the Bench as at February 2, 2012'. Online. Available: http://www.fja.gc.ca/appointments-nominations/judges-juges-eng.html (accessed 12 February 2012). (February 2012 figures).

41 National Women's Law Center (NWLC), 'Women in the Federal Judiciary: Still a long way to go'. Online. Available: http://www.nwlc.org/resource/women-federal-judiciary-still-long-way-go-1 (accessed 19 February 2012).

42 The Australasian Institute of Judicial Administration (AIJA), 'Judges and Magistrates (% of Women)'. Online. Available: http://www.aija.org.au/gender-statistics.html (accessed 12 February 2012) (2011 figures).

43 New Zealand Human Rights Commission (NZHRC), *New Zealand Census of Women's Participation 2010*, New Zealand: Human Rights Commission, 2010, p. 37 (2010 figures).

44 Northern Ireland Judicial Appointments Commission, *A Guide to Judicial Careers in Northern Ireland*, Belfast: Northern Ireland Judicial Appointments Commission, 2011 (2011 figures).

45 Alan Paterson, *Lawyers and the Public Good: Democracy in Action?* Cambridge: Cambridge University Press, 2012, p. 144.

46 Monique C Cardinal, 'Why aren't Women Sharia Court Judges? The Case of Syria', *Islamic Law and Society*, 17, 2010, 185, p. 186.

Court judiciary.[47] In Egypt, where until 2010 women were banned from sitting on the State Council, just 42 of the 12,000 strong judiciary are women.[48]

Traditionally, women have tended to be better represented in civil law countries – for example, France, Germany, the Netherlands – than in common law countries such as the United States, Australia, New Zealand, and England and Wales. There are two related reasons for this. Many civil law jurisdictions operate a so-called 'career judiciary', whereby potential entrants begin training to become a judge soon after their studies, rather than as a second career following success in the legal profession. Access to the judiciary is based on academic merit, which allows women lawyers to reap the benefit of an area where they typically excel over men. Judicial office (and its related benefits: parental leave, more flexible working hours and so on) is therefore an accessible and realistic career option for women. Indeed, women are often more able to achieve a prominent position in the judiciary than in large law firms.[49] However, women's success has not been without critics. In France, for example, 80 per cent of those entering the judiciary in 2003 were women, leading to the French Justice Minister to threaten to introduce quotas in order to restore the gender balance and to maintain public confidence in the system, particularly among male claimants and defendants.[50]

The second explanation for the greater representation of women relates to the prestige – or rather lack thereof – of the judiciary. Women tend to feature in larger numbers in the judiciaries of countries where a judicial career is less well regarded for example, where it is seen as part of the civil service.[51] The lower status (and remuneration) of judges, in comparison to other branches of the legal profession, means that many men opt for the kudos and income of commercial law over the 'boredom' of judicial office.[52] The greater presence of women on the Bench in these circumstances is likely to be because they are simply filling the void left by uninterested men. This in turn impacts on the prestige of judicial office. The more 'feminised' the judiciary (or indeed any profession) becomes, the lower status it

47 Indian Courts website. Online. Available: http://indiancourts.nic.in/ (accessed 12 February 2012).
48 Jailan Zagan, 'Egypt wrangles over whether women should be judges', *The Daily Telegraph*, 25 February 2010.
49 Eliane Botelho Junqueria, 'Women in the Judiciary: A perspective from Brazil' in Ulrike Schultz and Gisela Shaw (eds), *Women in the World's Legal Professions*, Oxford: Hart Publishing, 2003, p. 437; Laureline Duvillard, 'Women find no justice in law profession', *swissinfo.ch*, 13 May 2011.
50 Tilly Rubens, 'France has plenty of women judges – why don't we?', *The Times*, 9 March 2004.
51 Gisela Shaw, 'Women Lawyers in the New Federal States of Germany from Quantity to Quality' in Ulrike Schultz and Gisela Shaw (eds), *Women in the World's Legal Professions*, Oxford: Hart Publishing, 2003, p. 323, 334–337; Małgorzarta Fuszara, 'Women Lawyers in Poland under the Impact of Post-1989 Transformation' in Ulrike Schultz and Gisela Shaw (eds), *Women in the World's Legal Professions*, Oxford: Hart Publishing, 2003, p. 371, 375.
52 Schultz and Shaw, 'Introduction', p. xlviii.

enjoys.[53] The esteem in which an institution is held is, it seems, in direct inverse proportion to the number of women in it.

Women also tend to be better represented on courts with appointments processes that are structured to ensure a representative balance, that is where innovative policies and practices, uninhibited by traditional mechanisms, work to expand the recruitment pool and increase judicial diversity. This is often the case for inter- or multi-national courts or those in newer democracies.[54] This may explain the high levels of representation of women on the judiciaries in Eastern Europe, and on international courts such as the International Criminal Court (ICC) and the European Court of Human Rights (ECtHR).[55] However, a multi-national court does not always ensure the presence of women. As can be seen in Table 1.5, women make up less than 20 per cent of the European Court of Justice, just over 14.3 per cent of the International Court of Justice and a mere 4.8 per cent of the International Tribunal for the Law of the Sea.

Although in most judiciaries women are more likely to be found on the lower rungs of the judicial ladder, this is not always the case. For instance, women are in the majority or equal to men in the supreme courts, but not the judiciary overall, of Rwanda, Honduras, Bulgaria, Latvia and Romania.[56] Conversely, women are better represented on the Australian, Canadian and US Supreme Courts than in the judiciary as a whole. Generally, however, even in those judiciaries with a high overall proportion of women, men dominate the more prestigious and powerful courts. In Greece, for example, even though women make up around 51 per cent of the Supreme Court and Council of State – just four of the 22 court presidents or vice presidents are women. Similarly, in New Zealand the proportion of women judges falls from 26 per cent overall to 20 per cent in their Supreme Court and in Israel it drops by over a quarter to just 18.6 per cent. In Russia, just 16 of the 115 Supreme Court justices are women (13.9 per cent).[57] This is also the case in Scotland and Northern Ireland. The representation of women decreases to 14 per cent on the Court of Session in Scotland, while the Northern Irish High Court has no women judges. And, of course, the UK Supreme Court follows the same trend. The representation of women falls from, at best, 21.7 per cent of the judiciary of England and Wales as a whole to just 8.3 per cent of the UK Supreme Court.

53 Anne Boigeol, 'Male Strategies in the Face of the Feminisation of a Profession: The Case of the French Judiciary' in Ulrike Schultz and Gisela Shaw (eds), *Women in the World's Legal Professions*, Oxford: Hart Publishing, 2003, p. 401.

54 Malleson, 'Introduction', pp. 7–8.

55 Both the ICC and ECtHR have mechanisms embedded in their appointments processes to ensure a gender balance in the courts (Rome Statute of the International Criminal Court article 36 para 8(a)(iii) (ICC); Assembly Resolution 1366 (2004) (as modified by Resolution 1426 (2005) and Resolution 1627 (2008)) and Recommendation 1649 (2004) (ECtHR)).

56 DESA, *Trends and Statistics*, p. 121.

57 Trochev, 'Judicial Selection in Russia', p. 378 (2006 figures).

Table 1.5 Number of women and men on the highest national and international courts

	Women	Men	% Women
International Criminal Court (ICC)	11	9	57.9
Greece (Supreme Court and Council of State (combined))	154*	144	51.7
Rwanda (Supreme Court)	7	7	50.0
Croatia (Supreme Court)	20	21	48.8
Canada (Supreme Court)	4*	5	44.4
Australia (High Court)	3	4	42.9
European Court of Human Rights (ECtHR)	19	27	41.3
Serbia (Constitutional Court)	6	9	40.0
Uganda (Supreme Court)	2	3	40.0
Sweden (Supreme Court)	6	10	37.5
Norway (Supreme Court)	7	12	36.8
United States of America (Supreme Court)	3	6	33.5
Tanzania (Court of Appeal)	5	10	33.3
Germany (Federal Constitutional Court)	5	11	31.3
Austria (Constitutional Court)	4	9	30.8
Switzerland (Federal Supreme Court)	11	27	29.0
Argentina (Supreme Court)	2	5	28.6
Finland (Supreme Court)	5*	14	26.3
Denmark (Supreme Court)	5	14	26.3
Ireland (Supreme Court)	2	6	25.0
Nigeria (Supreme Court)	3	11	21.4
The Philippines (Supreme Court)	3	12	20
South Africa (Constitutional Court)	2	8	20
New Zealand (Supreme Court)	1*	4	20
European Court of Justice	7	29	19.4
Israel (Supreme Court)	3*	13	18.6
Mexico (Supreme Court)	2	9	18.2
Singapore (Supreme Court)	3	14	17.6
Spain (Constitutional Court)	2	10	16.7
China (Supreme People's Court)	2	12	14.3
Korea (Supreme Court)	2	12	14.3
International Court of Justice	2	12	14.3
Japan (Supreme Court)	2	13	13.3
Bangladesh (Supreme Court)	1	7	12.5
Brazil (Supreme Federal Court)	1	9	10.0
United Kingdom (Supreme Court)	1	11	8.3
India (Supreme Court)	2	24	7.7
Cyprus (Supreme Court)	1	12	7.7
Italy (Constitutional Court)	1	14	6.7
Egypt (Supreme Court)	1	18	5.3
International Tribunal for the Law of the Sea	1	20	4.8
Pakistan (Supreme Court)	0	16	0
Fiji (Supreme Court)	0	6	0

* includes a woman Chief Justice or President

Source: Court websites (February 2012).

Nonetheless, whichever way you look at it, it is clear that the judiciary of England and Wales is lagging behind in relation to both the judiciary as a whole and its Supreme Court. In 2009, the UK Supreme Court ranked 32nd out of 35 EU member states, above Cyprus, Portugal and Malta.[58] However, while the JAC and Ministry of Justice work to ensure that the judiciary in England and Wales catches up, concerns are beginning to be expressed in jurisdictions often seen as being at the vanguard of judicial diversity that gains are beginning to be lost.[59] In South Africa, for example, where the judiciary has been transformed since the end of apartheid, there is a concern that gender diversity has slipped off the political agenda.[60] In 2010, only 22.7 per cent of permanent judges were women, prompting the South African Judicial Services Commission to call for more women to apply.[61] Similarly, in Canada, where women judges make up around 31.9 per cent of the judiciary, there are concerns that the appointment of women judges is beginning to stall. In 2011, just eight women were appointed to the federal judiciary, compared to 41 men.[62] Similar concerns have been expressed in relation to the representation of women judges in New Zealand and the US.[63] The tide for diversity appears – at least in some places – to be turning not towards greater diversity but less.

So, where does this leave us? What this statistical and comparative account reveals is not only that increases in judicial diversity are hard won, but also that continued progress cannot be taken as a given. We cannot assume that just because *some* gains have been made that more will follow, or indeed that the gains secured so far will remain.[64] Part of the problem may be that it is assumed that the arguments *for* judicial diversity no longer need to be made: 'there is such a widespread assumption that increasing representativeness in the judiciary is an inherently good thing it is generally regarded as either unnecessary or politically questionable to ask why the change is required'.[65] The speed and level of progress in securing greater judiciary diversity belies this assumption. It is crucial that we continue to make the arguments for *why* judicial diversity is important. Not least, but not only, because, as we shall see, although the common arguments for

58 European Commission, *More Women in Senior Positions: Key to Economic Stability and Growth*, Directorate-General for Employment, Social Affairs and Equal Opportunities Unit G1, January 2010, p. 66.

59 Cheryl Thomas, *Judicial Diversity in the United Kingdom and Other Jurisdictions: A Review of Research, Policies and Practices*, London: The Commission for Judicial Appointments, 2005, pp. 71–98.

60 Franny Rabkin, 'Women need a foot in the judiciary door', *Business Day*, 28 April 2010.

61 Sapa, 'JSC wants more black female judges', *Times LIVE*, 20 April 2011.

62 Kirk Makin, 'Appointments of female judges slump under Harper's Tories', *Globe and Mail*, 11 November 2011.

63 NWLC, 'Women in the Federal Judiciary'; NZHRC, *Women's Participation 2010*, p. 37.

64 Clare McGlynn made the same point in relation to the progress of women lawyers in 2003 ('The Status of Women Lawyers in the United Kingdom' in Ulrike Schultz and Gisela Shaw (eds), *Women in the World's Legal Professions*, Oxford: Hart Publishing, 2003, p. 139).

65 Kate Malleson, *The New Judiciary: The Effects of Expansion and Activism*, Dartmouth: Ashgate, 1999, p. 106.

judiciary diversity – grounded in democratic legitimacy, equality of opportunity, and the inclusion of varied perspectives – all point towards the value of a diverse judiciary, they suggest different routes for how we might get there.

Arguments for judicial diversity

Why should we be worried about judicial diversity? Arguments for judicial diversity typically fall into three broad categories.[66] The first focuses on how diversity impacts on perceptions of the judiciary. These highlight the importance of diversity in ensuring the legitimacy and authority of the judiciary itself, as well as a means of shoring up public support and confidence, particularly among under-represented groups.[67] The second category encompasses arguments from equity and social justice. These focus primarily on the individual, maintaining that all suitably qualified candidates should have the same opportunity to become a judge, and that more diverse judges would act as role models, encouraging a broader range of candidates to apply to become judges. The final category is the most contentious. This sees the importance of diversity in the different perspectives a more diverse judiciary will have on judging and suggests that a judiciary and its decision-making is improved by a greater diversity of decision-makers.

Legitimacy and public confidence

Arguments for judicial diversity on the basis of democratic legitimacy are grounded in the view that it is strategically unwise and symbolically problematic for the judiciary to be dominated by heterosexual, white, middle-class, male barristers from private practice: 'In a democratic society, in which we are all equal citizens, it is wrong in principle for that authority to be wielded by such a very unrepresentative section of the population'.[68] The judiciary should not be – or be seen to be – the preserve of persons of a particular sex, race, social class or educational background. Diversity goes to the heart of the judiciary's legitimacy. In part, this is due to the changing role of the judiciary. Once the judiciary is recognised as an instrument of state enforcement and authority, making (at least in its upper levels) decisions of political and constitutional importance, it is clear that the judiciary can no longer rely, if it ever could, on deriving its legitimacy through deference to its legal experience and social superiority. Proponents of this view argue that it is

---

66 See, eg, Brenda Hale, 'Equality and the Judiciary: Why Should We Want More Women Judges?', *Public Law*, 2001, 489; Ministry of Justice, *Appointments and Diversity: 'A Judiciary for the 21st Century'*, CP19/2011, London: Ministry of Justice, 2011, pp. 8–9; Neuberger Report, [22–26].

67 Although this is not to suggest that public confidence and legitimacy amount to the same thing. There are ways of increasing public confidence in the judiciary that would not necessarily do the same for its legitimacy (see further Lizzie Barmes, Written evidence to the HL Select Committee on the Constitution Inquiry into Judicial Appointments Process, October 2011).

68 Hale, 'Equality and the Judiciary', pp. 502–503.

no more acceptable for the judiciary to be unrepresentative than it is for the cabinet, or parliament generally.[69] Increasing its representativeness is necessary for the judiciary to demonstrate its 'social accountability', which in turn 'amounts to an essential form of legitimacy'.[70]

Of course, this simply prompts a further question as to what it means to say that the judiciary is representative. Clearly, it cannot mean that judges should be the envoys or spokespersons of particular communities; that they should speak on behalf of a specific group or location in the same way as, say, members of parliament represent their constituents or as one might represent one's country at the World Cup or Olympic Games. Any suggestion that judges 'represent' a particular group (in the sense of acting or speaking for them) would have serious implications for understandings of judicial impartiality. Judges should not *represent* anyone.[71] And so, it may be that deploying the terminology of 'representation' is misleading. It is, perhaps, more accurate to say that the judiciary ought to *reflect* the community it serves, to allow for discussion and assessment of the judiciary's make-up 'without the appearance of the judiciary speaking or acting for one particular element of society'.[72] However, on either view, the suggestion is not that the judiciary should mirror society in every demographic detail, that the judiciary ought to reflect society in some 'crude, identikit way' – so that if five per cent of the population support Plymouth Argyle, then so too must five per cent of the judiciary.[73] Nor is it to suggest that all identity characteristics are of the same relevance or that we cannot distinguish between them.[74] On any measure, however, what a representative judiciary *does* entail is a membership that is comprised of individuals with 'a wide variety of backgrounds, cultures, opinions, styles, perspectives, values and beliefs',[75] that the judiciary should *not* be restricted to or dominated by a single group as it is at present by white, straight, men.

In addition, it is suggested that a varied Bench is essential to build and shore up public support and confidence in the judiciary. Giving evidence to the House of

69 Sean O'Grady, 'A Government of straight, white, privately educated men', *The Independent*, 7 August 2010.
70 Malleson, *The New Judiciary*, p. 114.
71 Thomas Legg, 'Judges for the New Century', *Public Law*, 2001, 62, p. 69; Malleson, *The New Judiciary*, p. 108.
72 Philip Leith et al., *Propensity to Apply for Judicial Office Under the Northern Ireland Judicial Appointments System: A Qualitative Study for the Northern Ireland Judicial Appointments Commission*, Belfast: Law School Queens University Belfast, 2008, p. 48.
73 Paterson, *Lawyers and the Public Good*, pp. 141–142.
74 See generally Davina Cooper, *Challenging Diversity: Rethinking Equality and the Value of Difference*, Cambridge: Cambridge University Press, 2004; Erika Rackley, 'Rethinking Judicial Diversity' in Ulrike Schultz and Gisela Shaw (eds), *Gender and Judging*, Oxford: Hart Publishing, forthcoming.
75 Department Constitutional Affairs (DCA), *Increasing Diversity in the Judiciary*, CP25/04, London: Department for Constitutional Affairs, 2004, p. 57.

Lords Select Committee on the Constitution Inquiry into Judicial Appointments Process in 2012, Lord McNally noted:

> I do not think that you can have a really harmonious society if the judiciary, however excellent, does not seem to reflect the society to which it is dispensing justice. You do not sacrifice quality for that aim, but I think that we are right to point in the direction of having a judiciary that in some ways reflects the society to which it is delivering justice.[76]

The importance of members of the public seeing 'people like them' on the Bench should not be underestimated. The impetus for this, however, is not to avoid discrimination. Despite the obvious disjuncture between the make up of the judiciary and the demographic profile of those who come before it, particularly in the criminal courts, the claim is rarely that judges are deliberately (or even unintentionally) biased against particular groups. Rather the motivation is one of perception. Research suggests that confidence in the judiciary (and the legal system more generally) is undermined when people do not – or only rarely – see themselves represented on the Bench.[77] It feeds a sense that judges are 'not like us', that they are 'out of touch' and don't know 'what is going on in the world'.[78] And, while it is tempting to dismiss these views as dated and stereotypical, so long as the composition of the judiciary, particularly at its most senior levels, remains unrepresentative, these views and their real, adverse impact on public confidence in the judicial system are difficult to counter. Also related to this are arguments suggesting that insofar as the judiciary is unrepresentative, this makes poor use of human resources: 'modern societies cannot afford to lose the intellectual power and energy of half the population . . . We need the wisdom, not only of wise men, but of our wise women'.[79] Finally, the absence of diversity fuels a perception of cronyism or self-interest in the appointments process. After all, it is more difficult to maintain

76 Oral evidence to the HL Select Committee on the Constitution Inquiry into Judicial Appointments Process, 18 January 2012, Q394. The committee's final report is clear that, in their view, 'a more diverse judiciary . . . would increase public trust and confidence in the judiciary' (Judicial Appointments Report [74]).

77 RG Hood, Stephen Shute and Florence Seemungal, *Ethnic Minorities in the Criminal Courts: Perceptions of Fairness and Equality of Treatment*, 2/03, London: Lord Chancellor's Office, 2003; Richard Moorhead, Mark Sefton and Lesley Scanlan, *Just Satisfaction? What Drives Public and Participation Satisfaction with Courts and Tribunals*, London: Ministry of Justice, 2008; Ruth Hunt and Sam Dick, *Serves you Right: Lesbian and Gay Expectations of Discrimination*, London: Stonewall, 2008, p. 12.

78 Hazel Genn, *Paths to Justice: What People Do and Think About Going to Law*, Oxford: Hart Publishing, 1999, pp. 239–244; Anon, 'What planet ARE judges living on?', *Daily Mail*, 31 May 2006; James Slack, 'The judiciary is out of touch with the public, says poll', *Daily Mail*, 8 March 2007; Rebecca Ley, 'Judges so out of touch with victim's lives', *The Sun*, 27 June 2007; Stephen Glover, 'Judges are unelected, out of touch and shockingly arrogant', *Daily Mail*, 21 May 2011.

79 Beverley McLachlin in Lady Hale, 'Making a Difference? Why We Need a More Diverse Judiciary', *Northern Ireland Legal Quarterly*, 56(3), 2005, 281, p. 286.

that everyone has an equal opportunity to become a judge, and that the best people are in fact being appointed, when they are all drawn from the same narrow group. As Shami Chakrabarti, Director of Liberty, notes:

> What if the current flow of likely candidates to the Bench, and senior judiciary in particular, has been so clogged by advantage, disadvantage and untested assumption (be it on the part of the feeder professions rather than judicial appointments in isolation), that there can be no real confidence that centuries of self-replicated professionals from the same gender and social strata were always the most suitable people to serve in the judicial branch.[80]

Equity

This brings us to the second broad group of arguments for judicial diversity: those grounded in equity. While the arguments outlined above take as their starting point a focus on the benefit of diversity for the judiciary as a whole, arguments from equity prioritise the rights and opportunities of the individual to become a judge. On this view, assuming that legal talent and ability are evenly spread among men and women, the over-representation of men in the judiciary is itself evidence of unfairness or disadvantage in the way judges are appointed.[81] The argument is essentially one of equal opportunities and fairness: all suitably qualified candidates should have a 'fair crack of the whip' when it comes to the processes of and criteria for judicial appointment.[82] So put, there seems to be little room for disagreement. Few would claim that judicial appointment should be the preserve of a favoured few or that everyone who is sufficiently qualified should *not* have the same opportunity *and prospect* of becoming a judge. Not least because, as Madame Justice Beverley McLachlin, Chief Justice of the Supreme Court of Canada, suggests: 'in a world where one of the primary functions of the judiciary is to promote equality and fairness, it would be anomalous if the very instrument charged with that goal should itself exclude women from its ranks'.[83]

However, while the argument that women should have the same opportunities to participate in public life as men is uncontroversial, it leaves those arguing for diversity on this basis with relatively few places to go. The difficulties in translating the straightforward and relatively uncontentious principle of equality into practical proposals for change are familiar.[84] The same goes for arguments grounded in

---

80 Shami Chakrabarti, 'The Judiciary: Why Diversity and Merit Matter' in *Judicial Appointments: Balancing Independence, Accountability and Legitimacy*, London: Judicial Appointments Commission, 2010, p. 67, 69.

81 Kate Malleson, 'Justifying Gender Equality on the Bench: Why Difference Won't Do', *Feminist Legal Studies*, 11, 2003, 1, p. 15

82 Hale, 'Equality and the Judiciary', p. 490.

83 Hale, 'Making a Difference?', pp. 285–286.

84 Malleson, 'Justifying Gender Equality', p. 15.

legitimacy and public confidence. Both stumble at the same hurdle: merit. The argument typically goes something like this: Of course, all things being equal, it would be better if the judiciary were more diverse, and appointing candidates from groups currently under-represented would achieve this. But this should not be at the cost of appointing weaker judges, that is, judges who will do the job of judging less well. What matters most is that we appoint the best, most able judges. A candidate's gender (or any other identity characteristic for that matter) does not and should not come into the reckoning when making appointments, as it has no bearing on their ability to do the job. This point was made forcefully by Lord Judge at the first 'Equality in Justice Day' organised by the Ministry of Justice in 2008:

> I suggest to you it is perfectly obvious that background, ethnicity, religion, sexuality and gender are utterly irrelevant to the ability of an individual to be a good judge, and therefore they are utterly irrelevant to the selection and appointment of any judge. The single most important consideration is always whether the individual in question has the quality, the aptitude and ability to take on and perform the individual office to which he or she is aspiring. I don't think I have said anything controversial; there can't be anyone here who disagrees.[85]

Faced with this type of argument, proponents of judicial diversity on the basis of legitimacy or equity appear to have little room for manoeuvre. Either they confront it head on and argue for appointments on some basis *other than* merit, or they acknowledge the primacy of merit and are reduced to claiming that the way we have gone about identifying merit has been distorted by misconceptions about what merit is and where it might be found, hoping that, when those misconceptions are addressed, a more diverse judiciary will follow. As we shall see in Chapter 6, arguments for diversity grounded in difference offer a way out of this impasse. For now, however, a brief outline of difference-based arguments for judicial diversity will suffice.

Difference

Arguments for judicial diversity on the bases of 'difference' or 'perspective' are grounded in the view there is a value in individual judges bringing their background and experiences to bear on their decision-making; that the benefit of increased diversity lies in the substantive difference it will make to how our judges judge. Without doubt, this argument is the most disputed of the three categories:[86]

85 Lord Judge, 'Equality in Justice Day', Royal Courts of Justice, London, 24 October 2008. He repeated this view to the House of Lords Constitution Committee: 'It is axiomatic that judges must be appointed on merit' (Judicial Appointments Report, [83]).
86 Malleson, *The New Judiciary*, pp. 106–112.

The view that diversity on the courts enriches judicial decision-making, that the interplay of perspectives of judges from diverse backgrounds and experiences makes for *better* judicial decision-making, especially on our appellate courts . . . invites some controversy . . . we start to get nervous about the idea that the inclusion of women and/or judges of color might lead to *different* or even *better* judicial decision-making.[87]

Difference arguments for judicial diversity not only go to the heart of understandings of who the judge is and what judges do, but also, as we shall see in Chapter 5, run the gauntlet of gender essentialism. They start from the position that, far from being extraneous, a judge's gender, ethnicity, sexuality and so on all have a bearing on the performance of their judicial role, and that as a result that *who* the judge is matters.[88] These arguments build from the observation that judging is more than the application of pre-determined rules, and hence requires, at times, the judge to make decisions guided by his or her own sense of what the law should be, the values and principles it should embody and promote. The claim then is that how the judge answers such questions will, at least in part, be a product of their background. Gender – as one relevant background characteristic – is amongst those factors which contribute to a judge's perception of what the law ought to be and hence which will make a difference to their judging.

One response to this has been to doubt whether it really is true to say that women judge any differently from men. For unless and until we can show that women are likely to differ in their judging, arguments for diversity on this basis cannot get off the ground. And even if we could show this, this does not as yet constitute an argument *for* judicial diversity. Indeed, on one view, insofar as greater diversity means that 'unrepresentative certainty' is replaced by the unpredictability of multiple, diverse perspectives, it appears to point in exactly the opposite direction.[89] So, for these and other reasons, there has been a tendency to downplay or dismiss difference-based-arguments from the arsenal of reasons for judicial diversity.

Nonetheless, difference may well be our best route to securing a representative Bench. In the first instance, one advantage of difference-based arguments for judicial diversity is that they appear to avoid the problems faced by legitimacy and equity arguments when faced with the commitment to appoint on merit. On this view diversity is relevant to merit because it goes directly to how judges judge, to the substantive impact a more diverse Bench will have on judicial decision-making, rather than simply to the gains of diversity in terms of public confidence and improved opportunities for those wishing to join. Moreover, as we shall see, one of the greatest obstacles women judges have faced is the perception that they are

87 Sherrilyn A Ifill, 'Judicial Diversity', *Green Bag*, 13, 2D, 2009, 45, pp. 49–50.
88 Sandra Berns, *To Speak as a Judge – Difference, Voice and Power*, Dartmouth: Ashgate, 1999, p. 8.
89 Malleson, *The New Judiciary*, p. 111.

indeed different from their male counterparts. The different approaches women judges have taken have often led to accusations of bias and impropriety. So long as this is the fate of the woman judge, the Bench will continue to be a place where women judges often feel unwelcome and where genuine equality will be out of reach. As such, there is reason to think that one precondition to achieving real diversity is an acceptance of the differences different judges can make. Here too difference arguments may provide a way forward. Whatever one's views on how often women judges will make a difference, on where and when gender does or should have an impact on judicial decision-making, progress toward a more diverse judiciary will be harder and slower unless and until differences in the way women judge, and the different perspectives and insights they can offer, are acknowledged and welcomed.

Chapter 2

Delivering diversity in the legal profession

There are no barriers to the advancement of women apart from those they choose themselves or those that are inherent in their biology.

(Martin Mears, former President of the Law Society, 1996)[1]

I don't think there are any barriers to women progressing through the profession, other than the barriers that they place on themselves such as having children. They don't have to have children if they don't want to.

(Male, fee-earner, 2010)[2]

There appears to be a consensus that a diverse judiciary is a good thing. And yet, as we have seen in Chapter 1, progress towards greater diversity has all but stalled. So why is this? Why do we not have a more diverse judiciary? Typically, two reasons are given: first, the lack of diversity in the legal profession and, second, inequities in the processes by which judges are selected. On this view, if we want a more diverse judiciary, these are the issues we need to address. The assumption is that once we do – once there are more women and other under-represented groups in the legal profession *and* once the judicial appointments process is fair and open – a diverse Bench will follow as a matter of course. However, as we shall see, things are not quite this simple. Women and other non-traditional lawyers continue to face significant structural and cultural barriers to their progression. These prevent them from reaching the upper levels of the profession from where they might join the Bench. Changing the make-up of the legal profession is proving to be a task even harder than increasing diversity on the Bench alone.

Rejecting the trickle-up argument

Diversity in the judiciary is directly linked to diversity in the legal profession. Even if everyone agrees that we want and need a more diverse judiciary and there is the

1 In Clare McGlynn, *The Woman Lawyer – Making the Difference*, London: Butterworths, 1998, p. 98.
2 In Richard Collier, *Men, Law and Gender: Essays on the 'Men' of Law*, London: Routledge, 2010, p. 176.

political will to push for it, we will not get it – cannot get it – unless there are (qualified) women available to appoint. Judges do not, to use Michael Beloff's words, 'spring like Botticelli's Venus full grown from a standing start'.[3] So long as we select judges from the legal profession, the make-up of the judiciary will largely reflect that of the profession. Accordingly a diverse legal profession is a prerequisite for a diverse judiciary. And herein lies the problem. Traditionally, the legal profession has been male dominated. Though formal barriers excluding women completely from the profession were removed by virtue of the Sex Disqualification (Removal) Act 1919, as recently as the mid-1970s male solicitors continued to outnumber their female counterparts by 20–1, and nearly half of all sets of barristers' chambers were still to have their first woman member.[4] Inevitably perhaps, this absence of women was replicated in the judiciary. In 1976, there were just 10 women working as full-time, salaried judges (around 2.3 per cent) and just two women sitting on the High Court bench.[5]

Of course, the converse of this argument is that once there *are* more women in the legal profession, then so long as the appointments process is fair, it will only be a matter of time before women 'trickle up' into the judiciary. And so all we need to do is to wait for them to get there. From the mid-1980s this 'trickle-up' argument was presented as both the explanation for the absence of judicial diversity and the solution as to how to get it.[6] It attracted many high profile supporters, particularly among the judiciary,[7] no doubt, at least in part, because it allowed

3   Michael Beloff, 'Sisters-in-Law: The Irresistible Rise of Women in Wigs', The Gray's Inn Reading 2009.

4   Albie Sachs and Joan Hoff Wilson, *Sexism and the Law: A Study of Male Beliefs and Judicial Bias*, Oxford: Martin Robertson, 1978, p. 174.

5   Helena Kennedy, 'Women at the Bar' in Robert Hazell (ed), *The Bar on Trial*, London: Quartet Books, 1978, p. 148, 149. Helena Kennedy strongly refutes the assumption that there were not sufficient women in the pool of potential judges to allow for the appointment of more women judges, even in 1976. She suggests that there were 80 women eligible for judicial appointment, of whom just 17 (21%) were appointed, compared to 53% of men in the same pool (p. 150).

6   See generally Kate Malleson, 'Prospects for Parity: the Position of Women in the Judiciary of England and Wales' in Ulrike Schultz and Gisela Shaw (eds), *Women in the World's Legal Professions*, Oxford: Hart Publishing, 2003, p. 175, 177–180.

7   See, for example, Lord Mackay, 'In the News', *New Law Journal*, 145, 14 April 1995, 514; Thomas Legg (Permanent Secretary of the Lord Chancellor's Department) in Home Affairs Select Committee, *Home Affairs Select Committee Report on Judicial Appointments Procedures*, London: HMSO, 1996 [79]; Lord Irvine, 'Speech to the Association of Women Barristers', The Barbican, London, 11 February 1998; Lord Bingham, HC Home Affairs Committee – Minutes of Evidence, 17 March 1998, Q124; Lord Irvine, HC Committee on the Lord Chancellor's Department – Minutes of Evidence, 2 April 2003, Q63; Lord Falconer, 'Foreword' to Commission for Judicial Appointments, *Annual Report 2003*, London: Commission for Judicial Appointments, 2003, p. 4; Lord Lloyd, Oral Evidence to the Constitutional Affairs Committee, Inquiry on Judicial Appointments and a Supreme Court (Court of Final Appeal), 27 November 2003, Q215 (HC 48-i Session 2003–04); Department for Constitutional Affairs, *Increasing Diversity in the Judiciary*, CP25/04, London: Department for Constitutional Affairs, 2004 [1.16] and more recently Lord Chancellor, House of Lords Select Committee on the Constitution, Annual Meeting with the Lord Chancellor, 19 January 2011, and Jonathan Sumption, Justice Committee 'Judicial Appointments Commission', Minutes of Evidence, HC 449-i, 7 September 2010, Q24.

them to talk confidently about progress in the not too distant future, while doing relatively little to bring it about. The trickle-up hypothesis underpinned Lord Taylor's bold prediction, speaking as Lord Chief Justice in 1992, that 'a substantial number of appointments' would be made in the next five years to redress the 'obvious' imbalance in the judiciary.[8] And also Lord Bingham's belief in 1998 that it would be a 'very short time' before a woman was appointed to the position of Lord Chief Justice.[9]

Neither Lord Taylor nor Lord Bingham's optimism was entirely without foundation (though in both cases the anticipated timescale was always improbable[10]). Since the mid-1980s women had been beginning to make their presence felt in both branches of the legal profession. The number of women enrolling at university law schools had been steadily increasing since the late-1970s and by 1987 women accounted for 46.6 per cent of law graduates in England and Wales.[11] From the outset female law students have outperformed their male counterparts, achieving a higher proportion of first class and upper-second class degrees. In 1986–1987, for the first time more women than men passed their professional exams to enter the solicitors' profession (with significantly more women passing first time) and, in the first eight months of this period, women secured half of all new training contracts.[12] In the same period, women accounted for 37 per cent of those called to the Bar, an increase from just 8.2 per cent in 1970.[13] By the early 1990s, these figures had continued to increase so that by 1992–1993 half of all law graduates and those entering the solicitors' profession[14] and 42.7 per cent of those called to the Bar were women.[15] And yet, despite this 'torrent' of women entering the pipeline,[16] three years after Lord Taylor's deadline had

8 Lord Taylor, *The Judiciary in the Nineties*, The Richard Dimbleby Lecture, 1992.
9 Lord Bingham, HC Home Affairs Committee – Minutes of Evidence, 17 March 1998, Q125. There has not yet been a female Lord Chief Justice.
10 The 'trickle-up' argument was never going to be a 'quick fix' solution to the lack of diversity in the judiciary. Even assuming broadly equivalent rates of progress, we could only expect equal numbers of women joining the legal profession to lead to equal numbers of women being appointed to the Bench after 20 years or so. Thus, we might only reasonably expect a *significant* increase in the number of women appointed, that is in addition to the appointments we might reasonably expect from a smaller pool, from the mid-2000s onwards. However, as Table 1.2 shows, even on its own terms, the rate of progress remains slow; women are not progressing onto the Bench in the same proportion to their presence in the legal profession.
11 Peter Marks, *Annual Statistical Report 1988*, London: Law Society, 1988, figures 6.2 and 6.4.
12 At the time these were called 'Articles'. Peter Marks, *Annual Statistical Report 1987*, London: Law Society, 1987, [0.2].
13 Bar Council figures (on file with author).
14 John Jenkins and Danielle Walker, *Annual Statistical Report 1993*, London: Law Society, 1993, tables 11.8 and 12.7.
15 Bar Council figures (on file with author).
16 Sally J. Kenney, 'Gender on the Agenda: How the Paucity of Women Judges Became an Issue', *The Journal of Politics*, 70(3), 2008, 717, p. 727.

passed, just 9.1 per cent of the judiciary were women, an increase of just 4.7 per cent on 1989.[17]

By the turn of the millennium, though the view still held sway among many judges and politicians, it was becoming increasingly apparent that the 'trickle-up' response to the problem of judicial diversity had largely failed to deliver.[18] Though there had been some limited progress, it was simply not happening fast enough. As Katherine Rake from the Fawcett Society, giving evidence to the House of Commons Constitutional Affairs Committee, noted:

> We talk about the trickle-up effect and when we come to the current system it has taken us 81 years to get from the first woman appointed to the Bar to the first woman Law Lord. In terms of getting parity we would be expecting – [relying] purely [on the] trickle-up – to wait for another century, maybe two centuries for that to happen.[19]

The 'upbeat rhetoric' of the early 1990s began to be significantly downgraded.[20] In 2003, Colin Campbell, then the First Commissioner for Judicial Appointments, indicated that it would be 'a hard job' and a further seven to 10 years before the balance between women and men in the judiciary was addressed.[21] In 2005, the then Lord Chancellor lowered expectations still further stating that within five years he wished to see every 'under-represented group applying in proportion to their presence in the pool',[22] a significantly lower target than Campbell's measure of parity. In the event, neither target was reached. More recently, the 2010 Advisory Panel for Judicial Diversity, chaired by Baroness Neuberger, gave itself a further 10 years in which to achieve its rather vague 'vision' of a 'much more diverse judiciary at all levels'.[23]

More recently, many senior policy makers, judges and politicians have made efforts to distance themselves from – or positively reject – the beleaguered

---

17 McGlynn, *The Woman Lawyer*, p. 173.
18 This is not to suggest that the 'trickle-up' argument was without critics before this. See, eg, JUSTICE, *The Judiciary in England and Wales*, London: JUSTICE, 1992; McGlynn, *The Woman Lawyer*, p. 174; Kate Malleson, *The New Judiciary: The Effects of Expansion and Activism*, Dartmouth: Ashgate, 1999, pp. 115–123.
19 Katherine Rake, Oral evidence to the Committee on Constitutional Affairs, 18 November 2003, Q152 (unrevised transcript).
20 Kate Malleson, 'Diversity in the Judiciary: the Case for Positive Action', *Journal of Law and Society*, 36(3), 2009, 376, 379.
21 Colin Campbell, Oral evidence to the Constitutional Affairs Committee, Inquiry on Judicial Appointments and a Supreme Court (Court of Final Appeal), 11 November 2003, Q4 (HC 48-i Session 2003–04).
22 Lord Falconer, 'Increasing Judicial Diversity: The Next Steps', Commission for Judicial Appointments, Institute of Mechanical Engineers, London, 2 November 2005.
23 Advisory Panel on Judicial Diversity, *The Report of the Advisory Panel on Judicial Diversity 2010*, London: Ministry of Justice, 2010, [15] (Neuberger Report).

trickle-up solution to judicial diversity.[24] In March 2011, Lord McNally, Minister of State for the Ministry of Justice and leader of the latest Judicial Diversity Taskforce, responding to a question on the progress made in improving gender and ethnic diversity in judicial appointments, categorically rejected the trickle-up argument: 'as far as I am concerned, the concept of trickle-up is not a response to the diversity problem that we face in the judiciary'.[25] In the same year, Lady Hale commented in an interview with *The Guardian* that more should be done to enable more women and BME candidates to join the judiciary: 'I don't think it's a matter of time . . . People have been saying it's a matter of time for a very long time'.[26]

Nevertheless, as we shall see in Chapter 3, while the trickle-up may no longer be presented as the solution to judicial diversity, vestiges of it remain. The lack of diversity in the legal profession continues to be deployed as an explanation for the slow progress toward judicial diversity. However, it is clear that the difficulties with the trickle-up response go deeper than the length of time it is taking to happen. The trickle-up argument fails to take into account complex structural and cultural factors within both the appointments process and legal profession which prevent women, and other non-traditional candidates from joining the Bench. It assumes that men and women, solicitors and barristers, experience the legal profession in the same way, that they have the same opportunities for progression and promotion. But this is not the case. For instance, one common example given for why there are fewer women and solicitors (of either sex) in the judiciary is the continuing de facto requirement of sitting as a recorder before appointment to the High Court. In 1996, this was identified by a number of witnesses to the Home Affairs Select Committee's inquiry into judicial appointments procedures as contributing to the lack of women and solicitors on the Bench,[27] and again, in 2011, in evidence to the House of Lords Constitution Committee Inquiry into Judicial Appointments.[28] Research suggests that for women barristers already 'trying to juggle the demands of practice and family-life', adding part-time judicial

24 Commission for Judicial Appointments, *Annual Report 2003*, [5.49], Brenda Hale, 'Equality and the Judiciary: Why Should We Want More Women Judges?', *Public Law*, 2001, 489, p. 492; Mrs Justice Dobbs, 'Diversity in the Judiciary – Lecture', Queen Mary University of London, London, 17 October 2007; Kenneth Clarke, Oral evidence to the HL Select Committee on the Constitution Inquiry into Judicial Appointments Process, 18 January 2012, Q380 (Constitution Committee Inquiry).

25 Lord McNally, Question on Judicial Appointments, House of Lords Main Chamber Debate, 726 (127), 17 March 2011 [348].

26 Owen Bowcott, 'UK Supreme Court's only female judge calls for more diversity in appointments', *The Guardian*, 25 October 2011.

27 Kate Malleson, *The New Judiciary: The Effects of Expansion and Activism*, Dartmouth: Ashgate, 1999, p. 117.

28 Thomas Legg, Written evidence to Constitution Committee Inquiry; Supporting Higher Courts Advocates, Written evidence to Constitution Committee Inquiry; Cordella Bart-Stuart, Oral evidence to Constitution Committee Inquiry, 23 November 2011, Q279 (uncorrected transcript).

appointment into this mix can seem like an 'impossibility',[29] while solicitors worry that their desire to undertake such work will be seen by their partners as indicating a lack of commitment to the practice. In particular, '[w]omen solicitors who had nevertheless become recorders thought that they had had to struggle to do so in the face of strong opposition from their firms, and had feared that they might be committing "career suicide"'.[30]

However, the crux of the difficulty with the trickle-up argument is that it rests on the assumption that once women enter the legal profession they will progress at more or less equal rates to men, and hence that, given time and weight of numbers, the composition of the senior levels of the legal profession will reflect that at entry level. In other words, the trickle-up approach to judicial diversity first requires a trickle-up in the legal profession. This has not happened. Women are not progressing through the legal professions in the same proportion in which they enter, or at the same rate as men. As a result, the increase in the number of women joining the legal profession has not been matched by a similar increase in the number of women in the pool of potential judges. Men continue to dominate the upper echelons of the legal profession. In fact, far from trickling-up, women lawyers are actually treading water – working hard to stay in more or less the same place.

Treading water – a statistical profile of women in the legal profession

Barristers

Historically, women have tended to become barristers rather than solicitors.[31] This meant that, though numbers were small, until the increase in the number of women joining the legal profession in the mid-1980s women were better represented at the Bar than in the solicitors' profession.[32] However, though women

---

29 Hazel Genn, *The Attractiveness of Senior Judicial Appointment to Highly Qualified Practitioners – Report to the Judicial Executive Board*, London: Directorate of Judicial Office for England and Wales, 2008, [75].
30 ibid.
31 The focus on women here is not to deny the importance of other diversity characteristics which are largely absent in the legal profession or the extent to which the *combination* of, say, gender *and* race work to further disadvantage many lawyers. However, many of the quantitative and qualitative surveys of the legal profession drawn on in this chapter consider identity characteristics in isolation, with the result that data on BME women or women from lower socio-economic groups is scarce and patchy. Hilary Sommerlad et al's *Barriers and Individual Choice* research for the Legal Services Board and the Bar Council and Bar Standards Board's *Barristers' Working Lives* report are excellent recent exceptions to this (Hilary Sommerlad, Lisa Webley, Liz Duff, Daniel Muzio and Jennifer Tomlison, *Diversity in the Legal Profession in England and Wales: A Qualitative Study of Barriers and Individual Choice*, London: University of Westminster, 2010; Geoff Pike and Dilys Robinson, *Barristers' Working Lives: A Biennial Survey of the Bar 2011*, London: Bar Council and Bar Standards Board, 2012).
32 Sachs and Wilson, *Sexism and the Law*, p. 174. Women have made up a larger proportion of the solicitors' profession since the mid-1980s.

have been joining the barrister's profession in equal or slightly larger numbers than men since 2000, their overall presence has stabilised at around 32–35 per cent.[33] In 2010, 34.8 per cent of the practising profession were women.[34] The Bar Council and Bar Standards Board *Working Lives* survey in 2011 found that one in eight women barristers (13 per cent) are from a BME background, compared to 8 per cent of male barristers.[35] Women barristers and those from a BME background were also more likely to have attended a state school and less likely to have studied at Oxford or Cambridge than their white, male counterparts.[36] One per cent of women barristers identified themselves as gay or lesbian.[37]

However, behind these headline statistics, figures suggest that women barristers still find it harder to find tenancy than their male counterparts. In 2009–2010, despite higher numbers of women than men completing the Bar Professional Training Course (BPTC), being awarded pupillage and being called to the Bar, 56 per cent of those gaining tenancy and newly employed barristers were men.[38] This difference was even more marked among BME candidates. In 2008–2009, 44 per cent of students on the BPTC were from a BME background, compared to

Table 2.1 Women entrants to the legal profession, 1970–2010

Year	Women called to the Bar	Women admitted to the Solicitors' Roll
1970	77 (8.2%)	62 (6.1%) (1965 figure)
1975	112 (11.2%)	283 (15.3%) (1973 figure)
1980	245 (28.4%)	959 (37%) (1983 figure)
1985	282 (29.8%)	1,111 (41.4%)
1990	484 (40.3%)	1,739 (46.6%)
1995	694 (43.5%)	2,466 (52.3%)
2000	648 (46.1%)	3,218 (53.1%)
2005	722 (49%)	4,438 (60.3%)
2010	976 (52.7%)	5,011 (59.1%)

Source: Bar Council and Law Society Annual Reports, with the exception of 1970–1985 solicitors' figures (McGlynn, *The Woman Lawyer – Making the Difference*, p. 95).

33 Bar Council figures (on file with author).
34 Jennifer Sauboorah, *Bar Barometer Trends in the Profile of the Bar*, London: Bar Council, December 2011, p. 13.
35 Pike and Robinson, *Barristers' Working Lives*, p. 13. BME barristers make up 10.1% of the practising profession (where ethnicity is known) (Sauboorah, *Bar Barometer*, Dec 2011, p. 38, 17).
36 Pike and Robinson, *Barristers' Working Lives*, p. 16. More than 2,900 practising barristers responded to this survey, and given this the report's authors are confident in the reliability of the results as the demographic profile of the respondents mirrors that of the Bar as a whole.
37 ibid., p. 81.
38 Sauboorah, *Bar Barometer*, Dec 2011, p. 7. Pupillage is a period of supervised practical training which must be completed in order to practise as a barrister in England and Wales. Securing 'tenancy' means being accepted as a permanent member of a particular set of chambers.

just 15.4 per cent of those registering for pupillage in 2009–2010.[39] Women are also under-represented, as a proportion, at the more prestigious self-employed Bar, from which the vast majority of Queen's Counsel (QC) and High Court judges are appointed (Table 2.2). In 2010, women made up around one-third of the self-employed Bar (32 per cent) compared to just under half of employed barristers (46.4 per cent).[40] The same is true of BME barristers, who make up just 9.7 per cent of the self-employed Bar.[41]

The disparity between women and men becomes even more pronounced among senior barristers. The number of women QCs remains significantly lower than men. Although the number of women QCs has more than doubled since the early 1990s, in 2010, of the 1,400 QCs at the self-employed Bar, a little over 150 were women (Table 2.3).[42] Though proponents of the trickle-up argument suggest that this is largely the result of the historical absence of women in the profession,

Table 2.2 Women at the self-employed Bar in England and Wales, 1955–2010

Year	Women	% Women
1921	20	–
1929	67	–
1955	64	3.2
1965	84	4.4
1970	147	5.7
1975	258	7.0
1986	747	13.6
1990	1,163	17.5
1995	1,900	22.4
2000	2,638	26
2005	3,543	30
2006	3,653	30.4
2007	3,731	30.9
2008	3,772	31.1
2009	3,860	31.5
2010	3,977	32

Source: Bar Council (figures on file with author), with the exception of 1921 and 1929 figures (Beloff, 'Sisters-in-Law'); 1955–1975 figures (Kennedy, 'Women at the Bar', p. 149).

39 Jennifer Sauboorah, *Bar Barometer Trends in the Profile of the Bar*, London: Bar Council, March 2011, p. 7; Sauboorah, *Bar Barometer*, Dec 2011, p. 41. There are no figures for BME women.
40 Sauboorah, *Bar Barometer*, Dec 2011, pp. 14–16.
41 ibid., p. 20.
42 ibid., p. 28. Queen's Counsel (QC) is an award of excellence in advocacy in the higher courts. Though the award can be made to both solicitors and barristers, in practice the vast majority of QCs are barristers.

Table 2.3 Women QCs at the self-employed bar, 1976–2010

Year	Women	% Women
1976	4	1.1
1986	20	3.6
1996	60	6.5
2006	118	9.2
2007	116	9.5
2008	127	10
2009	139	10.5
2010	152	10.8

Source: Bar Council (figures on file with author), with exception of 1976 figures (Sacks and Wilson, Sexism and the Law, p. 174).

the reality is not quite so simple. Even allowing for a slower progression of women through the profession, the number of women QCs does not reflect the number of women barristers in practice at the self-employed Bar with the appropriate level of experience. In 2002 just 8.3 per cent of QCs were women, despite women making up around 13 per cent of barristers of 20 years' or more call.[43] By 2010, though the number of women QCs has increased, this gap had widened: the percentage of practising women barristers with over 20 years' service was just under double (18.6 per cent) that of female QCs (10.9 per cent).[44]

It is clear then that the over-representation of men at QC level is not simply down to a lack of eligible women. There are – and have been for some time – a significant number of women barristers who fall within what may be considered the pool of potential QCs. One reason for this disparity is the continuing low number of applications from women. Despite changes to the appointments process in 2006, moving from a system of closed appointments to open applications, senior women barristers continue to under-apply. This low application rate is particularly worrying as, on average, barristers will make two or three applications before being successful. In the 2010–2011 QC appointments round, women made

43 Lord Chancellor's Department, *Judicial Appointments Annual Report 2001–2002*, London: Lord Chancellor's Department, 2002, [1.16]. Though this is a slight improvement on earlier figures. In 1992, women represented just 5.3% of QCs, despite accounting for 15.3% of barristers with 10 years' service or more and 11.88% of those with between 15–22 years of call (Lesley Holland and Lynne Spender, *Without Prejudice? Sex Equality at the Bar and in the Judiciary*, Bournemouth: TMS Management Consultants, 1992, p. 19).

44 Bar Council figures (on file with author). Ethnicity data is not broken down by sex; however, we know the proportion of QCs from a BME background at the self-employed Bar increased from just 3.6 per cent in 2006 to 4.9 per cent in 2010, despite 8.8 per cent of barristers at the practising Bar in 2010 at over 15 years' call having a BME background (Sauboorah, *Bar Barometer*, December 2011, p. 19, 30).

up just 16 per cent of applicants (41 applications),[45] despite 31 per cent (746) of barristers between 15–20 years' call being women, with the result that the number of men appointed outnumbered women by 3:1.[46]

Men also continue to dominate leadership and management positions. Just under 10 per cent of heads of chambers in England and Wales are women.[47] At the Inns of Court, women represent between 9.2 per cent and 15.5 per cent of elected Benchers,[48] averaging at 11.5 per cent,[49] and an increase from 6.1 per cent in 1996.[50] However, the proportion of women decreases to 10.6 per cent once honorary Benchers, typically eminent judges and lawyers from other jurisdictions, are included. At the Bar Council, which represents barristers in England and Wales, men make up 67.5 per cent of current council members, though in 2012 it has a woman vice-chair.[51] The Bar Council has had just one woman chair: Lady Justice Hallett in 1998.

Solicitors

Despite a significant increase in the number of women becoming solicitors and reports of 'record-breaking' appointments of women as partners,[52] men still continue to dominate the solicitors' profession at its most senior levels. Women have accounted for the majority of trainees since 1987–1988,[53] and between 2000–2010 the number of women holding practising certificates rose by almost 80 per cent, almost twice that of the legal profession as a whole.[54] In 2010, women represented 45.8 per cent of practising certificate holders, a slight decrease from 2009.[55] 13.8 per cent of women solicitors are from a BME group, compared to 8.8

---

45 ibid. It should be noted, however, that women applicants stand a better chance of success than their male counterparts. 66% of women were successful (up from 43% in the previous competition) compared to just 48% of men (Joan Higgins, 'Report of the Queen's Counsel Selection Panel for England and Wales 2010–11 Competition Awards', March 2011, [3.1–3.2]). By way of contrast BME lawyers made up 8% of applicants and 60% of appointees in the 2010–2011 competition (ibid., [3.1]).

46 Bar Council figures (on file with author).

47 As listed in A–Z of Barristers Chambers Online in the Barristers Magazine website (where sex is known) [accessed 11 August 2011].

48 Benchers are senior barristers involved in the running of the Inns of Court.

49 Figure provided by the Inns of Court, on file with author (July 2011).

50 McGlynn, *The Woman Lawyer*, p. 128.

51 Figures taken from the Bar Council website [accessed 13 February 2012].

52 Kit Chellel, 'Female partners defy glass ceiling in record numbers', *The Lawyer*, 8 September 2008.

53 John Jenkins, *Trends in the Solicitors' Profession – Annual Statistical Report 1994*, London: Law Society, 1994, table 9.9.

54 Nina Fletcher and Yulia Muratova, *Trends in the Solicitors' Profession: Annual Statistical Report 2010*, London: Law Society, 2011, p. 5.

55 Law Society, *Diversity Profile of the Profession: A Short Synopsis*, London: Law Society, 2011, p. 7.

Table 2.4 Women solicitors in England and Wales, 1950–2010

Year	Women	% Women
1950	26 (admitted to Roll in year, not total)	
1955	34 (admitted to Roll in year, not total)	
1960	672	2.9
1965	873	3.4
1970	1,360	4.5
1975	2,255	6.7
1980	5,883	11.8
1985	10,732	17.4
1990	16,728	24.0
1995	26,316	31.8
2000	39,183	37.5
2005	53,779	42.6
2006	57,249	43.6
2007	59,587	44.3
2008	63,169	45.2
2009	66,996	46.1
2010	53,966	45.5

Source: Law Society, *Number of Solicitors on the Roll and Practising Certificate Holders since 1950* – Fact Sheet information series and Law Society Annual Reports.

per cent of male solicitors.[56] Just 0.3 per cent of solicitors identify as a gay woman or lesbian.[57]

However, despite these figures, this has not been reflected in the number of women and BME solicitors reaching senior positions in the profession. In 2010, just over 21.1 per cent of women solicitors were partners, compared to 48.1 per cent of men,[58] and women made up just under a quarter of all partners.[59] Since 2000, the Law Society's *Trends in the Solicitors' Profession* annual statistical reports have noted that even after adjusting for level of experience women achieve partnership at a slower and lower rate than men.[60] As Table 2.5 shows, in 1992, 79 per cent of male solicitors with 10–19 years' experience were partners, compared to 53 per cent of women with the same experience. Ten years later,

56 ibid., p. 9. BME solicitors accounted for 11.1% of solicitors with practising certificates in 2010.
57 ibid., p. 10. The Law Society's 2009 Omnibus survey found that just over a quarter of solicitors had been privately educated (compared to a national average of 7%), and just over a third had one or both parents in a professional occupation. Just 7% of solicitors had attended the Universities of Oxford or Cambridge (compared to 14% in 1999) and, around 65% of BME solicitors had studied at post-1992 universities compared to 41.8% of their white counterparts (ibid., pp. 11–12).
58 Fletcher, *Trends in the Solicitors' Profession 2010*, p. 15.
59 Bill Cole, Nina Fletcher, Tara Chittenden and Joanne Cox, *Trends in the Solicitors' Profession: Annual Statistical Report 2009*, London: Law Society, 2010, [2.09] (2009 figures).
60 Law Society, *Trends in the Solicitors' Profession* Annual Statistical Reports 2000–2009 [2.10].

Table 2.5 Women and men solicitors in private practice who were either partners or sole practitioners 10–19 years after qualification as a percentage, 1992–2009

Year	% women	% men	% difference
1992	53.0	79.0	26.0
1997	63.1	87.7	24.6
2002	54.7	82.3	27.6
2003	52.1	78.7	26.6
2004	48.8	73.0	24.2
2005	45.4	67.8	22.4
2006	40.3	60.0	19.7
2007	49.2	77.8	28.6
2008	48.2	77.3	29.1
2009	46.7	74.7	28.0

Source: Law Society Annual Reports (1987–2009).

though the number of women with 10–19 years' experience who were either partners or sole practitioners has risen slightly overall, the gap between the percentage of men and women reaching these positions had widened. In 2010, men were still significantly more likely to become partners than their female colleagues.[61] And, although in the same year just over a quarter of BME solicitors are partners, they were more likely to be sole partners or partners in smaller (2–4 partner) firms.[62] BME solicitors represent five per cent of partners overall, a figure which has increased by just one per cent in the past six years.[63]

Women solicitors also tend to be paid less than their male colleagues. In 2010, women trainees were paid an average of 5.7 per cent – about £522 a year – less than their male counterparts.[64] The difference is greatest in the North East of England where male trainees earn, on average, £1,453 a year more than women trainees.[65] This gap increases further up the pay scale. A Law Society survey in 2007 revealed that male solicitors earned an average of £19,000 a year more than women solicitors. The median yearly salary for male solicitors was £60,000 compared to £41,000 for women, a pay gap of 31.85 per cent (although this decreases to 7.6 per cent once factors such as grade, size of firm, region, career breaks taken, area of law and hours worked are taken into account).[66] A similar

61 Cole et al, *Trends in the Solicitors' Profession 2009*, [2.10], chart 3.
62 Law Society figures (on file with author). There are no figures for BME women partners.
63 Dale McEwan, 'Ethnic minorities find top jobs out of reach', *The Lawyer*, 21 November 2011.
64 Cole et al, *Trends in the Solicitors' Profession 2009*, [8.14], table 8.13.
65 Anon, 'It still pays to be a man – annual traineeship stats published', *Solicitors Journal*, 5 April 2011.
66 Law Society, *Earnings and Work of Private Practice Solicitors in 2007 – Executive Summary*, London: Law Society, 2008, p. 5.

survey the following year revealed that the median pay gap had decreased to 28.9 per cent, and to 6 per cent once adjusted.[67] Explanations for the ongoing pay disparity differ. Responding to the 2008 figures, the Law Society tried – and failed – to distance itself from arguments of gender-based discrimination by suggesting that the difference is largely attributable to differences between women and men solicitors in terms of experience, grade and types of firms worked in.[68] As we shall see, these differences between women and men lawyers' career choices and paths are not gender-neutral. The fact that women are more likely to work in smaller firms and in areas of the law which attract lower pay and status simply prompts a further question as to why this is. Moreover, this still leaves 6 per cent of the pay gap attributable to '*possible* discrimination by employers'.[69] Little wonder that over 60 per cent of women lawyers surveyed in 2011 believed that they are paid less than their male peers – they probably are.[70]

Research has consistently shown that women solicitors are frustrated by the disparities within the profession in terms of pay and promotion. A survey of women solicitors in Scotland in 2000 found that 43 per cent of women solicitors thought recruitment practices within the profession favoured men, with 93 per cent believing that informal networks operated in favour of men.[71] A similar survey of solicitors in England and Wales in 2004 found that almost a quarter of women assistant/associate solicitors were either fairly or very dissatisfied with opportunities to obtain partnership, compared to just 12.8 per cent of their male counterparts.[72] This has been exacerbated by the introduction of a 'counsel' rank by the larger city law firms as an alternative to partnership, which creates a further opportunity for women to be sidelined with the effect that 'disproportionate numbers of women are found just below the glass ceiling or firmly on what is known in the US as the "mommy track"'.[73] Research published in 2010 suggested that '[t]he bigger the firm, the harder it is to make partner'.[74] Women represent

67 Law Society, *Gender and Earnings in Private Practice: Findings from the 2008 Salary Survey*, London: Law Society, 2009, p. 3. The position is even worse for women BME solicitors who often find themselves 'at the very bottom of the pile' when it comes to pay, hit with a 'double whammy' of the negative impact of ethnicity *and* gender (Law Society, *Ethnic Diversity in Law Firms – Understanding the Barriers*, London: Law Society, 2010, p. 69).

68 ibid., p. 4.

69 Law Society, *Gender and Earnings 2008*, p. 4 (my emphasis).

70 Jonathan Rayner, 'Women lawyers believe they are paid less than male peers', *Law Society Gazette*, 10 March 2011.

71 Fiona Raitt, Margaret Callaghan and Gerda Siann, 'Still a glass ceiling for women solicitors?', *Law Society for Scotland Journal Online*, 1 July 2000.

72 Jo Siems, *Equality and Diversity: Women Solicitors* (Research Study 48(1) (Quantitative Findings)), London: Law Society, 2004, p. 56.

73 Lizzie Barmes and Kate Malleson, 'The Legal Profession as Gatekeeper to the Judiciary: Design Faults in Measures to Enhance Diversity', *Modern Law Review*, 74(2), 2011, 245, 252.

74 Catrin Griffiths, 'The gender agenda' in *Diversity Report 2010*, London: The Lawyer, 2010, p. 10.

21.8 per cent of partners in the top 100 firms in the UK.[75] Of the top 10 firms in the UK by turnover, Eversheds comes top with 22 per cent of women partners.[76] To put these figures in context this means that on the best reading the percentage of female partners across all firms has increased by just over 8 per cent in 13 years.[77] Clare McGlynn's assessment of the progress of women lawyers through the solicitors' profession in the late 1990s appears prophetic:

> [What the] figures demonstrate is that, in time, women might just make-up one quarter of partnerships, but no more . . . Accordingly, it must be recognised that the mere passage of time will not ensure equality for women in the solicitors' profession and this myth must be exposed.[78]

Legal executives

There is a third, smaller branch of the legal profession. Legal executives are lawyers authorised to undertake 'reserved activities' by virtue of the Legal Services Act 2007. They specialise in specific areas of law, including civil litigation, family law and conveyancing. In practice, much of their day-to-day work is similar to that of solicitors, although at present legal executives do not have independent practice rights. Following the enactment of the Tribunals, Courts and Enforcement Act 2007, legal executives can now apply for appointment to the district bench as well as a number of tribunal positions. As legal executives do not need to be graduates, it offers a more accessible route into the legal profession. Fellows of the Institute of Legal Executives, that is those who have completed a period of qualifying appointment, have the option of going on to become solicitors after one or two years. Unsurprisingly, given this (and given too the lower status of legal executives in the hierarchy of legal professionals) women have made up around three-quarters of legal executives since 2000. In 2011, 74 per cent of legal executives were women.[79] However, it is likely that, given the male dominance of the other branches of the legal profession and the lower status of legal executives, women legal executives find themselves facing 'double marginalisation' both as women in the legal profession and as legal executives.[80] This is exemplified

---

75 ibid.

76 ibid.

77 At the same time, the number of female equity partners in the UK's largest firms is falling. For example, widespread cuts mean that Freshfields and Simmons now have 15% and 47% fewer female equity partners respectively than in 2006 (Matt Byrne, 'UK's top firms fail to increase female equity partner figures', *The Lawyer*, 14 September 2011).

78 McGlynn, *The Woman Lawyer*, p. 96.

79 Institute of Legal Executives, 'Diversity Statistics'. Online. Available: http://www.ilex.org.uk/about_ilex/equality_and_diversity/diversity_statistics.aspx (accessed 20 February 2012).

80 Andrew Francis, 'Legal executives and the phantom of legal professionalism: The rise and rise of the third branch of the legal profession?', *International Journal of the Legal Profession*, 9(1), 2002, 5, 20.

in a recent survey which found that women legal executives experienced confusion as to their role and saw themselves as being perceived as legal secretaries.[81]

Stagnating, not trickling-up

Thus, more than 30 years since women began to enter the legal profession in significant numbers, women continue to be under-represented in its upper eche-lons (see Table 2.6). Almost a decade after McGlynn's conclusion that women lawyers are 'under-represented, underpaid and marginalised', this continues to be true.[82] The statistics presented here, and more fully in the many reports on diver-sity in the legal profession, reveal a legal profession that is deeply 'segmented and stratified on gendered, raced and classed lines',[83] in which opportunities are not equally available to all, a profession marked by its 'white, male, middle-class history'.[84]

Even more worryingly, in the face of slow progress it seems that gains that were made over the last couple of decades are beginning to be lost. As such, we cannot assume that the gains that *have* been made will continue or that women will continue to progress. This has significant implications for judicial diversity. If women are unable to make it to the upper echelons of the legal profession, there will inevitably be fewer women in the pool from which judicial appointments are made.[85] Not only that but, given that women lawyers, and women barristers in particular, are typically more diverse (that is, there is a greater representation of BME and lower socio-economic backgrounds among women lawyers) progress toward diversity on all measures will be slower. The argument that given time women will 'trickle-up' to the top of the legal profession has been exposed as a myth. It is too slow, too passive, 'too simplistic'.[86] It rests on an assumption of structural neutrality within the legal profession, that the playing field between women and men lawyers is level. It is not. Research reveals the continuing pres-ence of institutional and cultural barriers preventing women from reaching the top levels of the legal profession and it is to these that we now turn.

81 Laura Manning, 'Ilex rebuts study saying legal execs get raw deal', *The Lawyer*, 28 February 2011.
82 Clare McGlynn, 'The Status of Women Lawyers in the United Kingdom' in Ulrike Schultz and Gisela Shaw (eds), *Women in the World's Legal Professions*, Oxford: Hart Publishing, 2003, p. 139, 156.
83 Sommerlad et al, *Barriers and Individual Choice*, p. 6.
84 ibid., p. 38.
85 This is not to suggest that those making judicial appointments should not be looking beyond this narrow pool for highly-qualified candidates.
86 McGlynn, *The Woman Lawyer*, p. 174.

Table 2.6 An overview of women in the legal profession, 1976–2010

Year	Law graduates	Admns to Solicitors' Profn	Solicitors	Partners in private practice	Called to bar	Self-employed barristers	+15 yrs' call at self-employed bar	QC	Salaried judiciary
1976	794 (29.7%)	22 (13%) (1973 figure)	2,296 (6.4%) (1974 figure)	–	166 (19.4%)	313 (8.1%)	80 (2.4%)	4 (1.1%)	10 (approx)
1980	968 (36.5%)	–	5,888 (11.8%)	–	245 (28.4%)	–	–	–	–
1986	1,186 (46.1%)	1,201 (44.1%)	11,924 (18.6%)	–	303 (32.3%)	747 (13.6%)	–	20 (3.6%)	–
1990	2,807 (49.4%)	1,739 (46.6%)	16,728 (24%)	2,937 (12.5%)	484 (40.3%)	1,163 (17.5%)	–	29 (4.3%)	34 (approx) (1989 figure)
1995	4,494 (52.4%)	2,466 (52.3%)	26,316 (31.8%)	3,954 (15.0%)	694 (43.5%)	1,900 (22.4%)	12% (1996 figure)	57 (6.4%)	–
2000	5,517 (59.2%)	3,218 (53.1%)	39,183 (37.5%)	5,418 (19.0%)	648 (46.1%)	2,638 (26%)	14% (1998 figure)	82 (7.6%)	10.4%
2005	7,692 (63.7%)	4,438 (60.3%)	53,799 (42.6%)	6,095 (22.6%)	722 (50%)	3,543 (30%)	1,024 (19.%)	92 (8%)	14.5%
2010	6,343 (63.4%) (2008 figure)	5,011 (59.1%)	53,966 (45.5%)	7,854 (24.7%) (2009 figure)	976 (52.7%)	3,977 (32%)	1,488 (22.6%)	152 (10.8%)	18.9%

Source: Law Society Annual Reports; Bar Council figures (on file with author); Lord Chancellor's Department; Judicial Appointments Annual Report 2001–2002; McGlynn, *The Woman Lawyer – Making the Difference*, p 148.

Commitment, choice and other old chestnuts

So what is preventing women from making their way to the upper echelons of the legal profession? Writing in 1978, Albie Sachs and Joan Hoff Wilson in their book *Sexism and the Law – A Study of Male Beliefs and Judicial Bias*, commented that:

> [t]he professions, like clubs and elite schools, were not simply institutions from which women happened to be absent. Their maleness became part of their character, so that the admission of women was seen as not merely adding to their number or introducing some novelty, but as threatening the very identity of the institutions themselves . . . [Men] shifted their control away from the point of entry towards the routes of advancement. To say this is not to suggest that men conspire as a secret brotherhood to exclude women – though male condescension may well be nearly universal and male hostility fairly common – or even that individual male's bigotry is the dominant bar to female advancement. Institutions tend to have machinery for their self-perpetuation, and all professions are structurally organised so as to maintain male domination and female subordination.[87]

The legal profession was – and continues to be – no exception. Formal barriers preventing women from *entering* the legal profession have been replaced with subtler, more complex forms of discrimination, which hamper their *progression* within it: 'discrimination is very subtle. Basically the higher you try to climb the more barriers seem to be put in your way'.[88] In 1992, the authors of the *Without Prejudice?* report commissioned by the Bar Council and Lord Chancellor's Department, examining gender discrimination at the Bar and in the judiciary, found that 60 per cent of women barristers had faced discrimination on the basis of their sex, with over 70 per cent considering that they were subject to greater pressure to perform and that their performance was more closely scrutinised than that of their male colleagues.[89] In a similar survey of solicitors in 2011, a remarkably similar proportion of women solicitors, 64 per cent, believed that their sex had put them at a disadvantage at some point in their career, compared to just 19 per cent of their male peers.[90] This figure increased to around 70 per cent of women partners in private practice and those working in commerce and industry,[91] with one respondent commenting, 'I was told in my three-month appraisal that it

87 Sachs and Wilson, *Sexism and the Law*, pp. 170–171.
88 Woman solicitor in Rachel Rothwell, 'What do men and women solicitors really think about discrimination?', *Law Society Gazette*, 15 April 2011.
89 Holland and Spender, *Without Prejudice?*, p. 7.
90 Rachel Rothwell, 'Gazette survey: work-based discrimination still rife, say women solicitors', *Law Society Gazette*, 14 April 2011.
91 ibid.

was just a fact of life that females have to work harder and achieve more than their male counterparts to impress male partners'.[92]

Almost a century after women were first admitted to the legal profession, research projects and reports continue to provide solid evidence of 'significant and ongoing barriers to the progress of women within the profession'.[93] Year on year, the *same* obstacles have been identified as the key barriers to women's progress: inflexible working practices, the existence of a hostile legal culture, disparity in the measurement of professional achievement, and the impact of (potential) motherhood.[94] This list should sound familiar. We know – and have known for some time – what is preventing women from progressing through the legal profession. And yet, given their apparent intractability and the reliance on the legal profession as part of the solution to ensuring greater judicial diversity, it is worth taking a moment to look at these barriers in more detail.[95]

Long hours and greedy employers

The inability to implement flexible working practices – such as working away from the office, job sharing, part-time work, being free to leave at a fixed time and work from home later in the evening – have consistently been identified as the most significant obstacle to women's ability to reach the upper levels of the legal profession. At its root lies the 'long-hours culture', typically involving 12–14 hour days and 7-day weeks. This culture manifests itself in various ways, including a heavy emphasis on 'presentism', of needing to be *seen to be* in the office – sometimes expressed as the 'jacket on the back of the chair' syndrome, whereby people leave their jackets on the back of their chairs to give the impression that they are still at work – as well as an expectation of constant availability to employers and clients, particularly those who are overseas and/or in the corporate or banking law fields.

---

92 Rothwell, 'What do men and women solicitors really think about discrimination?'.
93 Insight Oxford, *Obstacles and Barriers to the Career Development of Women Solicitors*, London: Law Society, London, 2010, p. 4 (Insight Oxford, *Obstacles and Barriers*).
94 See, eg, McGlynn, *The Woman Lawyer*, pp. 98–106, 149–158; Hilary Sommerlad and Peter Sanderson, *Gender, Choice and Commitment: Women Solicitors in England and Wales and the Struggle for Equal Status*, Aldershot: Ashgate, 1998; Liz Duff and Lisa Webley, *Equality and Diversity: Women Solicitors*, (Research Study 48(2) (Qualitative Findings and Literature Review)), London: Law Society, 2004; Siems, *Equality and Diversity*; Insight Oxford, *Obstacles and Barriers*; Sommerlad et al, *Barriers and Individual Choice*; Griffiths, 'The gender agenda'; Pike and Robinson, *Barristers' Working Lives*.
95 Though the legal profession is in many respects heterogeneous and differentiated – so that, for many purposes, talking about 'the Bar', 'solicitors' and 'the legal profession' overlooks important (socio-economic, demographic, regional) differences within these groups – Sommerlad et al note that despite this the strength and dominance of the legal culture is such that there is much uniformity in the barriers and obstacles facing women and other non-traditional lawyers across the legal profession (Sommerlad et al, *Barriers and Individual Choice*, p. 39). See further, Law Society, *Ethnic Diversity in Law Firms*; Law Society, *Law Society Survey of LGB Solicitors 2009: The Career experience of LGB Solicitors*, London: Law Society, 2010 (conducted by the InterLaw Diversity Forum for the Law Society and LGBT Network).

These working practices are deeply entrenched; the long-hours culture is said to 'seep through the brickwork'[96] of the large commercial law firms. And it is getting worse. According to a survey of law graduates in 2010 almost half of those applying for trainee positions expected to work over 50 hours a week and 10 hours a day, with a smaller percentage (15.3 per cent) expecting to work 55 hours a week.[97] There is, it is suggested, an 'unspoken rule' that long hours and 'all-nighters' are part of the job, part of a Faustian pact for starting salaries that are typically three times the average wage.[98] Thus, despite the recent proliferation of flexible working practices (alongside an increased awareness on the part of firms of their responsibility for the health of their associates[99]), participants in the Law Society's 2010 survey identified a disjuncture between expressed flexible policies and what is culturally acceptable, leading to 'a negative, uninformed and confusing view of flexible working: that is both acceptable and "not done"'.[100] While many male senior partners adopt flexible working arrangements, for example by working from home on Fridays, these are typically not considered 'flexible working' or they are being done 'under the radar', for example by presenting their attendance at their child's concert as 'being in a meeting'.[101] For the most part, there continues to be the perception that flexible working is incompatible with the long-hours culture of many law firms. Those taking advantage of flexible working arrangements feel guilty – 'if you have to leave early there's a walk of shame in every organisation and all women feel it'[102] – while their colleagues feel hard done by. As one male lawyer opined:

> If someone is on shorter time, you ask how committed are they? How much can they achieve in four days? This is a practical question, not gender-related . . . Could we run a firm if all our partners did it? It would be difficult.[103]

Without doubt, flexible working arrangements *are* resource intensive to set up. They *do* require a greater investment on the part of firms and supervisors to

96 Sophie Hamilton, former senior partner, quoted in Griffiths, 'The gender agenda', p. 12.
97 Corinne McPartland, 'Aspiring lawyers expect to work longer hours, says survey', *The Lawyer*, 22 April 2010.
98 Anon, 'Focus: Magic Circle work-life balance – work, rest and fair play', *The Lawyer*, 26 July 2010.
99 Alex Alridge, 'Are Law Firms Finally Addressing the Need for a Better Work-life Balance?', *The Guardian*, 1 July 2011; Alex Alridge, 'The case of the sleepless lawyers', *The Guardian*, 4 August 2011.
100 Insight Oxford, *Obstacles and Barriers*, p. 9; Sommerlad et al, *Barriers and Individual Choice*, p. 51. Law Society figures suggest that although 73% of men and women solicitors working in private practice have been offered flexible working, just 49% of solicitors overall and 56% of women solicitors are using it. This figure decreases further to 20% for solicitors overall and 28% among women solicitors working in large firms (81+ partners) (Law Society, *Flexible working and solicitors' work-life balance – Fact sheet series 2010*, London: Law Society, 2010).
101 Insight Oxford, *Obstacles and Barriers*, p. 9.
102 Nicola Kerr, SJ Berwin head of employment quoted in Griffiths, 'The gender agenda', p. 12.
103 In Ivana Bacik and Eileen Drew, 'Struggling with juggling: Gender and work/life balance in the legal professions', *Women's Studies International Forum*, 29, 2006, 136, p. 143.

manage their team effectively.[104] However, this is offset, supporters of flexible working suggest, by 'considerable' business benefits including increased productivity and staff retention:

> We don't have chargeable hours targets for partners or staff. It's about people knowing what people are doing and judging that rather than looking at metrics. As a result people are more comfortable, because they have confidence in themselves and the management team. That does have quite unexpected benefits.[105]

Figures show that the availability of flexible working arrangements and, crucially, a culture in which these opportunities can be taken up, has significant impact on retention and promotion rates among women lawyers. Research by *The Lawyer* in 2010, for example, found a direct correlation between the take up of flexible working arrangements and the number of women partners.[106] And so notwithstanding the obvious benefits for women themselves, and for firms keen to meet their diversity targets, flexible working practices also appear to make good business sense – not least because a conservative estimate puts the cost of replacing an associate solicitor at £125,000, not including intangible costs such as loss of institutional expertise and knowledge and disruption to working relationships.[107]

Of course, criticism of the long-hours culture and the accompanying demand for flexible working are not new (nor, as we shall see, do these come only from women). In fact, the 'greediness' of law firms has been noted since the late 1980s.[108]

---

104 Insight Oxford, *Obstacles and Barriers*, p. 14.
105 Pat Treacy, co-managing partner, quoted in Griffiths, 'The gender agenda', p. 12. See also Catrin Griffiths, 'Focus: Flexible working – now you see me . . .', *The Lawyer*, 1 February 2010. These benefits may be tempered by a concern that increased flexibility feeds the expectation of constant availability, meaning that some feel that they are never able to 'leave the office' or switch off from work.
106 Luke McLeod-Roberts, 'Part-time schemes help firms keep female partners working', *The Lawyer*, 1 February 2010. Women solicitors are five times more likely to work part-time than men. Just 1% of male solicitors working in commerce and industry work part-time, compared to 24% of their female colleagues (Law Society, *Flexible working fact sheet*).
107 Insight Oxford, *Obstacles and Barriers*, p. 20. A point also made by Clare McGlynn as chairwoman of the Young Women Lawyers group in 1997 (Grania Langdon-Down, 'More women equals more money', *The Independent*, 23 April 1997). This 'business case' for gender equality has been around for some time, see further Clare McGlynn, 'Strategies for Reforming the English Solicitors' Profession: An Analysis of the Business Case for Sex Equality' in Ulrike Schultz and Gisela Shaw (eds), *Women in the World's Legal Professions*, Oxford: Hart Publishing, 2003, p. 159 and more recently Jo Braithwaite, 'The strategic use of demand side diversity pressure on the solicitors' profession', *Journal of Law and Society*, 37(3), 2010, 442.
108 Carrie Menkel-Meadow, 'Feminisation of the Legal Profession: the Comparative Sociology of Women Lawyers' in Richard Abel and Philip Lewis (eds), *Lawyers in Society: Comparative Theories*, Berkeley: University of California Press, 1989, p. 239; See also Hilary Sommerlad, 'Researching and Theorizing the Processes of Professional Identity Formation', *Journal of Law and Society*, 34(2), 2008, 190.

Since then numerous reports and surveys have consistently supported the view that the 'blitz-mentality' of late nights and early mornings, far from being an inevitable part of being a lawyer, is rather 'a symptom of a lack of value for staff as human beings'.[109] Research published in the mid-1990s revealed widespread dissatisfaction among employees with the expectations placed on them by their firms.[110] A survey of trainees in 1998 found that both men and women trainees were feeling 'trapped, undervalued and frustrated'.[111] Around 39 per cent of the 200 trainees surveyed said they were 'wanting to get out' of the profession; 28 per cent indicated that if they were given the chance again they would not become lawyers: 'Considering the number of hours I work and the stress and responsibility I have for a considerably low wage . . . I would probably go into something totally different and which I enjoy – for example, interior design'.[112] Ten years later, little had changed.[113] In 2008, the Law Society's Junior Lawyer's Division concluded that

> [t]he popular belief that the life of a city lawyer is all about big bonuses, expensive holidays and flowing champagne is misguided. In fact, the career is more likely to end in emotional or physical breakdown . . . in anxiety, stress, depression, eating disorders and worse.[114]

Little wonder that nearly one in three lawyers surveyed in 2008 would discourage their children from joining the profession.[115]

Nor is the long-hours culture unique to the solicitors' profession. It is a similar story over at the Bar: 'every barrister knows, a successful full-time practice requires a great deal of work at evenings and weekends'.[116] Despite Bar Council guidelines on flexible working,[117] long and erratic hours are the norm (especially for junior counsel),[118] typically coupled with an expectation that barristers, when not in court, will be in chambers. The obvious exception to this is, of course, the (typically male) barrister who combines his legal practice with sitting as a

109 Duff, *Equality and Diversity*, pp. 30–31. See further Lisa Webley and Liz Duff, 'Women Solicitors as a Barometer for Problems Within the Legal Profession – Time to Put Values Before Profits', *Journal of Law and Society*, 34(3), 2007, 374, pp. 387–389.
110 McGlynn, *The Woman Lawyer*, p. 103.
111 Chris Fogarty, 'Trainees who bluffed their way in, want out', *The Lawyer*, 19 May 1998.
112 ibid.
113 Jonathan Rayner, 'Stress still high', *Law Society Gazette*, 19 May 2011.
114 Junior Lawyers Division, *Work-life balance policy*, London: Law Society, 2008, p. 2.
115 Jon Parker, 'Lawyers warn kids off career in law', *The Lawyer*, 1 July 2008.
116 Sylvia de Bertodano, 'Women used to talk about how little time they had taken off to have children', *The Times*, 4 June 2009.
117 Bar Council, *Equality and Diversity Code*, Annex G: 'Maternity, Paternity and Flexible Working Policy'.
118 Barristers at the self-employed Bar work on average 53 hours a week (Pike and Robinson, *Barristers' Working Lives*, p. 50).

part-time judge – although this is unlikely to be viewed as flexible working. Moreover, their self-employed status and the insecurity of their financial position, particularly when building up their practice, means that junior barristers need to take whatever cases are offered to them, often involving early starts, significant travelling and overnight stays, all typically at short notice. This combined with the competitive nature of the Bar works to 'foster an atmosphere which discourages flexible working'.[119] This is not to suggest that flexible working practices do not exist – they do – but rather that the *culture* of the Bar is such that it mitigates against their implementation. This high stress and high stakes culture fuels a life-style in which high-achieving barristers 'push themselves to the brink':

> [T]o be a successful barrister you have to put up an act. It is true that many barristers are natural performers, who revel in being on stage all day, many of whom see their job as much as to entertain the judge – or keep him awake – as to win the case. The profession naturally attracts self-confident extroverts and those who thrive in a competitive environment.[120]

Indeed, unlike their solicitor colleagues, 70 per cent of barristers surveyed for the *Working Lives* report in 2011 would still opt for the Bar if they started their career again.[121]

The extent to which the long-hours culture at both the Bar and in the solicitors' profession is simply 'part of the job' is a matter of debate. It may well be only when 'men . . . start saying "enough is enough" of this ridiculous hours culture we have . . . [that] people will listen'.[122] However, what *is* clear is that, insofar as the expectations that flow from it are entrenched, those who are unwilling or unable – typically, but not only, women – to meet these demands can find themselves at a disadvantage when it comes to progressing through the profession.

---

119 Entry to the Bar Working Party, *Final Report*, London: Bar Council, 2007, [333], see also Appendix 14. While the importance placed on flexible working arrangements has increased in recent years (just 6% of those leaving the Bar between 2001–2005 cited lack of flexible working as a reason for doing so), this has not been reflected in changes in practices at the Bar. 30% of those leaving the Bar in 2009, and 54% of women leaving who had children, suggested that they would have liked more flexible working arrangements (Electoral Reform Research, *Survey of Barristers Changing Practice Status 2001–9*, London: Electoral Reform Services, March 2011, [2.2.5] and [5.6.3] (prepared for the Bar Council).

120 Terry Kirby, 'Mark Saunders shoot-out: "It is a great life – but it is all acting"', *The Telegraph*, 20 August 2008. See also, Vanessa Lloyd Platt, 'The stress of being a female lawyer', *The Times*, 30 July 2009; Hilary Tilby, 'Stress at the Bar', *Counsel*, January 2010, pp. 18–19.

121 Pike and Robinson, *Barristers' Working Lives*, p. 76.

122 HR Director quoted in Collier, *Men, Law and Gender*, p. 182.

Old boys and mini-mes

Although one might not have expected a profession which had done its best to exclude women to be particularly receptive to their presence, it is clear that from the outset 'women have had to work much harder and endure many more secret humiliations, just to reach the position from which male lawyers start'.[123] Women lawyers still consider that they 'have to be better than, not equal to, men to succeed'; 'to work harder and longer to prove oneself'.[124] There continues to be a strong sense that the legal profession is 'male-shaped', not only in terms of its working practices and infrastructure, but also in relation to the culture that supports it: 'the male mindset and culture of the profession is very entrenched and very obstructive. It does not help women, only men'.[125] The view that the legal profession is 'an old boys' club' where partners and senior barristers continue to favour and promote 'mini mes'[126] (that is, people in their own image) persists, and is reinforced by informal practices and expectations which – whether for reasons of availability, disposition or even bias – men (or rather men of a certain class, ethnicity, sexual orientation, educational background and so on) find easier to negotiate than others.[127]

Examples abound. The most obvious and invidious is the, often unspoken, expectation of 'schmoozing' with clients over dinner or at the golf club, or with (senior) colleagues at formal networking events or at the bar after work. Despite reports that some firms are encouraging more 'feminised' activities, such as theatre trips or chocolate making workshops,[128] most of these events take place at venues that are male dominated or orientated, often bars or private members clubs, and typically involve sport and/or heavy drinking:[129]

> There might be 2–3 in a week and there's a terrific drinking culture that's associated with it as well and so they go on until closing time and then [say] where are we going now? If you say, well, actually I'm going home, they all look at you as if you're a lightweight. Ridiculous.[130]

---

123 Sachs and Wilson, *Sexism and the Law*, p. 178.
124 Insight Oxford, *Obstacles and Barriers*, p. 11.
125 ibid., p. 10.
126 Luke McLeod-Roberts, 'Minorities Report' in *Diversity Report 2010*, London: The Lawyer, 2010, 6, p. 8.
127 Sommerlad and Sanderson, *Gender, Choice and Commitment*, pp. 153–195; Law Society, *Ethnic Diversity in Law Firms*, pp. 38–40; Collier, *Men, Law and Gender*, pp. 172–177; Webley and Duff, 'Women Solicitors as a Barometer', p. 384.
128 Sommerlad et al, *Barriers and Individual Choice*, pp. 37–38; James Swift, 'Latham under fire for holding cooking event for female network', *The Lawyer*, 20 April 2012.
129 Insight Oxford, *Obstacles and Barriers*, p. 11; Sommerlad et al, *Barriers and Individual Choice*, p. 45; Richard Wachman, 'Sex and the City: Spearmint Rhino pulls bankers bearing bonuses', *The Guardian*, 20 February 2011.
130 Woman lawyer quoted in Webley and Duff, 'Women Solicitors as a Barometer', p. 387.

Of course, this is not to suggest that women never participate in these activities. They can and do – often to their advantage. As one woman equity partner commented to Sommerlad et al, 'we have a lot of male partners who play golf but no women so I thought . . . I can bring along my clients . . . another feather in my cap'.[131]

However, it is clear that, whether or not women are present, the *perception* of both participants and observers is that these are activities for men, and heterosexual ones at that:

> There is this sort of macho culture amongst lawyers, you know, taking clients out for drinks, taking clients to the rugby and so on and so forth. You know, there's nothing wrong with that per se, but there kind of can be an undercurrent that is almost implicitly homophobic.[132]

Thus, though women are not *formally* excluded from joining in these activities, their participation is not valued or viewed in the same way as men's. Their involvement is often 'deprofessionalised': 'We have our golf days, a jolly boys' outing . . . then there's a dinner at night . . . the women go then. But you turn up as if you're a trophy on someone's arm, rather than actually taking part'.[133] Lesbians and gay women often experience this objectification and sexualisation even more acutely:

> The really macho partners, they don't want to know, if you don't want to drink pints in the pub with them and eye up women, and talk about your sexual conquests and flirt with the secretaries, and play squash, you're not really going to go anywhere.[134]

Research by the InterLaw Diversity Forum for the Law Society in 2009 found that lesbian and gay women were more likely to report that their sexual orientation had adversely affected their career progression, compared to their gay male counterparts.[135]

Despite the apparent prominence and centrality of these activities in both branches of the legal profession, little attention is paid to their real value, to what these networking events actually achieve in terms of work for the firms or chambers. Participants in both the Law Society and Legal Services Board's surveys in 2010 questioned the success of such activities in actually bringing business in or persuading clients of their professional abilities. As one woman partner commented:

---

131 See Sommerlad et al, *Barriers and Individual Choice*, pp. 61–62.
132 Gay male partner quoted in Tara Chittenden, *Career Experiences of Gay and Lesbian Solicitors* (Research Study 53), London: Law Society, 2006, p. 53. See also, Law Society, *Law Society Survey of LGB Solicitors*.
133 Sommerlad et al, *Barriers and Individual Choice*, p. 40.
134 Lesbian, employed sector, quoted in Chittenden, *Career Experiences of Gay and Lesbian Solicitors*, p. 54.
135 Law Society, *Law Society Survey of LGB Solicitors*, p. 5.

It's always slightly disappointing that nobody seems to see through that, that the huff and the puff and the bluster of look at me, I'm having a marvellous game of golf, doing this, having lunch with so and so. Nobody stops to then follow that back up and say, well what did you achieve? It's all about sort of presence and profile and sort of an office concept like that.[136]

Nevertheless, notwithstanding concerns about their value as effective business strategies, internal and external networking remain essential to career development and progression. Building personal relationships both within the firm and potential clients, and over at the Bar with senior barristers as well as clerks and solicitors, is crucial. Those who are unable – or unwilling – to participate in these events are often doubly disadvantaged. Not only are they unable to establish and benefit from important networking opportunities, but their reluctance or inability to engage in these extra-curricular activities counts 'against' them for progression and promotion purposes. Their failure to participate is seen as evidencing their 'lack of commitment' to the firm *or indeed their own career* – a desire to step off the partnership track.[137] As Hilary Sommerlad and Peter Sanderson noted in their study of women solicitors in the late 1990s:

> [a] woman can work hard, perform exceptionally in examinations, become an expert in her field, only to discover that she is regarded as 'a good techni-cian', a 'back room girl', since what may be required for partnership material is someone who is 'clubbable', or 'ladsy' or attractive.[138]

The same point was made almost 10 years later by a woman equity partner in Sommerlad et al's research for the Legal Services Board:

> . . . Clubbable: it's the sort of person who will go to the bar afterwards on a Friday evening with them and that sort of thing, and generally enjoy sort of relaxed social chit chat with the other people . . . Women find that difficult because they've got other responsibilities, so they can't join in with that sort of thing . . . if you've got a larger firm where you've got say a tradition of going out for a drink together on a Friday, and you've got some members there who've got family responsibilities, or who don't want to do that, they're nearly always going to be female, and they're going to be left out of that bit. And that's going to affect it, I think, it has to affect their visibility.[139]

There is a further point to make here. One might expect that a woman who *does* show the requisite level of 'commitment', who *does* stay after work, who schmoozes

136 Sommerlad et al, *Barriers and Individual Choice*, p. 44.
137 ibid., p. 27.
138 Sommerlad and Sanderson, *Gender, Choice and Commitment*, p. 17.
139 Sommerlad et al, *Barriers and Individual Choice*, p. 44.

clients and brings in work for the firm would be rewarded for doing so *in the same way as her male colleagues.* However, it remains the case that, however 'clubbable' or visible a woman is, however much she may aspire to match the image of the ideal-ised lawyer, she will rarely meet it.[140] Masculinity remains '*the* core cultural capital of the professions'.[141] Professional achievement continues to be measured against criteria which are 'male-orientated'.[142]

This significantly impacts on women's ability to progress within the legal profes-sion in at least two ways. First, both branches of the legal profession continue to be divided along gender lines. Not only are women trainees more likely to work outside London, and in smaller firms,[143] women solicitors are also found in greater numbers in the 'shelter'[144] of in-house positions, such as local government, the advice service or educational establishments.[145] Women lawyers, both in private practice and at the Bar continue to be less likely than their male counterparts to practise in business and commercial law fields and more likely to be found in less prestigious and less well-remunerated specialisms such as social security, employ-ment, education and family law, or in the 'softer' areas of 'male' specialisms, such as sex cases in criminal law.[146] The proportion of women barristers at the self-employed Bar working in family law is twice that found in any other area of prac-tice.[147] This segregation has important consequences for women lawyers' career progression and development. Not only do they find it harder to meet their targets, to bring in the 'big money', there is also continuing evidence that within the same specialisms male lawyers are allocated the more complex cases making it signifi-cantly easier for them to meet their targets, while gaining important expertise and experience to allow them to progress within the profession.

It is important to note here that, although the absence of women from certain areas of law is usually presented as a result of women's 'choice' (that, for example, women *choose* to work in family law and the like) in reality this choice is often extremely limited. Research in 2010, for example, found that many women solicitors had felt 'bullied' into working in a particular area of practice.[148] Over at the Bar, the *Without Prejudice?* research in 1992 found that 67.6 per cent of women, compared to 88.6 per cent of men, were working in their preferred area of practice.[149] More recently, women barristers have highlighted the need to

---

140 McGlynn, *The Woman Lawyer*, pp. 99–100.
141 Sommerlad and Sanderson, *Gender, Choice and Commitment*, p. 17.
142 Insight Oxford, *Obstacles and Barriers*, p. 15.
143 Cole et al, *Trends in the Solicitors' Profession 2009*, Tables 8.9 and 8.11.
144 Sommerlad et al, *Barriers and Individual Choice*, p. 27.
145 Law Society, *Women Solicitors – Fact sheet series 2009*, London: Law Society, 2010.
146 Law Society, *Categories of work undertaken by solicitors – Fact sheet series 2010*, London: Law Society, 2010; Law Society, *The Work of Solicitors: Law Society Individuals Omnibus Spring 2010*, London: Law Society, 2011.
147 Pike and Robinson, *Barristers' Working Lives*, p. 45.
148 Sommerlad et al, *Barriers and Individual Choice*, pp. 25–30.
149 Holland and Spender, *Without Prejudice?*, p. 9 and Appendix F1.

'reinvent' themselves professionally on returning from maternity leave by expanding into other areas of law in order to find enough work.[150] Others point to the extent to which prejudice and stereotypes continue to affect the allocation of briefs by clerks:[151]

> In criminal defence they wouldn't trust you with nice juicy stuff. The only time I ever got to do exciting murder or drugs cases was when I was being led by a more experienced male barrister. So, I think it is harder to crack the so-called serious stuff in crime. In immigration there's no problem.[152]

The second way in which the male-orientation of the legal profession hinders women lawyers' ability to progress relates to expectations in the way that they perform their role. These differ between men and women. Traits typically displayed by men – such as hustling for business, competitiveness, risk-taking and so on – are valued *and rewarded* over those typically displayed by women – for example, nurturing and growing existing client relationships, teamwork, communication skills and so on.[153] The expectations and qualities of a good lawyer play to (typically) male strengths so that it is harder for women to (be seen to) display them.[154] Others suggest the fault lies with the women themselves: 'women are failing to push themselves forward . . . we don't promote ourselves'.[155] Similar reasons were also given by female barristers for not applying for silk:

> Men and women approach things differently. Men look down a list of criteria and say 'yes, that's me'. But women are more circumspect. Women need more encouragement than men do . . . Women want to be sure before they apply whereas men will take a punt.[156]

And who can blame them? Women who adopt the typically 'male' traits do so at their peril. They are often derided – by both men and women – as 'ball-breakers' or even 'anti-role models', happy to 'actively kick others off the ladder':[157]

---

150 Maya Sikand in Anon, 'The law of motherhood', *The Guardian*, 28 April 2011.

151 Rosaline Sullivan, *Barriers to the Legal Profession*, London: Legal Services Board, July 2010, p. 17.

152 Female, white academic/barrister in Sommerlad et al, *Barriers and Individual Choice*, p. 25. Again, this is not a new source of potential discrimination. The *Without Prejudice?* Report noted, in 1992, the 'strong incentive' for clerks to give work to those who they considered a 'safe pair of hands' (Holland and Spender, *Without Prejudice?*, p. 9).

153 Insight Oxford, *Obstacles and Barriers*, p. 15.

154 Webley and Duff, 'Women Solicitors as a Barometer', p. 386.

155 Insight Oxford, *Obstacles and Barriers*, p. 17. There is a body of literature that shows that the necessity for self-promotion disadvantages women (Sommerlad et al, *Barriers and Individual Choice*, p. 37, fn 134).

156 Kate Malleson and Fareda Banda, *Factors affecting the decision to apply for Silk and Judicial Office* (Lord Chancellor's Department Research Programme 2/00), London: Lord Chancellor's Department, 2000, pp. 24–26.

157 Insight Oxford, *Obstacles and Barriers*, p. 18.

'I use the term female loosely, you know it takes a certain type of female to succeed in this environment' . . . 'It tends to be more aggressive women . . . you know, acting just like men . . . which can mean [they are] even more scary creatures than an aggressive man'.[158]

Women in the legal profession have, it seems, a very particular image to maintain. The profession has failed to keep pace with societal changes, particularly in relation to gender equality: '. . . whilst girls [sic] generally don't have to fight as hard for equality as their predecessors, this is not the case in the legal world'.[159] The legal profession continues to be characterised by out-dated and, at times, patronising assumptions about women including expectations about the way they should dress,[160] conjecture about their desire for children, as well as prejudice and stereotyping about their career aspirations and abilities. Women especially, but not only those from a BME background, continue to be asked inappropriate questions at interview grounded in assumptions about their gender and ethnicity. Several of the Asian female respondents in the Legal Services Board survey in 2010 had been asked at interview whether they would be able to attend functions after work or if their mother would mind them being out late. Another relayed the experience of a friend interviewed at a law firm in the North East of England:

She had recently become widowed and she was asked about children because of her age and references were made to her wedding ring. And it is something that you associate with a bygone era. She was recently bereaved and was forced to say well children aren't going to happen.[161]

But what of the women who do have children? Where do they fit into the mix?

Invisible pregnancies and self-raising families[162]

In 1987 Robert Perkins, a solicitor at Moore & Blatch in Southampton, wrote to *The Lawyer* outlining the 'basic' necessities needed by a 'lady lawyer' if she was successfully to combine motherhood, marriage and lawyering:

---

158 Male fee earners quoted in Collier, *Men, Law and Gender*, p. 173.
159 Insight Oxford, *Obstacles and Barriers*, p. 11.
160 Jonathan Russell, 'Your skimpy skirt and high heels just won't do, trainee solicitors told', *The Telegraph*, 8 April 2011. As Clare McGlynn notes, commenting on similar articles in 1998: 'undue concentration on the personal attributes of women diverts attention away from the vital issues of occupational and professional status, ideologies and recruitment patterns which effectively discriminate against women' (*The Woman Lawyer*, p. 3).
161 Sommerlad et al, *Barriers and Individual Choice*, p. 34. Again, over half of the women responding to the *Without Prejudice?* Report had been asked at interview about their plans to get married, have children or stay at the Bar (Holland and Spender, *Without Prejudice?*, p. 8).
162 Woman barrister, Letter to *The Independent*, 26 November 1990 in McGlynn, *The Woman Lawyer*, p. 150.

Lady lawyers understandably and properly seek equality in status and remuneration. The basic necessities for a mother and wife to take on the responsibilities and put into effect the dedication that is required of a successful lawyer
must include: a) A first-rate trained career nanny with regular back-up for
nanny's off-time, holidays etc – not the teenage daughter of the neighbours
who helps out. b) Proper domestic arrangements concerning gardening,
cleaning and cookery. c) Possibly a willingness to pay boarding school fees.
d) An understanding and co-operative husband.[163]

While we might bristle at Perkins's terminology and tone, over 20 years later his
key point remains true: a woman lawyer's success rests on the extent to which she
is able to ensure the invisibility of her family. Although the view that 'firms cannot
afford "to nurse [women lawyers'] practices while they nurse their brats"' may no
longer be openly expressed,[164] maternity and child-care responsibilities continue
to be a major obstacle to women's progression within the legal professions. CP
Hawkes's advice to women lawyers in 1930 appears prophetic: 'it would seem as
though a married lady-barrister would have to forgo the joys of family life and
mother-hood, for the law is a jealous lover and admits of no divided allegiance'.[165]

Though men are increasingly sharing child-caring responsibilities, research
suggests that primary responsibility for child-care still falls disproportionately on
women. In the period 1998–2009, working mothers spent on average 155 minutes
a day engaged in primary child-care, compared with an average of 43 minutes for
working fathers.[166] The Bar Council's Working Lives survey in 2011 found that
two-thirds of women barristers with dependent children took primary responsibility for providing or arranging child-care, compared to just four per cent of
men.[167] The Law Society survey in 2010 noted that women participants expressed
'[m]uch frustration . . . at male counterparts having full domestic support':

> 'they all have wives full time at home' . . . which many argued further drives
> or facilitates the maleness of the profession. Juggling is a heavy burden and
> participants described some men as 'sleepwalking their way through life'.[168]

---

163 Robert Perkins, Letter to *The Lawyer*, 13 August 1987 quoted in Luke McLeod-Roberts, '20 years
of The Lawyer: Diversity', *The Lawyer*, 5 December 2007.
164 Sachs and Wilson, *Sexism and the Law*, p. 176.
165 CP Hawkes, *Chambers in the Temple: Comments and Conceits 'in Camera'*, London: Methuen & Co,
1930, p. 75. In 2011, women barristers are twice as likely as male barristers to be single. They are
also less likely than their male counterparts to have children (Pike and Robinson, *Barristers'
Working Lives*, p. 14).
166 Miranda Veerle, *Cooking, Caring and Volunteering: Unpaid Work Around the World* (OECD Social,
Employment and Migration Working Papers, No. 116), Paris: OECD Publishing, 2011, p. 19.
167 Pike and Robinson, *Barristers' Working Lives*, p. 14.
168 Insight Oxford, *Obstacles and Barriers*, p. 18. See also the comments of *male* lawyers who felt disadvantaged *compared to other male lawyers* because their wives were also in full-time employment
(Collier, *Men, Law and Gender*, p. 168).

Whether we like it or not, to the extent that the cultural and institutional barriers discussed above intersect with child-care and other caring responsibilities they continue to impact disproportionately on *women* lawyers.[169] Thus, insofar as attempts to de-gender criticisms of, for example, the difficulties in maintaining a good work–life balance present the obstacles faced by women in the legal profession as gender-neutral, this may in the long-run make it even *harder* for women to progress. While many men lawyers may now *prefer* to share child-care responsibilities, and may find it difficult (and on occasions *more* difficult) than women to negotiate how to do this,[170] paternity – let alone the *potential* of paternity – unlike maternity rarely, if ever, prevents men from developing their careers. Sachs and Wilson's observation in the late 1970s still holds true: 'maternity has replaced delicacy as the major justification for keeping women out of the professions, [while] paternity . . . works the other way – men should be given opportunities because they have children to support'.[171]

So just how invisible do a woman lawyer's caring responsibilities need to be? Or, put another way, just how family-*un*friendly is the legal profession? Central to answering this are particular understandings of a woman lawyer's 'choice' and 'commitment'. Writing in 1998, McGlynn had this to say about the reasons why women solicitors leave the profession:

> The conclusion is drawn that it is not the fault of the firm that a woman solicitor leaves because, for example, her request to work part-time is refused or because of the firm's negative attitude towards her second pregnancy. This is seen as the woman's choice to leave, despite the fact that she may have invested years in her career and may not have wished to leave the firm. Although in the end it was she who handed in her notice and walked out the office door, her 'choices' were constrained by the actions and attitudes of the firm, to the extent that, in effect, she was left with no choice.[172]

The gendered reality of the woman lawyer is reframed as one of *individual* preferences and responsibilities. It is her *choice* that sets in motion the subsequent chain of (negative) events. And, if she doesn't like the way it turns out, well then she has only herself, her decisions, to blame. Over a decade later, this view continues to

---

169 Sommerlad et al, *Barriers and Individual Choice*, p. 36. See also Hilary Sommerlad, 'Women Solicitors in a Fractured Profession', *International Journal of the Legal Profession*, 9(3), 2002, 213, pp. 217–222.

170 Collier, *Men, Law and Gender*, pp. 170–172; Law Society, *Law Society Survey of LGB Solicitors*, p. 7.

171 Sachs and Wilson, *Sexism and the Law*, p. 177. There is continuing evidence that higher male salaries are justified by their 'breadwinner' role across high status professions (Sommerlad et al, *Barriers and Individual Choice*, p. 40).

172 McGlynn, *The Woman Lawyer*, p. 99.

hold considerable sway among members of the legal profession. It is presented as a fact of (legal) life, just the way things are:

> The only problem for women is for those who leave to have children and then come back. You cannot go part time or have time out whatever your reason or sex and expect to keep up with those who do not – it is a factual thing not a discriminatory one . . . As such women get the raw end of this – they have to make the awful decision whether to have children or to get the absolute maximum from their careers. This seems highly unfair but I honestly can't see a way around it.[173]

The rhetoric of *choice* is used to explain – to justify – any number of disparities in the way women and men experience the legal profession. Women lawyers *choose* to work in particular areas of practice, they *choose* to move in-house or to join the employed bar, to have a family. And, like all decisions, these choices have consequences. In the context of the legal profession, these decisions demonstrate a *lack of commitment* on the part of the woman lawyer to her career and/or to her employer, hence her lower professional status, pay, promotion opportunities and so on.[174] In the 'human capital theory' of female choices, women are responsible for their own lack of progression.[175] Of course, the reality is that the identification of an individual's choices and commitment are highly gendered,[176] not least because, as we have seen, the *same* activities are often interpreted differently depending on whether it is a man or woman lawyer performing them.

Against this backdrop, any assessment of an individual's choices and level of commitment is likely to be contentious. It is clear that while some choices are viewed positively, such as working long hours or hustling for business at the bar after work, others are automatically seen as evidencing a reduced level of commitment – however strong the evidence to the contrary.[177] Top of this list, at least for women lawyers, is starting a family. Indeed, such is the strength of this assumption that even the *possibility* of such an eventuality is enough to start alarm bells ringing. Participants in the Law Society's survey of women solicitors in 2010 believed that passing references to marriage or engagements or children even other people's – would be interpreted by colleagues as 'being broody' and thereby indicate a lack of commitment to the firm:[178]

173 Male solicitor quoted in Rothwell, 'What do men and women solicitors really think about discrimination?'.
174 Clare McGlynn, 'The Business of Equality in the Solicitors' Profession', *Modern Law Review*, 63, 2000, 442, pp. 443–444.
175 Webley and Duff, 'Women Solicitors as a Barometer', p. 377.
176 Sommerlad and Sanderson, *Gender, Choice and Commitment*, pp. 215–227.
177 Duff and Webley, *Equality and Diversity*, p. 20.
178 Insight Oxford, *Obstacles and Barriers*, p. 11. In contrast, marriage continues to be viewed as 'increasing men's commitment' (Sommerlad et al, *Barriers and Individual Choice*, p. 40).

When I became engaged, the assumption was that I would stop working after I married. I realise now that the elder statesmen running the department were frightened that I would get pregnant on their time and be off for a year. They needn't have worried, as they managed to make life so unbearable that I left of my own accord. The same treatment was given to other females in the department. Any woman who clung on was swiftly moved into professional support work – a dead end job, with no partnership prospects. Their careers were over.[179]

Although firms and chambers are no longer able to avoid the problem altogether by not employing women in the first place,[180] research continues to highlight the negative impact having a family can have on a woman lawyer's career. A brief overview here will suffice. Despite the proliferation of equal opportunities and maternity leave policies (but not maternity pay), over half of men and women barristers do not think the Bar is family-friendly.[181] It is not uncommon for women barristers to return, often after a relatively short period of maternity leave, to find that their previously buoyant practice has all but disappeared.[182] The reality of returning to practice requires considerable investment of time and energy to pick up the pieces and start again.[183] Thus, although, in theory, her self-employed status allows her to limit her hours, in practice the returning woman barrister is unlikely to be in a position to do this. The nature of the profession means that it is not usually possible for her to plan ahead and the vulnerability of her practice and finances means she is unlikely to be in a position to turn work down. Moreover, the timing of chambers meetings (typically in the early evening or at weekends) can mean that barristers with caring responsibilities can find themselves excluded from management and decision-making processes. At the Bar in London, the continuing lack of child-care facilities within the Inns of Court, recognised as a priority since the early 1990s,[184] is emblematic of the lack of institutional support for (predominantly women) barristers with caring responsibilities.[185] In 2009 28 per cent of women leaving the self-employed Bar stated that they were doing so because of child-care responsibilities (compared to just 3 per cent of men) and,

---

179 Anon quoted in Anon, 'The law of motherhood'.
180 Holland and Spender, *Without Prejudice?*, p. 11.
181 Pike and Robinson, *Barristers' Working Lives*, p. 72.
182 Comment from the Bar Council's Exit Survey reproduced in Appendix 14 of the Entry to the Bar Working Party, *Final Report*, London: Bar Council, 2007.
183 Maya Sikand quoted in Anon, 'The law of motherhood'.
184 Holland and Spender, *Without Prejudice?*, p. 15; Anon, 'Women and the Bar', *Law Society Gazette*, 27 June 1990.
185 Rowenna Davis, 'Why Children Must be Called to the Bar', *The Guardian*, 15 June 2010. The latest application was rejected by the Middle Temple in June 2010 on the grounds that more income could be generated if the proposed location was used for other purposes.

of these, just under half suggested that crèche and child-care facilities would have been 'useful'.[186]

The same is true in the solicitors' profession. Despite claims that 'forward-thinking' firms are 'bending over backwards' to accommodate flexible working for women *and* men,[187] women solicitors who make it back from maternity leave[188] often find that the promise of flexible working does not reflect the reality. For example, a woman's request for flexible working may not be matched by a reduction in her billable hours with the result that[189] 'you have to fit a full-time job into the flexible working, whilst getting paid for 80 per cent'.[190] Others find that even a very brief career break or period of flexible working serves to 'de-professionalise' them.[191] They are no longer considered to be 'proper lawyers' or are seen to have somehow 'lost their edge'.[192]

Of course, this is not to suggest that women cannot successfully combine motherhood and a legal career. It is possible to 'win at both'.[193] However, what is clear is that many of the women who do, do so because they have to be willing and able to emulate the male model of success, to 'hide' their change in status, to render their family responsibilities *invisible*. As one male BME trainee solicitor commented:

> [t]here are a few [women] partners who have had kids, when a partner would ask them a personal question, how are you doing, etc, they would deliberately never bring that issue up, for instance, they'd never talk about it; it would always be about work and how they were looking forward to the next deal or whatever . . . it's not really normal, you wouldn't really think that's a normal kind of response.[194]

This compartmentalisation of work and family life often comes at a price. Participants in the Law Society's survey of women solicitors in 2010 spoke of the

186 Electoral Reform Research, *Survey of Barristers Changing Practice Status 2001–9*, [5.4].
187 Sofia Lind, 'Bending over backwards – how City law firms are handling the flexible working question', *Legal Week*, 22 September 2010.
188 When asked to explain why they had not renewed their practising certificates, over two-thirds of women surveyed in 2003 indicated that concerns about the misgivings of employers and colleagues about their home responsibilities interfering with their work commitments were deterring them from returning (Siems, *Equality and Diversity*, p. 104).
189 Sommerlad et al, *Barriers and Individual Choice*, p. 36.
190 Insight Oxford, *Obstacles and Barriers*, p. 7.
191 Sommerlad et al, *Barriers and Individual Choice*, p. 37.
192 Duff and Webley, *Equality and Diversity*, p. 20; See also Siems, *Equality and Diversity*, pp. 85–93.
193 The extent to which women lawyers can 'have it all' continues to play out in the legal and national press. See, eg, Anon, 'The law of motherhood'; Felicity Gerry, 'Bar v Family: how to win both', *The Guardian*, 4 May 2011; Griffiths, 'Focus: Flexible Working'; Lloyd Platt, 'The stress of being a female lawyer'.
194 In Sommerlad et al, *Barriers and Individual Choice*, p. 49.

difficulty of 'juggling' their professional and personal lives,[195] and of their feelings of guilt and inadequacy at not being able to perform to the highest level in all areas of their life, perpetuated by 'impossible role models ... making fairy cakes for school or fancy dress costumes at two in the morning'.[196] Others have suggested that the reluctance of women who *are* making it work to draw attention to the extent to which they are working flexibly has 'inadvertently' created a problem of a lack of visible role models proving that it *is* possible to have a successful family life and career.[197]

For many women the real, or anticipated 'pressure of motherhood' or, more accurately, the rigidity of legal practice – is too much.[198] As early as 1987 over half of the women who had been admitted to the solicitors' profession 10 years earlier had either left it altogether or had moved into the public sector or in-house positions (compared with just 14 per cent of men).[199] While over at the Bar, the *Without Prejudice?* report in 1992, noted that survival rates of women barristers for each year of call since 1970 averaged at 28.5 per cent.[200] While it might be expected that a profession unused to 'accommodating' women would need some time to adjust, the number of women leaving both branches of the profession has not abated. In 2010, the proportion of women solicitors leaving private practice within 9 years of qualifying stood at 40 per cent.[201] The combination of the lack of women at partnership level and seeing women partners who have '"given up" so much' is, it is suggested, leading to a 'mass exodus' of younger (women) lawyers, seeking to pre-empt the difficulties discussed above by voluntarily stepping off the partnership track or by 'opting-out' of private practice early in order to build their careers in-house or in the public sector.[202] Similarly, a Bar Council study in 2005 of barristers ceasing self-employed practice found that almost twice as many women who began a tenancy between 1988 and 1998 had ceased to practise between their sixth and tenth years of call than men.[203] Women continue to be more likely than

195 Insight Oxford, *Obstacles and Barriers*, p. 18.
196 ibid.
197 Griffiths, 'Focus: Flexible Working'.
198 Luke McLeod-Roberts, 'A fifth of female lawyers choose kids over career', *The Lawyer*, 8 February 2010.
199 Marks, *Annual Statistical Report 1987*, p. 7. In 1989, it was noted that the percentage of women still holding practising certificates declined as the number of years since admission increased (Stephen Harwood, *Annual Statistical Report 1989*, London: Law Society, 1989, p. 9).
200 Holland and Spender, *Without Prejudice?*, p. 3. The survival rate for male barristers was not much better (33.9%).
201 Luke McLeod-Roberts, 'A&O set benchmark for part-time work', *The Lawyer*, 1 February 2010.
202 Insight Oxford, *Obstacles and Barriers*, p. 17; Sommerlad et al, *Barriers and Individual Choice*, p. 27. This exodus is not limited to women lawyers. Increasing numbers of male lawyers are leaving the profession in order to achieve a better work-life balance – the '"carrot" of partnership' is no longer enough (Richard Collier, 'Work-life balance: ladies only?', *The Lawyer*, 23 May 2005; see also Collier, *Men, Law and Gender*, pp. 183–187).
203 Karon Monaghan, 'Neuberger and the "F" word', Paper presented at Durham University, 22 February 2008, [14] (on file with author) referring to the Bar Council's Equality and Diversity Committee Exit Survey for Barristers Changing Practice Status Report 2005.

men to leave the Bar or to change practice status. In 2009, women made up around a third of current practitioners (32 per cent) and accounted for 42 per cent of all leavers.[204] Over half the women leaving the self-employed Bar had practised for seven years or less (51 per cent), compared with just 28 per cent of the male leavers.[205] In 2010 just 24.8% of women called to the Bar in 2003 remained at the self-employed Bar.[206]

Of course, motherhood is not the only reason that women leave the legal profession. In fact, any one of the barriers explored in this chapter may well be a reason to leave. As one legal consultant commented:

> The overall issue is that at the top end the law is a really difficult place for women to succeed. Even if you're not a woman who wants children it's almost inevitable you won't be in the club with the boys.[207]

And, whatever the reason (or combination of reasons) for leaving, the upshot is the same. Women are not only not trickling-up the legal profession, they are trickling-*out*. And this has serious implications for the diversity not only of the legal profession, but also for the judiciary.

Moving beyond the trickle-up argument

When women began entering the legal profession in large numbers, it was easy to assume that in time change would follow; that as increasing numbers of women entered the legal profession they would eventually trickle-up to its senior levels, rebalancing the pool of potential judges and ensuring a more diverse Bench. And it is easy to see why so many in the legal profession and beyond were – and still are – 'seduced' by the trickle-up argument. After all, it makes relatively few demands. Its logic is straightforward: so long as the judiciary is drawn from the legal profession, if there are fewer women than men in the legal profession, as has historically been the case, then the same will be true of the judiciary. Once this is remedied – that is, once more women join the legal profession – a more diverse judiciary will follow. In the meantime, all we need do is wait. It is an argument for change grounded in inaction. The trickle-up argument enables its proponents to be seen to be 'doing something' about diversity, while doing nothing at all. And, of course, depending on your viewpoint, herein lies the rub:

> The view that time and the example set by a growing number of very able women at the Bar will dispel discrimination is a seductive one. It absolves

---

204 Electoral Reform Research, *Survey of Barristers Changing Practice Status 2001–9*, [5.1].
205 ibid., [5.3.2].
206 Bar Council figures on file with author.
207 Byrne, 'UK's top firms fail to increase female equity partner figures'.

individuals and the profession from taking action. There is little evidence, however, within the profession or elsewhere, that the laissez faire approach is effective . . . Time [is] no great healer.[208]

And so it has proven. Despite increasing numbers of women entering the legal profession and creating pressure on the pipeline, the much-fêted trickle-up has failed to materialise. The composition of the legal profession at its upper levels remains stubbornly resistant to change.

And what is more, we know, for the most part, why this is. We know why men continue to dominate at partnership and QC level as well as in the Inns of Court and professional bodies. We know the barriers facing women seeking to make their way through the legal profession. We know that the equality between women and men lawyers, taken for granted by the trickle-up argument, does not exist. We know that women in the legal profession continue to encounter discrimination, in both its passive and more blatant guises. We know that women not only fail to progress through the legal profession at the speed or rate of their male colleagues, but also that, in many cases, they are not even on the same track, since women are more likely to be working in low status, low paid, low profile positions and areas of law. We know that women lawyers are more likely to leave, to trickle-out of the legal profession than their male colleagues. And we know that the reasons for all of this will be presented as the result of 'choices' women lawyers have made.

In the face of this slow progress and continuing discrimination, the trickle-up argument has no response. As Sally Kenney notes, a 'torrent in the pipeline . . . creates pressure, to be sure. It creates a large group of interested parties whose ambitions are thwarted'.[209] A mass of entrants failing to make their way to the upper echelons of the profession might also make it easier to point to ongoing obstacles and barriers hindering their progress, but, as we are seeing, this will not *in and of itself* alter the composition of the judiciary.[210] Instead, the trickle-up argument relies on those largely responsible for what the Commission for Judicial Appointments identified in 2003 as wide and 'systemic bias in the way in which the legal profession . . . conduct[s] business',[211] to introduce the structural and institutional changes necessary to ensure that women lawyers progress at the same rate as men. The trickle-up argument shifts responsibility for diversifying the judiciary onto those invested in maintaining the status quo. It allows the legal profession to dictate the pace of change in the judiciary. And while its leaders might no longer feel quite so confident as Martin Mears in 1996 to lay the blame publicly for women lawyers' lack of progression on their biology, it is clear that the

208 Holland and Spender, *Without Prejudice?*, p. 6.
209 Kenney, 'Gender on the Agenda', 727.
210 ibid.
211 Commission for Judicial Appointments, *Annual Report 2003*, [5.50–5.51].

sentiment remains.[212] The legal profession remains a bastion of maleness in which women are merely 'fringe-dwellers'.[213] And, moreover, the 'brutal truth' is that men not only continue to dominate more senior positions within the legal profession, but are becoming even more resistant to change.[214] So long as our judges continue to be appointed from the upper echelons of the Bar, those charged with bringing about greater judicial diversity have few levers by which they may exert pressure on an 'embattled profession' that has shown itself to be adept at resisting change.[215] The legal profession is able to act as a 'gatekeeper' to the judiciary, as efforts to increase judicial diversity are, in practice, 'subordinated to upholding the interests of particular sections of the legal profession'.[216]

So where does this leave us? Certainly so long as the legal profession continues to restrict the flow of women into the pool of potential judges, the task of changing the make-up of the judiciary is made harder. And insofar as there has been a general reluctance effectively to confront the legal profession about this, it is hard to resist Lizzie Barmes and Kate Malleson's conclusion that, whatever else we do in relation to judicial diversity, 'however neutral and meritocratic the judicial appointments process, diversity will remain elusive while the demonstrably false premise obtains that appointments are from an equally neutral, meritocratic legal profession'.[217] Clearly, the continued disparity between women and men in the pool of potential judges makes it harder for those seeking to remedy the imbalance between them on the Bench. Unless and until there are more women, and other non-traditional candidates, at all levels of the legal profession, this is unlikely to be mirrored in the judiciary. This is a problem and is a problem which, as we are

212 The concern that the next generation of male lawyers are adopting the mindset of their more senior colleagues (Insight Oxford, *Obstacles and Barriers*, p. 11) is given credence by the comment of a trainee that the additional hurdles women face is 'because *they go and have kids*, they get penalised for it, it's as simple as that' (Collier, *Men, Law and Gender*, p. 176).

213 Margaret Thornton, *Dissonance and Distrust: Women in the Legal Profession*, Oxford: Oxford University Press, 1996, pp. 3–4.

214 Collier, *Men, Law and Gender*, pp. 188–189.

215 ibid., p. 190. They could, of course, as Lady Hale and others have suggested, make more of an effort to identify the highly-qualified candidates who are engaging in less 'visible' forms of legal practices rather than just top QCs (Bowcott, 'UK Supreme Court's only female judge calls for more diversity in appointments'). Lord McNally giving evidence to the Constitution Committee Inquiry into the Judicial Appointments Process appeared to be willing to tackle the legal profession's grip on judicial appointments: 'With no disrespect to such a distinguished profession . . . this [reminds] me of the old story of meeting the sleeping pig on the road. You give it a kick to move it, it gives a contented grunt and then goes back to sleep. Somehow we have to get buy-in . . . from the professions themselves . . . I will concede to the Lord Chancellor that his profession is not inherently prejudiced, but there are problems which need to be unstitched. Other professions have done it, so why not the law?' (18 January 2012, Q379).

216 Barmes and Malleson, 'The Legal Profession as Gatekeeper', p. 249. See also House of Lords Select Committee on the Constitution, *Judicial Appointments* (HL Paper 272), 2012 [120–125] (Judicial Appointments Report).

217 ibid., p. 256.

seeing, has no quick fix. Until this is resolved, until men and women are able to progress and compete equally in the legal profession, the diversity of the judiciary is unlikely to change. However, while to this extent the prospects of a diverse judiciary rest on resolving problems in the make-up of the legal profession, it does not follow that, until these problems are resolved, there is nothing more we can do. The fact that we cannot put *everything* right does not mean that we cannot put *anything* right. In fact, where this leaves us is with the second factor often cited for the lack of judicial diversity: the process of appointing judges. And this is something which we *can* do, and have been doing, something about.

Chapter 3

How we appoint judges

I don't think the Judicial Appointments Commission has made a blind bit of difference to [judicial diversity] – that is a personal opinion. There is more diversity now than when it was set up, but I don't think it has gone any faster than you would have expected it to do under the old arrangements anyway.

(Kenneth Clarke, Minister of State for Justice and Lord Chancellor)[1]

Typically, two explanations are given for why we do not have a more diverse judiciary and why it is taking so long to get one: first, the homogeneity of the pool from which judges are selected, explored in the previous chapter and, second, the process by which judicial appointments are made. As we can see, improving levels of diversity in the legal profession is not proving straightforward. The composition of the senior levels of the legal profession has so far proven resistant to change, with the result that men continue to dominate the traditional pool of potential judges. But what of the second explanation for the lack of diversity: an appointments process that has traditionally worked against those women who *are* able to make it into this pool? Here too progress toward greater judicial diversity is proving harder than was anticipated. Indeed, significant changes in the appointments process and the promise of further modifications, although welcome, appear unlikely to yield greater diversity in the near future.

Judicial appointment? Not for the likes of me . . .

For centuries judges were appointed through a secretive and closed process. Judicial appointment was by invitation only. Responsibility for choosing the judges fell to the Lord Chancellor, a senior member of the government and then head of the judiciary, who would 'tap' the shoulder of those he thought were

1 Kenneth Clarke, Oral evidence to the House of Lords Select Committee on the Constitution, 'Annual Meeting with the Lord Chancellor', 19 January 2011, Q27 (unrevised transcript).

suitable for judicial appointment from members of the Bar. Historically the senior Bar, and hence the pool of potential appointees, was small enough for the Lord Chancellor to know most of them personally (especially as he was also likely to have been involved in their earlier appointment to QC). However, as the Bar grew, the Lord Chancellor, and in turn the appointments process, became increasingly reliant on views of potential candidates garnered through a process of informal consultation with senior members of the judiciary and legal profession. This sought to gather as much information as possible about the candidates from across the legal profession, while also incorporating a 'valuable element of peer-appraisal'.[2]

However, the process attracted strong criticism from both outside and within the legal profession.[3] At issue was whether an assessment of the suitability and competence of the potential candidate could 'fairly be done, and fairly be seen to be done'[4] through such a wide-ranging and largely secretive exercise. At best, it was argued, the process encouraged capricious or ill-informed comments about the candidates; 'nothing is more arbitrary, I promise, than being able in confidence to put down your views about colleagues with no come-back'.[5] And, at worst, it was (or at least was seen to be) 'a licence to discriminate' against anyone who was not a 'safe pair of hands',[6] allowing the judiciary to be run as if it were 'the private fiefdom of a very narrow kind of white, heterosexual male'.[7] Either

2 Lord Mackay, 'Selection of Judges Prior to the Establishment of the Judicial Appointments Commission in 2006' in *Judicial Appointments: Balancing Independence, Accountability and Legitimacy*, London: Judicial Appointments Commission, 2010, p. 67.

3 See, for example, Lord Bingham, HC Home Affairs Committee, Minutes of Evidence, 17 March 1998, Q128–130; Colin Campbell, Oral evidence to the Constitutional Affairs Committee, Inquiry on Judicial Appointments and a Supreme Court (Court of Final Appeal), 11 November 2003, Q53 (HC 48-i Session 2003–04); HC Constitutional Affairs Committee, *Judicial Appointments and a Supreme Court (Court of Final Appeal)*, (First Report of Session 2003–04, Volume 1) HC 48-1, 2004, [147–153]; Clare Dyer, 'Solicitors boycott "old-boys' network"', *The Guardian*, 28 September 1999. Indeed, in 1991, Geoffrey Bindman, former legal adviser to the Race Relations Board and Commission for Racial Equality, suggested that the reliance on informal consultation in the appointments process amounted to indirect discrimination contrary to the Sex Discrimination Act 1975 and the Race Relations Act 1976 (Geoffrey Bindman, 'Is the system of judicial appointments illegal?', *Law Society Gazette*, 27 February 1991, 24–25). This was strongly refuted by the then Lord Chancellor, Lord Mackay, as 'wrong in theory and fact' (Anon, 'Lord Mackay hits out on judicial appointments', *Law Society Gazette*, 30 July 1991).

4 Law Society, *Broadening the Bench: Law Society proposals for reforming the way judges are appointed*, London: Law Society, October 2000, p. 10.

5 Lord Lester quoted in HC Constitutional Affairs Committee, *Judicial Appointments and a Supreme Court (Court of Final Appeal)*, [148].

6 Male BME barrister quoted in Kate Malleson and Fareda Banda, *Factors affecting the decision to apply for Silk and Judicial Office* (Lord Chancellor's Department Research Programme 2/00), London: Lord Chancellor's Department, 2000, p. 14.

7 Adrian Fulford quoted in Frances Gibb, 'Men in grey suits asked if I had some kind of unspeakable sexual interest', *The Times*, 21 January 2009.

way, it seemed unlikely that this method of appointing judges would deliver a diverse Bench in the near future.

In 1992, the *Without Prejudice?* report jointly commissioned by the Bar Council and Lord Chancellor's Department concluded that the judicial appointments process depended on 'patronage, being noticed and being known' and as such was 'unlikely . . . to offer equal access to women'.[8] Judicial appointment turned on the visibility and reputation of the would-be judge. There was a sense among potential applicants, especially those from non-traditional groups, that judicial appointments were *really* made on the basis of who one knew, what chambers one came from, what judges one had appeared before and so on.[9] The appointments process, it was suggested, was weighted in favour of white, male barristers who, as we saw in the previous chapter, were more likely to be in positions where they would be 'known' or 'noticed', and against women and other candidates who were less visible, who were more likely to be outside traditional networks. These views were given credence not only by the lack of diversity on the Bench, but also by the fact that the current incumbents were selected from a small group of favoured chambers. Research by the Association of Women Barristers in 1996 found that in the previous 10 years, just under a third of all appointments to the High Court and above came from just seven sets of chambers, representing three per cent of sets in London and two per cent of sets across England and Wales.[10]

Little wonder that research by Kate Malleson and Fareda Banda for the Lord Chancellor's Department in 2000 found a 'high level of criticism' and a 'significant degree' of dissatisfaction with the judicial appointments process among women, solicitors and members of BME groups.[11] In fact, for these groups the lack of openness and transparency, as well as continuing patronage and the need to be 'known', were not simply weaknesses in the process itself but also reasons *not to apply in the first place*. As a result, they were simply less likely to 'opt-in' to the process. After all, there was little point in engaging with a process that was weighted against – or in favour of – certain candidates, in applying to join an institution that would 'never have the likes of me'.[12] As a result, highly-qualified women and BME candidates under-applied for judicial appointment.[13]

8 Lesley Holland and Lynne Spender, *Without Prejudice? Sex Equality at the Bar and in the Judiciary*, Bournemouth: TMS Management Consultants, 1992, p. 26.
9 Malleson and Banda, *Factors affecting the decision to apply for Silk and Judicial Office*, pp. 24–25.
10 Clare McGlynn, *The Woman Lawyer – Making the Difference*, London: Butterworths, 1998, p. 178. In a written answer from the Lord Chancellor's Department to the House of Commons in November 1999, it was suggested that between 1996–1999 just nine sets of chambers had more than one member appointed to the judiciary (including the circuit bench) (11 November 1999).
11 Malleson and Banda, *Factors affecting the decision to apply for Silk and Judicial Office*, p. 39.
12 Lord Irvine, 'Speech to Minority Lawyers Conference', London, 29 November 1997.
13 Figures from the Lord Chancellor's Department support this. By way of example, in 1999, women made up just 17% of applicants and 16% of appointments to the position of assistant recorder (a key entry post into the senior judiciary), despite comprising 22% of the pool of potential appointees (Malleson and Banda, *Factors affecting the decision to apply for Silk and Judicial Office*, pp. 6–7).

By the turn of the millennium, while opinions differed over whether the problem lay in the system itself or in women's perception of the system, it was clear that unless and until more women applied for judicial office, the number of women judges would continue to be low. Something needed to be done. And, fortunately, radical reform of an increasingly discredited appointments process appeared, at last, to be on the political agenda.

From Lord Chancellor to Judicial Appointments Commission

Although Lord Hailsham and Lord Mackay introduced some changes to the appointments process during the mid-1980s to early 1990s,[14] it was not until Lord Irvine's appointment as Lord Chancellor following the general election in 1997 that far-reaching reform of the judicial appointments process appeared a real possibility.[15] The newly-elected Labour Party had been a long term supporter of some form of judicial appointments commission and Lord Irvine himself, just five years earlier, had described arrangements for the appointment of judges as 'outdated, secretive and elitist'.[16] However, it was not to be. After just one year in office, Lord Irvine was of the view that the arrangements – although in need of some 'improvement' – were 'basically sound'.[17] In particular, he had 'no intention of abolishing' the widely-derided system of 'secret soundings'[18] – a moniker he rejected as inaccurate: the process neither involved 'soundings' nor was 'secret' (not least because 'it is no secret that they happen').[19] Almost as soon as it had arrived, wholesale reform of the judicial appointments process was once again off the political agenda.

This is not to say that there were no changes to the judicial appointments process during Lord Irvine's tenure. As researchers and campaigners continued to make the case for changes to the appointments process and, in particular, for

14 See further, Mackay, 'Selection of Judges', pp. 11–30; 'Timeline of Judicial Initiatives in England and Wales' in Advisory Panel on Judicial Diversity, *The Report of the Advisory Panel on Judicial Diversity 2010*, London: Ministry of Justice, 2010, Annex 3 (Neuberger Report) (prepared by Cheryl Thomas).

15 Robert Lindsey, 'Women lawyers to push Lord Irvine over judicial selection', *The Lawyer*, 7 January 1997.

16 Lord Irvine, 'Setting New Bench Marks', *The Guardian*, 4 March 1992.

17 Lord Irvine, 'Speech to 1998 Women Lawyer Conference', London, 25 April 1998.

18 ibid. The sounding process was not without supporters see, eg, the views of white male barristers interviewed by Malleson and Banda who were 'broadly accepting of current process' especially when it came to identifying weak or inappropriate candidates: 'we all know each other terribly well and the judges know us terribly well . . . everybody gossips like crazy of course and even know everybody else's weak points so its very transparent within the system' (Malleson and Banda, *Factors affecting the decision to apply for Silk and Judicial Office*, p. 28).

19 Lord Chancellor's Department Press Release, Discrimination in Judicial Appointments – Irvine's Statement, 29 November 1997.

appointments to be made by an independent judicial appointments commission,[20] he sought to address concerns over the lack of transparency in the appointments process by taking a number of less radical steps to ensure that the process was 'open, fair, effective, and – just as important – accessible',[21] including advertising vacancies in the High Court.[22] In March 2001, in line with a recommendation made by Leonard Peach in his assessment of the judicial and QC appointment processes in 1999,[23] the Commission for Judicial Appointments was established. Unlike its similarly named successor, its remit was not to participate in the appointments process itself, but rather to investigate complaints and to provide an independent review of the processes by which judges and QCs were appointed. Its findings were published in often highly critical annual reports.[24] By 2003, having repeatedly urged women and BME candidates to put themselves forward with the mantra 'Don't be shy; apply',[25] Lord Irvine's 'improvements' were complete. Just two months before leaving office, and echoing the comment of his predecessor, Lord Hailsham, almost 20 years earlier, that the judicial appointments process was 'almost as foolproof as it could be',[26] Lord Irvine told the Select Committee on the Lord Chancellor's Department, that he believed the existing system 'has been brought to the best state that is reasonably achievable in a system of this kind'.[27]

20 For example, Cheryl Thomas and Kate Malleson, *Judicial Appointment Commissions: The European and North American Experience and the Possible Implications for the United Kingdom*, (Lord Chancellor's Department Research Series 6/97), London: Lord Chancellor's Department, December 1997; Leonard Peach, *An Independent Scrutiny of the Appointment Processes of Judges and Queen's Counsel*, London: HMSO, 1999 (Peach Report); Law Society, 'Broadening the Bench'; Law Society, 'Judicial Appointments Commission: A Discussion Paper', January 2000.

21 Lord Irvine, 'Speech to 1998 Women Lawyer Conference'. See, generally, Mackay, 'Selection of Judges', pp. 24–29.

22 Although in truth this did little to restrict the Lord Chancellor's discretion. It merely created a 'long list' from which the Lord Chancellor could – should he wish – make selections for judicial appointment. He retained the power to appoint those not included on this list. Between 1999 and 2003, 64% of appointments, 23 out of 36, were by invitation from the Lord Chancellor (HC Constitutional Affairs Committee, *Judicial Appointments and a Supreme Court (Court of Final Appeal)*, [153]).

23 Peach Report, Recommendation 13, pp. 24–27.

24 During its five-year existence, the Commission for Judicial Appointments was consistently and openly critical of the soundings or consultation process, which it viewed as 'fatally flawed' and ripe for abolition. See, eg, Commission for Judicial Appointments, *Annual Report 2005*, London: Commission for Judicial Appointments, 2005 [2.24]; Commission for Judicial Appointments, *Annual Report 2004*, London: Commission for Judicial Appointments, 2004, [3.27–3.28].

25 Lord Irvine, 'Speech to 1998 Women Lawyer Conference'; Lord Irvine, 'Speech to the Association of Women Barristers', The Barbican, London, 11 February 1998; Lord Irvine, 'IBA World Women Lawyers Conference', Old Hall Lincoln's Inn, London, 1 March 2001; Lord Irvine, 'Speech to the Association of Women Solicitors', Painter Stainers Hall, London, 23 March 2001.

26 In Jon Robins, 'Women, ethnic minorities and solicitors; the courts need you', *The Lawyer*, 5 December 2005.

27 Lord Irvine, Select Committee on the Lord Chancellor's Department, Minutes of Evidence, 2 April 2003, [75].

Enter Lord Falconer, a Secretary of State for Constitutional Affairs and Lord Chancellor ready not only to go 'boldly' but also 'further and faster' than any previous Lord Chancellor in his pursuit of judicial reform.[28] In July 2003, the newly renamed Department for Constitutional Affairs consulted on the appointments process, resurrecting the possibility of an independent judicial appointments commission.[29] The following year, in his address to the Labour Party Annual Conference, Lord Falconer promised to deliver 'real change' to the judiciary:

> We are going to take steps to increase diversity in the judiciary. Judges must be and will continue to be appointed on merit. But it can't be lack of merit, can it, that means it's taken until this Labour government to appoint the first-ever woman judge in the House of Lords? Or ... for the first-ever member of an ethnic minority to become a High Court judge?[30]

A month later, in October 2004, a further consultation paper on judicial appointments was published: *Increasing Diversity in the Judiciary*.[31] It confirmed the establishment of a judicial appointments commission, which would be charged not only with increasing the transparency and accountability of the appointments process but with 'open[ing] up the Bench to more candidates'.[32] For the first time, increasing judicial diversity was seen as a focus, rather than simply a desirable by-product, of changes to the appointments process. The success or otherwise of the appointments process was to be measured not simply by the fairness and transparency of its processes, but also by its outcome, in the diversity of the applicants and of the appointments made.

28 Lord Falconer, 'Increasing Judicial Diversity: The Next Steps', Commission for Judicial Appointments, Institute of Mechanical Engineers, London, 2 November 2005.

29 Department for Constitutional Affairs, *Constitutional Reform: A New Way of Appointing Judges*, CP 10/03, London: Department for Constitutional Affairs, 2003; Department for Constitutional Affairs, 'Summary of Responses to the Consultation Paper, Constitutional reform: A new way of appointing Judges' (January 2004). In the same month the Department for Constitutional Affairs also released a consultation paper on proposing to replace the House of Lords with a new Supreme Court of the UK, which argued for appointments to the new court by a recommending commission (Department for Constitutional Affairs, *Constitutional Reform: A Supreme Court for the United Kingdom*, CP 11/03, London: Department for Constitutional Affairs, 2003).

30 Charlie Falconer, 'Opening up our Institutions for the Future', Speech to the Labour Party Conference, 29 September 2004.

31 Department for Constitutional Affairs, *Increasing Diversity in the Judiciary*, CP25/04, London: Department for Constitutional Affairs, 2004.

32 ibid., p. 8. A provision for a judicial appointments commission responsible for recruiting and selecting judges was included in the Constitutional Reform Bill, introduced to the House of Lords by the Lord Chancellor in February 2004.

All in all, indications were good. As the parliamentary processes continued, Lord Falconer continued to make the case for the necessity of a more diverse judiciary:

> My strong view is that, over time, we will not continue to have the best judges, as we do now, unless we increase their diversity. We will not, over time, continue to have judges, as we do now, who understand the communities they serve unless we increase their diversity. We will not continue to have judges, as we do now, who carry the confidence of their communities unless we increase their diversity. Diversity matters. Diversity is not an afterthought – something we do at the end of the process to see whether we have got things 'roughly right'. Nor is it a politically correct gesture – something we do to tick boxes to prove how forward thinking we all are . . . I believe that the case for greater judicial diversity is clear. A more diverse judiciary is a better judiciary. And a better judiciary means better justice.[33]

How did he propose to deliver this better, stronger, more diverse, judiciary? The first thing to note is that Lord Falconer's aforementioned boldness only went so far. Judicial appointments would continue to be made on merit. Any use of positive action, such as quotas or targets, to speed up the representation of certain groups, and notwithstanding the improvements to the quality of justice Lord Falconer considered they might bring, continued to be off the table. Moreover, Lord Falconer's expectations as to the composition of a diverse Bench were relatively low. Unlike Lord Taylor who, as Lord Chief Justice in 1992, had spoken of a 'substantial number' of appointments of women and BME candidates within the next five years,[34] Lord Falconer gave himself a further 13 years *after* Lord Taylor's deadline, until 2010, to ensure under-represented candidates were being appointed 'in proportion to their presence in the pool',[35] a considerably lower target. Nevertheless, change was afoot. Lord Falconer appeared to be willing to take (at least some) 'positive steps' necessary to deliver a diverse judiciary.[36] And his primary foot-soldier to aid him in this mission was the newly inaugurated Judicial Appointments Commission (JAC). Buoyed by reports in the press that the number of women and BME judges was 'rocketing',[37] expectations were high; a more diverse Bench seemed – at last – to be a real possibility.

33 Lord Falconer, 'Increasing Judicial Diversity', Women Lawyers' Forum, London, 5 March 2005. See also Lord Falconer, 'Increasing Judicial Diversity: The Next Steps'.
34 Lord Taylor, *The Judiciary in the Nineties*, The Richard Dimbleby Lecture, 1992.
35 Lord Falconer, 'Increasing Judicial Diversity: The Next Steps'.
36 ibid.
37 Frances Gibb, 'More women join the judiciary', *The Times*, 1 February 2006.

The JAC: new broom, same old cobwebs

The JAC started work in 2006, dramatically altering the way judges were appointed in England and Wales. For the first time, members of the judiciary were selected by an independent commission, rather than a government minister.[38] The process of appointing judges also changed. Secret soundings and taps on the shoulder were replaced (for the most part) by application forms, qualifying tests and interviews. And yet, despite this (not so) 'quiet revolution'[39] in the personnel choosing the judges and how they are selected, as we saw in Chapter 1, relatively little has changed in relation to the *outcome* of the process, in the judges who are being chosen. A diverse judiciary, particularly at its senior levels, seems as far away as ever. In fact, a snail could crawl the entire length of the UK – and a quarter of the way back again – in the time the Equality and Human Rights Commission predict it will take for there to be parity between women and men in the senior judiciary.[40]

So, what has gone wrong? Why did Lord Falconer's mission end in failure? A number of factors have contributed to the JAC's inability to alter, or indeed challenge, the status quo. The combination of antipathy and suspicion of the legal profession and certain elements of the judiciary, at least when the JAC was first set up, statutory provisions restricting who can be appointed and the basis for appointments, as well as overly ambitious expectations as to what the JAC could achieve and the length of time it would take to meet its objectives have certainly contributed to a sense that the JAC was perhaps destined to disappoint. However, the criticisms are not all one way. The JAC has made some poor choices both in terms of its selection processes and in its relationship with the other key stake-holders in the judicial appointments process, most notably those high up in the legal profession. And so, while without doubt the JAC was dealt a rather poor hand, its progress to date has not been helped by the relatively conservative way it has chosen to play it.

38 The composition of the JAC is set out in Schedule 12 of the Constitutional Reform Act (CRA) 2005. Six of the 14 commissioners, including the chair, must have a non-legal or lay background. Of the remaining commissioners, five must be drawn from the judiciary, alongside one member from each branch of the legal profession, one tribunal member and one lay justice member. There is no statutory requirement of diversity among the commissioners. In February 2012, at the time of writing, six of the 15 commissioners are women.
39 Baroness Prashar, 'Speech to Chartered Institute of Patent Attorneys Congress', 30 October 2008; Baroness Prashar, 'Sweet & Maxwell Judicial Review Conference', 21 November 2008.
40 The Equality and Human Rights Commission used the example of a snail crawling nine times around the M25 (the motorway that circles London) (Equality and Human Rights Commission, *Sex and Power 2008*, London: Equality and Human Rights Commission, 2008, p. 5). The 2011 *Sex and Power* report suggests it will take another 45 years (up from 40 years in 2007, although down from 55 years in 2008) (Equality and Human Rights Commission, *Sex and Power: 2011*, London: Equality and Human Rights Commission, 2011, p. 3).

Setting the ground rules

Despite its name, the JAC does not make judicial appointments.[41] Rather, the Constitutional Reform Act 2005 gives the JAC the task of *recommending* candidates for judicial appointment, by identifying a single candidate for each appointment for consideration by the Lord Chancellor, who can then appoint the candidate, ask the JAC to reconsider their recommendation or reject the candidate outright.[42] Within this broad remit, the JAC is largely free to determine how it selects the candidates for recommendation, subject to the statutory requirements of appointment on merit and of encouraging diversity in the pool.[43] To this end, the JAC has developed and published the five core 'qualities and abilities required for judicial office',[44] which, along with the statutory requirements for each post, are used to determine a candidate's suitability for judicial appointment, as well as establishing a significant outreach programme. The nomination – or selection (as the JAC describes it) – process varies slightly according to the level of the court and each is considered here in turn.

41 Judicial appointments, depending on the level, are either made by the Lord Chancellor or by the Queen (on the recommendation of the Prime Minister).

42 The JAC is responsible for all judicial appointments, except for those at the very top (to the Supreme Court) and very bottom (the appointment of lay magistrates) of the judicial hierarchy. The process varies according to the level of appointment and are set out in the CRA (ss 26–31 and schedule 8 (Supreme Court); ss 67–84 (senior appointments); ss 85–94 (High Court and below)). One notable omission from the JAC's remit is the appointment of deputy High Court judges. Previously, responsibility for the selection and appointment of these recorders and circuit judges who are authorised to sit in the High Court, rested with the Lord Chief Justice (or nominee) under s 9(1) of the Senior Courts Act 1981. The JAC is required to 'concur' with nominees which, in 2010–2011, it did in respect of 22 individuals (Judicial Appointments Commission, *Annual Report 2010/11 Building the Best Judiciary for a Diverse Society*, London: Judicial Appointments Commission, 2011, p. 8). Beyond this, there is no publicly available information as to either the identity or diversity of appointments at this level. Insofar as appointment to the position of deputy High Court judge appears to be an important step towards securing full-time senior judicial appointment (the JAC notes that over 80% of those it has selected for appointment to the High Court have had this experience) it is right that this position is brought within the JAC's purview (as suggested in Ministry of Justice, *Appointments and Diversity: 'A Judiciary for the 21st Century'*, CP19/2011, London: Ministry of Justice, 2011, [42–50]) and that future appointments are actively used as a means of ensuring a more diverse pool of potential High Court appointments.

43 CRA s 63(2); s 64(1). In addition, the JAC must select candidates of 'good character' (CRA s 63(3)) and must have regard to guidance issued by the Lord Chancellor, issued under s 65, including for the purposes of 'the encouragement of diversity in the range of persons available for selection' (CRA s 65(3)), although to date no guidance has been issued.

44 These are intellectual capacity; personal qualities; an ability to understand and deal fairly; authority; and communication skills and efficiency (JAC website, 'Qualities and Abilities'. Online. Available: http://jac.judiciary.gov.uk/application-process/112.htm) (accessed 23 February 2012). Merit is discussed in detail in Chapter 6, pp. 187–195.

Appointments up to and including the High Court

The selection process for appointments up to and including the High Court is a mixture of old and new.[45] Without doubt it is a much more open and transparent process than its forerunner. The process utilises a variety of recruitment tools including written applications, qualifying tests, interviews, role-plays, candidate presentations and what the JAC calls 'situational questioning' in which the candidate is tested on how he or she would respond to 'real-life' issues. And, while the process is not fully independent of executive control and the influence of the senior judiciary, the role of both is significantly curtailed.[46] Similarly, although innovations such as the qualifying test were, and still are, controversial, particularly among members of the Bar and tribunal members,[47] this allows for the transparent assessment of candidates' relative qualities at the shortlisting stage, while the use of role-plays and situational questioning enables candidates to demonstrate their abilities in ways which go beyond the usual scope of a traditional interview.[48]

45 The selection process is outlined in detail on the JAC website (JAC website, 'Selection Process Overview', Online. Available: http://jac.judiciary.gov.uk/selection-process/352.htm) (accessed 23 February 2012).
46 Before making its recommendation to the Lord Chancellor, the JAC is statutorily obliged to consult the Lord Chief Justice and another person who has held the post, or has relevant experience of the post, about the candidate(s) it is minded to select (CRA, s 88(3); s 94(3)). And, although the JAC need not follow the recommendation of these statutory consultees, when making its report to the Lord Chancellor it must state whether it has done so and, if not, give its reasons as why this is the case. The Ministry of Justice has consulted on whether responsibility for appointing judges to the High Court and below (including the power to request reconsideration or reject nominations) should be transferred from the Lord Chancellor to the Lord Chief Justice (as head of the judiciary) (Ministry of Justice, *Appointments and Diversity*, Q1). While there are concerns that this will remove an aspect of political accountability and may be seen to increase the influence of the judiciary, this is unlikely to have any significant impact on the appointments process. The HL Constitution Inquiry into Judicial Appointments recommended that this power be transferred to the Lord Chief Justice for appointments below the High Court and that a review of whether this should be extended to appointments to the High Court should be held in 3–5 years' time (House of Lords Select Committee on the Constitution, *Judicial Appointments* (HL Paper 272), 2012, [34] (*Judicial Appointments Report*).
47 See, eg, Joshua Rosenberg, 'Lawyers who merit judicial appointment are not reaching the bench' *Law Society Gazette*, 2 February 2010 as well as written evidence to the HL Select Committee on the Constitution Inquiry into the Judicial Appointments Process, October 2011 (Constitution Committee Inquiry). From Anne Arnold (district judge (magistrates' courts) and recorder), the Legal Services Board, Alison McKenna (principal judge, first-tier tribunal (CHARITY)), Sheba Haroon Storey (principal judge, Asylum Support) and the Chancery Bar Association. In his most recent Annual Report, the Judicial Appointments and Conduct Ombudsman noted a decrease in the number of complaints about the qualifying test indicating, in its view, that 'applicants are getting used to this form of sift criteria' (Judicial Appointments and Conduct Ombudsman, *Annual Report 2010–11*, London: Stationery Office, 2011, p. 8).
48 The Advisory Panel on Judicial Diversity (APJD) in 2010 made a number of recommendations relating to the JAC's selection process, including putting the qualifying tests online, providing effective feedback and streamlining the processes that are currently being considered by the JAC (Neuberger Report, Recommendations 25–34, 39–40; Ministry of Justice, *Improving Judicial Diversity: Progress Towards Delivery of the 'Report of the Advisory Panel on Judicial Diversity 2010'*, London: Ministry of Justice, 2011, pp. 37–45, 49–50) (McNally Report)).

Nevertheless the JAC has, it seems, some way to go before the ghosts of the appointments process past are fully exorcised. Vestiges of the old system – in particular in its decision to seek 'JAC nominated' references in addition to those nominated by the candidates – remain. The criticisms of the use of such consultations should by now be familiar. The uniformity of the consultees – the make-up of the current Bench means that the vast majority are likely to be white men from a limited professional and socio-economic background – both *disadvantages* and disempowers non-traditional candidates and works to the *advantage* of candidates who are known to the judiciary – who are 'already "in the club"'[49] – typically white, male barristers.[50] As Anne Morris notes in a different context:

> Not all those who discriminate do so consciously. The white middle-class who still predominate the boardrooms, committee rooms and courts may instinctively and unconsciously prefer and select those who 'embody' what they consider to be the 'requirements' for the job. It need not be as obvious as the old school tie or a shared University education, or even connections of friendship or family. It may simply be that people are more comfortable with the kind of reflection they see in the mirror.[51]

This is precisely why an open and transparent appointments process is essential. Moreover, even if efforts are made to reduce the possibility of discrimination, the benefits of an extensive consultation process *for selectors* are limited in large recruitment exercises for junior judicial positions where the senior judiciary are unlikely to know the candidates.

While the changes to the appointments process have generally been well-received – three-quarters of the respondents to research commissioned by the JAC looking at continuing barriers to judicial appointment agreed that establishing the Commission had been a positive step – there continues to be a perception of underlying bias (among both under- and over-represented groups) in the process.[52]

---

49 Neuberger Report, [120]. Disappointingly, the APJD was of the view that the statutory consultation process provided an important 'safeguard' in the appointments process and that coming, as it does, *after* the JAC has made its provisional decision ensures that all candidates *up to this point* are considered on their merit, regardless of whether or not they are known by members of the judiciary. Rather than recommending their abolition, the APJD recommended that the importance and purpose of the statutory consultation needed to be conveyed to candidates as part of a concerted campaign of 'myth-busting' (Neuberger Report [121]).

50 This view is given credence by recent High Court appointments. Of the judges currently in the High Court, appointed between 2000–2010, over a quarter (27%) came from just seven chambers (June 2011 figures).

51 Anne Morris, 'Embodying the Law: *Coker and Osamor v The Lord Chancellor and the Lord Chancellor's Department* [2002] IRLR 80 (Court of Appeal)', *Feminist Legal Studies*, 11, 2003, 45, pp. 52–53.

52 Anthony Allen, *Barriers to Application for Judicial Appointment Research*, London: BMRB Social, 2009, pp. 1, 3.

Almost the same proportion of respondents (72 per cent) believed it was harder for some candidates to be successful than others, with BME candidates more likely than any other group to agree that it is harder for certain types of people to apply successfully for judicial appointment.[53] Higher court experience, being known by senior judiciary, being a barrister, and having the right education and social network were all viewed as having a strong positive influence on appointment.[54] A third of all respondents – and 38 per cent of women – still indicated that a judicial career was 'not for people like them'.[55] Women continue to be more likely than men to be unsure both that they have the skills to apply for judicial office, *and that the selection process will recognise them*.[56] A similar survey of lesbian, gay, bisexual and transgender (LGBT) lawyers in 2010 found that 70 per cent of respondents – and 100 per cent of lesbian respondents – believed that there was prejudice in the selection process (compared with 55 per cent of those interviewed by the JAC).[57]

The appointments system may therefore be more open and transparent than ever before but, as the JAC is learning, the process needs not only to *be* fair, but also to *be seen as* fair. And with figures suggesting that 24 per cent of respondents interviewed for the JAC disagree and a further 37 per cent unsure that this is the case,[58] there is clearly still work to be done. With this in mind, the opaqueness of the appointment process to the Court of Appeal Bench and to other senior judicial positions is even more troubling.

Appointments to the Court of Appeal and leadership positions

The JAC also has responsibility for recommending candidates for appointment to the Court of Appeal and for the position of Lord Chief Justice, the various heads of division and senior president of tribunals. In contrast to the openness of the appointments process for the other positions for which the JAC has responsibility, the process of appointments to the Court of Appeal, outlined in a note agreed by

53 ibid., p. 61. Data relating to ethnicity is not further broken down by sex.
54 ibid., p. 3.
55 ibid., p. 31.
56 ibid., p. 6.
57 Leslie J Moran and Daniel K Winterfeldt, *Barriers to Applications for Judicial Appointment Research: Lesbian, Gay, Bisexual, and Transgender Experiences*, London: InterLaw Diversity Forum, 2011, p. 41.
58 A high proportion of LGBT lawyers also believe the appointments process is unfair (40%, with an additional 33% answering 'don't know') (Moran and Winterfeldt, *Barriers to Application*, p. 39). Interestingly, although women, BME candidates and solicitors are more likely to think that the appointments process was unfair, a significant proportion of white, male or barrister respondents also thought this was the case, suggesting that some changes to the appointments process designed to increase diversity are seen by some members of these groups as tantamount to positive discrimination (Allen, *Barriers to Application*, p. 58).

the JAC and Judicial Executive Board, is somewhat opaque.[59] When a vacancy arises all serving High Court judges are deemed to have applied for appointment, unless they have specifically informed the Lord Chief Justice that they do not wish to be considered. While this ensures that all suitably qualified *High Court judges* are considered regardless of seniority, it limits the pool of potential candidates to the High Court bench, despite the statutory criteria for appointment to the Court of Appeal allowing for direct appointments of those who have been *eligible* for judicial office in the past seven years.[60] In other words, the process by which appointments to the Court of Appeal Bench are made or, more accurately, the *absence* of a process of application for those *not* already High Court judges, restricts the pool of potential appointees. No doubt aware that this, at least at face value, appears to ignore the statutory obligation to have regard to the need to encourage diversity in the pool of potential appointees, the note confirms that the JAC 'vigorously' carries out its statutory duty and is 'enthusiastically' supported in this by the Judicial Executive Board and Lord Chief Justice.[61] However, it continues, appointments to the Court of Appeal should 'normally' be made from the High Court bench. It gives two reasons for this: first, the nature of the work of the Court of Appeal means that it is essential that its members have practical experience as a trial judge. Second, it ensures the quality of the High Court bench by requiring that 'the best candidates accept the responsibilities of a High Court Judge and do not simply wait to be appointed directly to the Court of Appeal'.[62]

While it is difficult to argue against the view that experience as a High Court judge is helpful to the role of Court of Appeal judge, nonetheless the de facto requirement that all Court of Appeal appointments come from the High Court is problematic. So, one argument for why those outside the High Court should not be appointed directly to the Court of Appeal is that candidates have a 'responsibility' to work their way up the judicial hierarchy and that it is unfair if those who have remained in (typically lucrative) practice are able to 'leapfrog' those who have served their time on the High Court bench. The problem with this argument is that it is inconsistent with the JAC's statutory duty of appointment on merit. Its implication is that the best candidate – that is the candidate who will perform the

59 'Process for Appointments to the Court of Appeal', JAC and JEB Note (on JAC website, Senior Appointments: http://jac.judiciary.gov.uk/about-jac/142.htm (accessed February 2012)). There is no similar note for appointments to Lord Chief Justice and other senior judicial/leadership positions.

60 Senior Courts Act 1981 s 10(3), as amended by Tribunals, Courts and Enforcement Act 2007, schedule 10(1) [13(2)]. A person satisfies the judicial-appointment eligibility condition on a seven-year basis if she or he has been a solicitor of the senior courts of England and Wales, or barrister in England and Wales, for at least seven years; and has been gaining experience in law during the post-qualification period.

61 'Process for Appointments to the Court of Appeal', Judicial Appointments Commission and Judicial Executive Board Note.

62 ibid.

role of being the judge most effectively – will not be appointed unless and until he or she have served in a lower court. So long as we are committed to appointment on merit, this sort of argument should be rejected outright. Of course, appointment on merit is not threatened if the best candidates are always to be found in the High Court. But we cannot simply assume this to be true. Moreover, as we have seen, this was not parliament's assumption when it set down the qualifications necessary for appointment to the Court of Appeal. The recent appointment of Jonathan Sumption QC directly to the Supreme Court suggests that there may indeed be cases where the best candidate is indeed to be found outside the High Court bench.[63] As such, we risk excluding meritorious candidates who are not High Court judges and reinforcing the mistrust of those who doubt the transparency of the appointments process. Moreover, crucially, as the JAC and JEB's note recognises (albeit tangentially), limiting the pool of potential candidates for appointment to the Court of Appeal to those already sitting in the High Court will do little to increase the representation of non-traditional groups among our Court of Appeal judges – let alone on the Supreme Court Bench – in the near future.[64]

There is a further problem with this process of appointing Court of Appeal judges. Unlike judicial appointments up to and including the High Court and to the Supreme Court, there is no application form or letter in which a candidate can make his or her case for appointment against (published) criteria for appointment (although it appears that shortlisted candidates may at some point be asked to provide a copy of their CVs and relevant judgments). Nor is there the opportunity for candidates to provide references in support of their application. Instead the Master of the Rolls, the Lord Chief Justice's current nominee as the judicial member of the Court of Appeal selection panel, invites *all* the members of the Court of Appeal (over 50 judges) and any others that the panel thinks are appropriate, to comment on the suitability for higher judicial office of those currently sitting on the High Court bench. Although these comments are required to be

63 The opposition of some senior members of the Court of Appeal to Sumption's earlier attempt to 'leapfrog' into the Supreme Court is well known. See the series of articles by Frances Gibb in *The Times* ('"Leapfrog" lawyer who raised the Bar', 18 January 2012; 'Supremely judicial choice – shame about the backbiting', 25 March 2010; 'Supreme ambition, jealousy and outrage', 4 February 2010; 'Brain "size of a planet" is not big enough for top court, say judges', 15 October 2009).

64 Rosemary Hunter has argued that, given that Supreme Court justices typically spend between 12–17 years in the High Court and the Court of Appeal the current High Court and Court of Appeal judges will have a monopoly on Supreme Court appointments until 2020–2025. Supreme Court justices typically spend between 12–17 years in the High Court and the Court of Appeal. (Rosemary Hunter, 'Appointment of a New Supreme Court Justice – A Missed Opportunity', *The Barrister*, 8 June–30 July 2010, p. 32). Thus, on these figures, the earliest a BME judge might join the Supreme Court is 2016, although this is somewhat optimistic given that the most senior BME judge in the High Court (Mrs Justice Dobbs) has not yet been promoted to the Court of Appeal.

supported by relevant evidence, once again the benefits of such a broad consultation are doubtful. The comments of the Court of Appeal are then summarised and passed to the panel together with copies of the evidence, CVs and judgments of shortlisted candidates, who, after consulting further with the heads of division and *possibly* interviewing the candidates, make their decision.

This process should sound familiar. It is, in effect, a variation on the system of informal consultation which underpinned the previous appointments process. And, like that process, its lack of transparency means that, as the Advisory Panel on Judicial Diversity in 2010 acknowledged, it 'runs the risk' of being 'perceived, rightly or wrongly, as unfair'.[65] In particular, there is a concern that the level of involvement by the senior judiciary may encourage 'self-perpetuat[ion]', identified by JAG Griffith as a judicial trait in the mid-1970s,[66] causing the selection panel to 'subconsciously recruit in their own image'.[67] Experience to date appears to support this concern. Just two of the 18 judges appointed to the Court of Appeal since 2006 have been women; none of the appointees has been selected from a minority ethnic group. Of course, it may well be that all the candidates appointed were the best candidates for the job. However, so long as the process remains closed, both in terms of the candidates who can apply and the information that is given to the panel, then suggestions or concerns otherwise are difficult to rebut. The process of appointing judges not only needs to be, but also be seen to be, fair. As it is, the appointments process for senior judicial appointment and to the Court of Appeal is neither.

Unsurprisingly, the lack of openness and transparency in the Court of Appeal appointments process, as well as the extent of the involvement of the senior judiciary, was criticised by the Advisory Panel on Judicial Diversity. It recommended that appointments to senior judicial office should be 'made on an evidence base provided by the applicant and their referees in response to published criteria'.[68] Given the concerns discussed above, it is disappointing that the Judicial Diversity Taskforce led by Lord McNally, charged with tracking the implementation of the Advisory Panel's conclusions, focused only on appointments to the High Court (despite the original Advisory Panel recommendation coming directly under the heading 'Appointment to the Supreme Court and Court of Appeal'). On this

65 Neuberger Report [139].
66 JAG Griffith, *The Politics of the Judiciary*, 5th edn, London: Fontana Press, 1997, p. 22.
67 Neuberger Report [139]. At present, the Constitutional Reform Act also appoints the Lord Chief Justice (or his or her nominee) as chair, giving her or him the casting vote in case of a tie. Although this requirement has never been used, the APJD in 2010 recommended that membership of the selection panels for senior judicial appointments be increased to five in order to alleviate the need for the casting vote provision (Neuberger Report, Recommendation 42 [140]). This is included in the Ministry of Justice's *Appointments and Diversity* consultation paper (Q4).
68 Neuberger Report, Recommendation 41. It is interesting to compare the Advisory Panel's position on consultation in the context of the senior judiciary with its response to the role of statutory consultation for junior judicial positions, which it views as vital to the appointments process (Neuberger Report [121]).

(partial) basis the Taskforce concluded that the appointments process was 'in line with this recommendation in all respects' and that no further action is needed.[69]

Appointments of Supreme Court justices (including President and Deputy President)

Supreme Court justices are currently selected by an ad hoc panel comprised of representatives from the judicial appointments commissions of England and Wales, Scotland and Northern Ireland, as well as the President and Deputy President of the Supreme Court.[70] As with other judicial appointments, the selection panel is free to determine its own appointments process, subject to the usual requirement to appoint 'on merit'.[71] There is no accompanying 'good character' requirement or expectation that the panel have regard to the need to encourage diversity in the pool of potential applicants (as for other judicial appointments). However, the panel is obliged to ensure that together 'the judges will have knowledge of, and experience in, the law of each part of the United Kingdom'.[72] The appointment of Lord Reed in February 2012 confirms the expectation that the previous convention that two of the Law Lords (now justices of the Supreme Court) are Scottish and one is from Northern Ireland will continue.

All Supreme Court justices are statutorily required either to have held high judicial office for at least two years (in the Court of Appeal or High Court), to satisfy the judicial-appointment eligibility condition on a 15-year basis or, in the case of candidates from Northern Ireland or Scotland, to have been a qualifying practitioner for at least 15 years.[73] In practice Supreme Court justices, like the members of the House of Lords, are usually appointed from the Court of Appeal Bench.[74] Unlike the closed system used to appoint members of the Court of

---

69 McNally Report, p. 53.
70 The composition of the selection panel for senior judicial appointments forms part of both the Ministry of Justice's *Appointments and Diversity* consultation and the Constitution Committee Inquiry, with the latter recommending that the size of the panel be increased to allow for greater lay representation (Judicial Appointments Report [144–157]).
71 CRA s 27(5). In addition, under s 27(9) the selection panel must have regard to any guidance given by the Lord Chancellor, subject to any other provision in the Act.
72 CRA s 27(8). By convention this extends to Scotland and Northern Ireland only. Constitutional, linguistic and equity-based arguments for specific Welsh representation in the Supreme Court have been unsuccessful (see, further, Timothy Jones, HC Constitutional Affairs Committee, Minutes of Evidence, 2 December 2003, Q325–327).
73 CRA s 25(1).
74 Although, historically, direct appointments to the Court of Appeal and House of Lords from the Bar or even political office were relatively common, Jonathan Sumption QC's appointment in 2011 was the first appointment directly from the Bar to what is now the Supreme Court since the appointments of Lord Reid (1948) and Lord Radcliffe (1949) (Louis Blom-Cooper, Brice Dickson and Gavin Drewry (eds), *The Judicial House of Lords 1876–2009*, Oxford: Oxford University Press, 2009, Appendix 4 (pen portraits of the Lords of Appeal).

Appeal, the selection process is relatively open. Vacancies are advertised on the Supreme Court's website together with an information pack detailing the criteria for appointment and selection process. The selection process adopts a mixture of modern and traditional recruitment methods similar to those used for appointments up to and including the High Court. Applications are made by way of CV and letter, with supporting evidence in which the candidate is expected to set out how he or she meets the following appointment criteria:

> Knowledge and experience of the law; intellectual ability and interest in the law, with a significant capacity for analysing and exploring legal problems creatively and flexibly; clarity of thought and expression, reflected particularly in written work; an ability to work under pressure and to produce work with reasonable expedition . . . social awareness and understanding of the contemporary world; an ability to work with colleagues, respecting their views, but also being able to challenge and debate in a constructive way; a willingness to participate in the wider representational role of a Supreme Court Justice . . . [and] vision, coupled with an appreciation of the role of the Court in contributing to the development of the law.[75]

Judicial applicants are asked to submit copies of up to three judgments which they think demonstrate their judicial qualities, while other applicants are asked to provide other forms of writing: articles, opinions or such like. All applicants are also asked to provide the names of two referees able to comment on aspects of the applicant's judicial qualities not, or less likely to be, known by the (extensive) statutory consultees. The selection panel is statutorily obliged to consult all senior judges who are not members of the panel and who are not willing to be considered for selection,[76] as well as the Lord Chancellor, the First Minister in Scotland, the First Minister for Wales and the Secretary of State for Northern Ireland.[77] The information pack indicates that a long-listing exercise may take place before this consultation and leaves open the possibility of further consultation as the panel

---

75 Information Pack – Vacancy for Two Justices of the Supreme Court, July 2011, p. 4.
76 CRA s 27(2). 'Senior judges' are Supreme Court justices, the Lord Chief Justices of England and Wales and Northern Ireland, the Master of the Rolls, the Lord President of the Court of Session, the Lord Justice Clerk, the Presidents of the Family Division and Queen's Bench Division and the Chancellor of the High Court (CRA s 60).
77 As Alan Paterson and Chris Paterson illustrate, this means in relation to the most recent appointments to the Supreme Court (in which two justices were appointed – one-sixth of the court), 'the major input as to the merits of each and every candidate came from up to 24 white men and one white woman . . . If this was the HR procedure for a post in a private company or organisation of any kind, it would be considered untenable. Instead it was the most recent appointment process for the body at the apex of one branch of government in the UK' (*Guarding the Guardians? Towards an independent, accountable and diverse senior judiciary* (London: CentreForum, 2012) p. 74).

'deems appropriate'.[78] 'Leading' candidates are invited to meet with the panel before the final short-listing takes place. Short-listed candidates are then invited to interview, which includes a short presentation, after which the panel makes its decision.[79] One candidate is selected for each vacancy.

This is not, however, the end of the selection process. Once the panel has made its recommendation to the Lord Chancellor, she or he is then obliged to consult with *those already consulted* by the panel for its views on the chosen candidate.[80] If, following this, the Lord Chancellor disagrees with the panel's recommendation she or he has the same limited power of rejection or reconsideration as for all judicial appointments.[81] Once a decision has been reached, the Lord Chancellor recommends the candidate to the Prime Minister, who in turn recommends the candidate to the Queen, who makes the appointment.[82]

The role of the Lord Chancellor in the appointments process as a whole, particularly in relation to senior appointments, has, therefore, been significantly curtailed. The Lord Chancellor plays no role in the short-listing or selection process, and is not able, for example, to recommend her or his preferred candidate over one nominated by the selection panel. Nonetheless, although by the time of the Constitutional Reform Act 2005 it was clear that judicial appointment on the authority of a single senior politician (albeit, or perhaps especially, one informed by a team of omniscient advisers) had become untenable, it was never the intention that the Lord Chancellor's role in the process should be downgraded to that of the selection panel's messenger.[83] The Constitutional Reform Act 2005 deliberately gives the Lord Chancellor an important 'backstop' role in the appointments process – including the ability, right at the end of the process, to veto a

78 Information Pack – Vacancy for Two Justices of the Supreme Court, July 2011, p. 5.
79 Lord Mance, in his submission to the Constitution Committee Inquiry, noted that it had not been the practice of the Supreme Court selection committee to interview all short-listed candidates (Written evidence, Constitution Committee Inquiry, p. 188, [12]).
80 CRA s 28(5). Jenny Rowe, the chief executive of the Supreme Court concluded in her review of the Supreme Court selection process in 2011 that there is little need for the Lord Chancellor to conduct a second round of consultation following the panel's recommendation. Instead, the chair of the selection panel should be under an obligation to inform the statutory consultees of his or her recommendation to the Lord Chancellor (*Supreme Court Annual Report and Accounts 2010–2011*, HC 976, London: Stationery Office, 2011, p. 16).
81 CRA ss 29–30 and explanatory notes.
82 CRA s 26(2) and 26(3) and explanatory notes. The Constitutional Reform and Governance Bill 2010 included a provision to remove the Prime Minister from the appointments process (schedule 12). This was removed from the final Act during the final parliamentary stages of the Bill. The Ministry of Justice's *Appointments and Diversity* consultation contains the same provision, and so it is likely that the Prime Minister will no longer be involved in any judicial appointments in the future (Q12).
83 See, eg, HC Constitutional Affairs Committee, Minutes of Evidence, 6 January 2004, Q523 and 532 and discussion between Lord Mackay, Lord Falconer and Jack Straw giving oral evidence to the Constitution Committee Inquiry, 12 October 2011, Q121–130.

particular candidate. And while the desire for increased openness and transparency means that the Lord Chancellor's ability to exercise this power is not limitless – and nor should it be – but neither was it intended to be toothless, not least because the democratic accountability of the appointments process (such as there is) relies on the Lord Chancellor playing (or at least being seen to play) an active role.[84] Of course, one difficulty is that the most obvious way for the Lord Chancellor to do this is by rejecting, or raising doubts about, the selection panel's nominee. So long as she or he agrees with the selection panel's nomination, or any disagreement is unpublished, it is harder for the Lord Chancellor to be seen to be exercising the 'backstop' role.[85] In other words, the greater the level of agreement between the selection panel and the Lord Chancellor, then the more likely that the ad hoc selection panel (the JAC for that matter in relation to other senior appointments) will be seen as the de facto *appointing* body.[86]

This has not gone unnoticed. Inevitably perhaps, at a time when the Supreme Court is increasingly called upon to decide sensitive political issues, the 'democratic deficit'[87] in the way the justices are appointed, and in particular the absence of effective political involvement in the selection and appointment process, has been subject to intense scrutiny and criticism. And so, just five years after the JAC started work, changes to the judicial appointments process are once again being mooted.[88]

84 Peter H Russell, 'Conclusion' in Kate Malleson and Peter H Russell (eds), *Appointing Judges in an Age of Judicial Power: Critical Perspectives from Around the World*, Toronto: University of Toronto, 2006, p. 429; Kate Malleson, 'Parliamentary Scrutiny of Supreme Court Nominees: A View from the UK', *Osgoode Hall Law Journal*, 44(3), 2006, 557.

85 The JAC's written evidence to the Constitution Committee Inquiry indicated that the level of rejections of JAC recommendations, or requests for reconsideration (presumably across all levels) have averaged at around one a year (Written evidence, Constitution Committee Inquiry, October 2011). The current Lord Chancellor, Kenneth Clarke, has described exercising his right of veto as 'an Exocet missile that I would never fire unless there was some compelling reason' (Oral evidence, Constitution Committee Inquiry, 18 January 2012, Q374).

86 Robert Hazell and Kate Malleson, Written evidence, Constitution Committee Inquiry, October 2011; Richard Cornes, 'Gains (and Dangers of Losses) in Translation – the Leadership Function of the United Kingdom's Supreme Court, Parameters and Prospects', *Public Law*, 2011, 509.

87 Malleson, 'Parliamentary Scrutiny of Supreme Court Nominees', p. 563.

88 In fact, changes to the appointments process – including giving the Lord Chancellor the power to set targets – had already been considered as part of the package of measures included in the Draft Constitutional Renewal Bill in March 2008 (Ministry of Justice, *The Governance of Britain – Judicial Appointments*, Cm 7210, London: Ministry of Justice, 2007). However, in June 2009, the government concluded that, save from removing the Prime Minister from the appointments process (see note 80 above), further reform of the appointments was 'premature' and that a comprehensive review of the process should wait until after the JAC was fully established (Government response to the Report of the Joint Committee on the Draft Constitutional Renewal Bill, Cm 7690, 2009, [141]).

A work in progress – reinventing the new wheel

In response to continuing dissatisfaction with the judicial appointments process,[89] in 2011 the House of Lords Select Committee on the Constitution conducted a wide-ranging inquiry into the appointments process across all levels of the judiciary. Accepting the consensus that appointments should be made on merit alone, it set itself a broad remit, including consideration of the constitutional arguments for judicial diversity as well as 'the respective roles of the independent selection commissions, ministers, the judiciary and parliament'.[90] Toward the end of the Select Committee's review, the Ministry of Justice announced its own consultation on amendments to the statutory and regulatory frameworks for judicial appointments and proposals to improve judicial diversity.[91] The possibility of further reform, particularly an increase in the political scrutiny of and involvement in senior judicial appointments, and even the possibility of the use of positive action, appeared to be on the cards.

Although for centuries judicial appointments were wholly in the hand of a single politician – the Lord Chancellor – historically fears of a move toward US-style politicisation of the appointments process have meant that there has been limited appetite for parliament to have a significant role in the appointments process. The possibility of parliamentary confirmation hearings was raised and dismissed by the House of Lords Select Committee on the Constitutional Reform Bill in 2004,[92] and again by the Labour Government in its *Governance of Britain* consultation in 2007.[93] However, it emerged again during the Select Committee on the Constitution's inquiry. This is likely due to a combination of factors, including the perceived weakness of the Lord Chancellor's current role in the appointments process as outlined above and the changing role of the judiciary, particularly at the Supreme Court level. Insofar as judges, particularly in the senior judiciary are making decisions with political ramifications and which affect the governance of the state, it follows that the process of judicial appointment should be conducted

---

89 In 2010, against the backdrop of the Coalition Government's so-called 'bonfire of quangos', the Lord Chancellor had conducted an 'end to end' internal review of the judicial appointments process. Although it raised a number of practical issues for the JAC to address, it confirmed the JAC as a 'valued independent' body. The review also highlighted a number of 'constitutional' questions, which formed the starting point for the Constitution Committee Inquiry ('Letter to Baroness Jay, dated 4 January 2011, in Justice Committee, Se*cond Report of Session 2010–2011: Appointment of the Chairman of the Judicial Appointments Commission*, HC 770, 31 January 2011).

90 House of Lords Select Committee on the Constitution, 'The Judicial Appointment Process: Call for Evidence', May 2011. The final report was published in March 2012 (*Judicial Appointments Report*).

91 Ministry of Justice, *Appointments and Diversity*. The manuscript for this book was submitted before the Government's response was published in May 2012. The Crime and Courts Bill, containing measures relating to judicial appointments, was introduced in the House of Lords in May 2012.

92 House of Lords, *Constitutional Reform Bill – First Report* (Volume I, HL Paper No 125-I), 2004, [408–420]. Although it did recognise the benefit of a joint Parliamentary Committee 'to act as a bridge between Parliament and the judiciary' [420].

93 Government response to the Report of the Joint Committee on the Draft Constitutional Renewal Bill, Cm 7690, 2009, [108].

with this in mind. The process of appointing judges becomes then a question of how to construct a judiciary best equipped to discharge its constitutional function.

On this view, effective political oversight of the judicial appointments process, through an increased role for parliament, serves at least three purposes: first, the 'overt political accountability' it offers, particularly in the appointment and selection of the senior judiciary, enhances the democratic legitimacy of the appointments process.[94] Second, to the extent that it leads to greater transparency, not only of the appointment process itself but also of those appointed to the Bench – their motivations, values, competences and so on – it increases public trust and confidence in the judiciary as a whole. Finally, insofar as greater political input in the appointments process reinforces public confidence in the legitimacy of the judiciary, this in turn strengthens the individual judge's decision-making. It is suggested that while US Supreme Court justices might not enjoy the confirmation hearing 'experience', their judicial position is reinforced by it.[95]

However, even if we agree that there is a role for parliament in the appointments process, the question remains as to what this role should be. There are broadly two options. Either parliament has a supervisory role, overseeing the running and remit of the appointments process, or it has a role in deciding which candidate to appoint. The first option would allow for greater parliamentary scrutiny of the appointments process. This might include requiring those involved in making appointments to report, and be accountable, to a joint parliamentary committee, a post-appointment meeting between the candidate and parliamentarians, or even the setting of diversity targets.[96] These recommendations have the benefit of strengthening the legitimacy and transparency of the appointment process, informing the public about the candidates and even setting a broad strategy for appointments, while leaving the decision of who to appoint free from political interference.

The second option provides for greater political involvement in the selection and/or appointment of individual judges. Again there are a number of options. An additional round to the appointments process might be introduced, in the form of parliamentary confirmation hearings or pre-appointment meeting with a joint parliamentary committee.[97] Alternatively, the current structure of the

---

94 Alexander Horne, *The Changing Constitution: A Case for Judicial Hearings*, London: Study of Parliament Group, 2010, pp. 28–30.

95 Mary L Clark, 'Introducing a parliamentary confirmation process for new Supreme Court justices: its pros and cons, and the lessons learned from the US experience', *Public Law*, 2010, 464, pp. 472–473.

96 See further Written evidence to the Constitution Committee Inquiry from Robert Hazell and Kate Malleson, InterLaw Diversity Forum for Lesbian, Gay, Bisexual and Transgender (LGBT) Networks, Judicial Executive Board, Aileen McColgan, Karon Monaghan and Rabinder Singh, and the Society of Asian Lawyers.

97 These would be along similar lines to those for major public appointments – see, eg, the meeting between the Justice Committee and the new chair of the JAC (Justice Committee, 'Chair of the Judicial Appointments Commission', Minutes of Evidence, HC 770-I, 31 January 2011).

appointments process would remain but with the inclusion of the Lord Chancellor[98] or parliamentarians on the selection panels for senior judicial appointments or the submission of (possibly ranked) short-lists to the Lord Chancellor.[99] While there continues to be little stomach among the judiciary and legal profession for parliamentary hearings in any form,[100] the latter two options appear to be less controversial.[101] The introduction of short-lists, particularly for senior judicial appointments, would serve a dual purpose: it would both reinforce the involvement and authority of the Lord Chancellor in the appointments process – who would not only make but be seen to be making the final decision as to who to recommend for appointment – and would also improve the democratic legitimacy of those appointed. Expanding the membership of those involved in either putting together the short-list, or selecting the appointee, would also have the additional benefit of countering or limiting the influence of the current members of the judiciary on the appointments process, particularly in relation to appointments to the Supreme Court.[102]

98 As suggested in the *Appointments and Diversity* consultation paper (Ministry of Justice, *Appointments and Diversity* [76] Q10) and included in schedule 12 of the Crime and Courts Bill.

99 See further Written evidence to the Constitution Committee Inquiry from Baroness Hale, Robert Hazell and Kate Malleson, Graham Gee, Thomas Legg and Alan Paterson.

100 See, eg, the discussion between Lord Kerr and Lord Justice Etherton, Oral evidence, Constitution Committee Inquiry, 13 July 2011, Q47–50, and comments of the Lord Chancellor, Oral evidence, Constitution Committee Inquiry, 18 January 2012, Q384, as well as written submissions to the Constitution Committee Inquiry from the Association of Women Barristers (p. 22), the Equality and Diversity Committee of the Bar Council of England and Wales, the JAC and Law Society. There is, however, greater support for increased parliamentary or executive involvement prior to appointment among academics (see further written submissions to the Constitution Committee Inquiry from Mary L Clark, Robert Hazell and Kate Malleson, Graham Gee and Alan Paterson); Clark, 'Introducing a Parliamentary Confirmation Process'; Alan Paterson, *Lawyers and the Public Good: Democracy in Action?* Cambridge: Cambridge University Press, 2012, pp. 150–152.

101 Although not completely, see, eg, Lord Phillips, Oral evidence, Constitution Committee Inquiry, 19 October 2011, Q173; Baroness Prashar, Oral evidence, Constitution Committee Inquiry, 30 November 2011, Q308–309. In fact, both of these options were rejected by the Constitution Committee (*Judicial Appointments* Report, [22-26] and [36-37]).

102 There is a strong element among the judiciary that they 'know best' when it comes to assessing a candidate's potential as a judge (see, eg, Robert Carswell, Lord Chief Justice of Northern Ireland, HC Constitutional Affairs Committee, Minutes of Evidence, 9 December 2003, Q365). The concern is that this may lead to self-replication. It is crucial therefore that the selection panel has a significant lay element able to challenge this assumption. At the moment all but one member of the selection panel for Supreme Court appointments may be drawn from the judiciary. The APJD recommended reducing the number of serving justices on the panel to reduce the judiciary's influence (Recommendation 43). This is currently being considered by the House of Lords Select Committee on the Constitution Inquiry into Judicial Appointments Process and the Ministry of Justice is committed to consulting on the issue 'once a suitable legislative vehicle has been identified' (McNally Report, p. 53).

But what of the other aspects of the Constitution Committee and Ministry of Justice inquiries? In particular, where do efforts to increase judicial diversity come into the changes to the appointments process? While it is clear that the process of appointing judges must be fair and open, and that a greater role for parliament would improve the accountability of the process as a whole and public confidence in those appointed, it is also clear that neither of these things, in and of themselves, will lead to greater diversity in the appointments actually made.

Delivering judicial diversity: high hopes and false expectations

How did we get to the position where, despite over two decades of changes to the judicial appointments process, there has been little improvement when it comes to the diversity of those appointed? One answer lies in the motivation for the changes. Crucially, despite Lord Falconer's desire to put diversity 'at the heart' of the appointments process, for many parliamentarians and senior members of the legal profession and judiciary, the primary motivation for reforming the appointments process was not to increase the representation of non-traditional candidates on the Bench but rather to improve the transparency of the process *so that they could better defend the appointments that were being made*. The revamped appointments process introduced in the mid-2000s is the result of 'two decades of competing demands for, and resistance to, change in the appointments process'.[103] The result is an uneasy compromise between those who viewed the introduction of a more transparent appointments process as a judicious, but essentially cosmetic, exercise and those hoping that it would bring substantive change to the appointments made. Indeed, for a body fêted as central to delivering a diverse judiciary, the JAC has no statutory duty to do so.[104] The JAC was not intended as – and was not given the remit or ability to be – a panacea for the 'problem' of judicial diversity. Its primary purpose was never to redress the gender, or any other form of, imbalance on the Bench in the manner of the so-called diversity 'task forces' in Canada and the US.[105] When it came to selecting judges, the objective of the JAC was the same as the Lord Chancellor's before it: to select the best candidates for the job. The Constitutional Reform Act 2005 has very little to say about diversity. Insofar as the JAC has a diversity remit it is limited, under section 64(1), to encouraging

103 Cheryl Thomas, Oral evidence, Constitution Committee Inquiry, 6 July 2011, Q1.

104 The JAC simply 'must have regard to the need to encourage diversity in the range of persons available for selection for appointment' (CRA s 64(1)).

105 See, eg, Cheryl Thomas, *Judicial Diversity in the United Kingdom and Other Jurisdictions: A Review of Research, Policies and Practices*, London: The Commission for Judicial Appointments, 2005, pp. 78–87.

diversity in the pool of candidates eligible for appointment.[106] Diversity and merit each has its own distinct zone: 'diversity in the field; merit in the selection'.[107] So, while the success of the JAC is judged, at least in part, on its ability to deliver a more diverse Bench, we might doubt whether it has ever really been in a position to achieve this.[108] As Lord Falconer's successor, Jack Straw conceded, the expectation that 'the establishment of the Judicial Appointments Commission would lead to a more diverse judiciary' was always unrealistic.[109]

Of course, as we shall see, this is not to suggest that the JAC could not have done – and still could do – more to improve the diversity of those it selects. Nor is it to imply that the members of the JAC were or are impervious to the desire for greater diversity among those appointed to the Bench. Indeed, in an early meeting with the House of Commons Constitutional Committee, the then chair of the JAC, Baroness Prashar, went so far as to suggest that, if the JAC's appointments were *not* diverse, something would be 'drastically wrong' with the appointments processes the Commission had put in place (although she would not be drawn further on quite why this should be the case).[110] Lord Justice Auld, speaking in the same meeting, put the matter in a rather different light, suggesting that '[t]he object of the Commission is to appoint judges on merit. It is not to appoint a more diverse judiciary'.[111] Diversity, he continued, was simply 'a means to securing the appointment of more judges on merit'[112] – a phrase Baroness Prashar was later to borrow in a lecture addressed to the London School of Economics' Student Law Society.[113]

Despite Baroness Prashar's confidence, early indications as to the JAC's ability to deliver a more diverse judiciary were not promising. By May 2008, just under

---

106 This is in contrast to the Northern Ireland Judicial Appointments Commission, which is required 'so far as it is reasonably practicable to do so, to secure that a range of persons reflective of the community in Northern Ireland is available for consideration by the Commission whenever it is required to select a person to be appointed, or recommended for appointment, to a listed judicial office' (Justice (Northern Ireland) Act 2002 s 5(10)(b) as amended by the Justice (Northern Ireland) Act 2004 s 3).

107 Baroness Prashar, 'Judicial Appointments: A New System for a New Century', Centre for Crime and Justice Studies, King's College London, March 2007 [65].

108 This point was made by a number of witnesses during the consultation process prior to the enactment of the CRA. See, eg, Lady Justice Hale, HC Constitutional Affairs Committee, Minutes of Evidence, 9 December 2003, Q203 and Barbara Cahalane, HC Constitutional Affairs Committee, Minutes of Evidence, 9 December 2003, Q127. See generally, Lizzie Barmes and Kate Malleson, 'The Legal Profession as Gatekeeper to the Judiciary: Design Faults in Measures to Enhance Diversity', *Modern Law Review*, 74(2), 2011, 245.

109 Jack Straw, Justice Committee, Minutes of Evidence, 13 May 2008, Q60.

110 Baroness Prashar, HC Constitutional Affairs Committee, Minutes of Evidence, 18 July 2006, Q18.

111 Lord Justice Auld, JC Constitutional Affairs Committee, Minutes of Evidence, 18 July 2006, Q36.

112 ibid.

113 Baroness Prashar, 'Speech by Baroness Prashar', London School of Economics' Student Law Society, 22 February 2007.

a year since the JAC started making appointments, judicial diversity had not only failed to improve but appeared to be going backwards. In the JAC's first year the proportion of women appointed to the judiciary as a whole fell from 41 per cent to 34 per cent, while the appointments of BME candidates almost halved.[114] This was compounded by a series of early appointments which saw 10 white, male, barristers joining the High Court bench.[115] Faced with an appointments process that threatened to be *worse* at delivering diversity than its predecessor, Straw was quick to act. In April 2009, he established the Advisory Panel on Judicial Diversity, chaired by Baroness Neuberger. Its brief was 'to identify the barriers to progress on judicial diversity and make recommendations . . . on how to make speedier and sustained progress to a more diverse judiciary at every level and in all courts in England and Wales'.[116]

Of course, we have been here before. In fact, the panel's report tells us relatively little that we did not already know. Numerous reports have highlighted the particular difficulties faced by non-traditional groups in relation to judicial appointment.[117] We know, and as we saw in the previous chapter, that women and other non-traditional groups have a harder time making it to the upper echelons of the legal profession and that, as a result, they are under-represented in the pool of potential judicial applicants. Similarly, we know that the expectation of having to go 'out on circuit', as well as the use of certain non-statutory criteria for appointment, such as fee-paid experience, restricts the number of women, solicitors and public sector lawyers who *have* made it to the upper echelons of the profession from applying for judicial appointment. And we also know, and have for some time, that many of the same obstacles affecting women solicitors and barristers in the legal profession – in particular difficulties relating to balancing competing

114 Department for Constitutional Affairs, *Judicial Appointments 2005–2006*, Judicial Competition Statistical Tables, Summary Tables for 1 April 2005–31 March 2006; Judicial Appointments Commission, *Annual Report 2007–2008: Selecting on Merit and Encouraging Diversity*, London: Judicial Appointments Commission, 2008, p. 36. However, the number of women and BME judges at entry level positions has increased slightly (JAC News Release, 'Women continue to succeed in judicial appointments, 1 December 2011), as discussed in Chapter 1 this has not been reflected in the higher courts or leadership roles (Ministry of Justice and Judicial Appointments Commission, Statistical Digest of Judicial Appointments of Women and BME Candidates from 1998–99 to 2008–09, July 2010 and Statistical Digest of Appointments of Solicitors from 1998–99 to 2008–09, July 2010).

115 Clare Dyer, 'First 10 high court judges under new diversity rules', *The Guardian*, 28 January 2008.

116 Neuberger Report [12].

117 See, eg, Holland and Spender, *Without Prejudice?*; JUSTICE, Judiciary in England and Wales; Law Society, 'Broadening the Bench'; Commission for Judicial Appointments, *Annual Report 2003*, [5.50–5.51]; Opinion Leader Research, *Judicial Diversity: Findings of a Consultation with Barristers, Solicitors and Judges – Final Report*, London: Department for Constitutional Affairs, 2006; Hazel Genn, *The Attractiveness of Senior Judicial Appointment to Highly Qualified Practitioners – Report to the Judicial Executive Board*, London: Directorate of Judicial Office for England and Wales, 2008; Allen, *Barriers to Application*.

expectations of work and family life and an overly masculine legal culture – deter highly-qualified applicants from applying for judicial office. As a result, many of the 53 recommendations made by the advisory panel, including its call for improved mentoring and support for under-represented groups, measures to expand the pool of potential candidates, a 'pro-active' myth-busting campaign, an increased emphasis on progression through the judiciary, and for systematic and consistent monitoring of judicial data make for familiar reading.

The same is true of its central argument that '[d]elivering a more diverse judiciary is not just about recruiting talent wherever it may be found, important though that is, but about retaining talent and enabling capable individuals to reach the top'.[118] As we are seeing, a judicial appointments commission in and of itself will make little difference here, making the appointments process more transparent and seeking to widen the pool of potential candidates is not enough. If we are serious about changing the make-up of the Bench, diversity needs not simply to be at the heart of the appointments process, but recognised as an essential requirement of a strong judiciary.[119] Thus while the advisory panel, like Lord Falconer before it, recognises the need for 'a fundamental shift in approach' – a movement from a focus on outreach and recruitment to one where the importance of diversity is addressed systematically throughout all aspects of the judicial role, and which 'embed[s] diversity throughout the system: through attracting, appointing, retaining, developing and promoting the best talent'[120] – its recommendations are unlikely to make this a reality. Indeed, to date, despite high-profile rhetoric as to the co-operation between the legal profession, the JAC and the judiciary,[121] and increased monitoring, the signs are not good.

---

118 Neuberger Report, [5]. The Neuberger Report is premised on a shift in focus from judicial appointments to the concept of a 'judicial career' (as opposed to a career judiciary) (Recommendation 1, [35–40]). This argument has been made in various forms on a number of occasions. There are, however, a number of difficulties with this strategy as a means of increasing diversity including its reliance on candidates 'trickling-up' the judicial hierarchy (when we know that women and BME lawyers have higher attrition rates), the difficulties in dismantling the structural and cultural barriers to allow progression from the circuit to High Court bench (and from the tribunal to the district bench), as well as issues relating to timing, increased bureaucracy, complexity and inflexibility.

119 Although the Neuberger Report acknowledges that there is a 'strong case for [judicial] diversity' ([1]), in reinforcing diversity as a means of preserving rather than *improving* the status quo it misses the opportunity to make it (Neuberger Report, [15]).

120 Neuberger Report, [39].

121 See, eg, the JAC Diversity Forum, set up in February 2008, bringing together the JAC, Ministry of Justice, the judiciary and professional bodies with the intention of making 'a concerted effort to improve diversity within the judiciary and legal profession . . . by coordinating activities and by identifying new opportunities for action' (JAC website 'Diversity Forum'. Online. Available: http://jac.judiciary.gov.uk/about-jac/257.htm). However, in December 2011, the Law Society's Gazette reported that the 'Solicitors in Judicial Office Working Group', which was created to follow through on the recommendations of the APJD in relation to solicitors, had not met in two years (Jonathan Rayner, 'City judicial diversity forum has not met in two years', *Law Society Gazette*, 15 December 2011).

One year on, although some progress has been made, it continues to be too slow. Without, in Lord McNally's words, 'a much greater sense of urgency and commitment',[122] we are unlikely to achieve the advisory panel's 'vision' of a 'much more' diverse judiciary *at all levels* by 2020.[123] So, if we are serious about wanting to alter the current profile of the judiciary, where does this leave us?

Grasping the nettle – quotas, targets and other forms of diversity-engineering

On one view the solution is clear: if we really want a judiciary that is diverse, then the appointments process needs to be focused on making sure this happens. Simply (re)stating the desirability of having a diverse judiciary and hoping that it materialises is, as we are seeing, unlikely to make much difference. And while, of course, making sure that the appointments processes are fair and open and targeted outreach to encourage qualified candidates from under-represented groups to apply are vital, we also need to look beyond the usual options. So what could the JAC and Ministry of Justice be doing?

One option is to introduce quotas requiring that women (and those from other under-represented groups) make up a particular proportion of judges appointed, or of applicants in the pool, across the judiciary as a whole, or at each level. Quotas provide a guarantee of diversity: women judges have to be appointed. And, while we might wish they were not necessary, the same point can be made of quotas as has been made of women-only shortlists for parliamentary appointments: '[t]hey may not be "fair", they may grate against liberal principles, they may, as critics claim, cast aspersions on the merit of the women [appointed], but one thing cannot be denied, measures that guarantee women's [appointment] work, and work quickly'.[124] So, if our aim really were simply to get more women on the Bench, or even in the pool of potential applicants, one of the most effective ways of doing this would be to use quotas.

---

122 Lord McNally, 'Advisory Panel on Judicial Diversity Annual Report: Written Statement', House of Lords, 9 May 2011.

123 Neuberger Report, [15]. Baroness Neuberger in her evidence to the Select Committee on the Constitution Inquiry into Judicial Appointments Process expressed her frustration at the lack of progress that had been made following her report, suggesting that 'considerably greater progress could have been made on most of what [the Report] said' (2 November 2011, Q217).

124 Sarah Childs, Joni Lovenduski and Rosie Campbell, *Women at the Top 2005: Changing Numbers, Changing Politics?*, London: Hansard Society, 2005, p. 96.

And, for a time, it appeared that the traditional tide *against* the use of quotas (and positive action more generally) in this context might be beginning to turn.[125] After all, it is harder to argue that proactive change was *not* needed in the face of over 20 years of slow progress and empty promises. As Kate Malleson notes:

> The easy gains have been won and either the goal of real and substantive change must be dropped, in the way that class equality has largely been abandoned by mainstream politics, or more radical and potentially higher-risk, higher-benefit strategies must be adopted. Without these there is very little prospect of moving from token appointments of non-traditional candidates to the fundamental refashioning of the composition of the judiciary.[126]

As the Advisory Panel on Judicial Diversity started work, nothing it appeared, including quotas, was off the table.[127] In the event, however, it was business as usual. Their report states simply: '[t]here should not be diversity quotas or specific targets for judicial appointments' (albeit while setting out its 'vision' – a target, perhaps – of a more diverse judiciary by the end of the next decade).[128] Of course, there are good reasons for not pursuing quotas as a means of redressing judicial diversity. Insofar as quotas work against the recruitment of those best able to do the job of judging, or fall foul of employment law and related legislative frameworks, their introduction would, at best, be counter-productive and, at worst, unlawful.[129] However, while few would wish to argue against Lord Irvine's view that the judiciary cannot be run 'as some kind of social experiment and [that] you cannot run risks with the administration of justice for us all simply to

---

125   The view that 'we won't have quotas' (Falconer, 'Increasing Judicial Diversity: The Next Steps'), that they are 'wrong in principle' (Anthony Clarke, 'Open Societies and the Rule of Law', Atkin Lecture 2008, The Reform Club, London, 13 November 2008, [18]) and 'demeaning' to non-traditional candidates (Kenneth Clarke, HL Select Committee on the Constitution, 'Annual Meeting with the Lord Chancellor', 19 January 2011, Q27) is firmly entrenched among many members of the judiciary, legal profession and general public. See, generally, discussion between Kenneth Clarke and Lord McNally giving oral evidence to the Constitution Committee Inquiry, 18 January 2012, Q375–376 and *Judicial Appointments* Report (102–105). However, arguments for the use of quotas and/or other forms of positive action to readdress the gender and ethnicity balance in the judiciary have been made. See, eg, Holland and Spender, *Without Prejudice?*; Seamus Taylor, HC Constitution Affairs, Minutes of Evidence, 18 November 2003, Q151; Mrs Justice Dobbs, 'Diversity in the Judiciary – Lecture', Queen Mary University of London, London, 17 October 2007; Kate Malleson, 'Diversity in the Judiciary: the Case for Positive Action', *Journal of Law and Society*, 36(3), 2009, 376; Kate Malleson, 'Gender Quotas for the Judiciary in England and Wales', in Ulrike Schultz and Gisela Shaw (eds), *Gender and Judging*, Oxford: Hart Publishing, forthcoming.
126   Malleson, 'The Case for Positive Action', p. 402.
127   Tom Whitehead, 'Quotas could be introduced for judges to increase ethnic minorities and women', *The Telegraph*, 28 April 2009.
128   Neuberger Report, Recommendation 5, [43–47].
129   Although see Malleson, 'The Case for Positive Action', pp. 395–396.

correct gender and other imbalance on the Bench',[130] the extent to which the merest whiff of *any* form of positive action leads to a knee-jerk reaction against *all* measures aimed at widening the pool of potential judges requires greater justification.

With this in mind, it is disappointing that both the Advisory Panel on Judicial Diversity and the subsequent Judicial Diversity Taskforce saw 'little difference' between quotas and specific, non-binding targets.[131] The imposition of targets has long been recognised as an effective way of encouraging and measuring progress toward diversity.[132] Unlike quotas, targets are aspirational. They are commonly used both in business and government to articulate goals and set benchmarks against which progress can be measured.[133] Thus, while critics argue that targets 'artificially increase the pace of change' and negatively impact on 'the quality of applications and the perception of the appointments system and the judiciary as a whole',[134] others suggest the introduction of clear and measurable targets would be a positive step towards increasing judicial diversity.[135] After all, as Baroness Falkner recently argued in response to a question on judicial appointments in the House of Lords, '[i]f that other bastion of male privilege, the City of London, can have targets, is it not time that the senior judiciary did as well?'[136] Targets signal a real and determined commitment to effect change, kick-starting the process of diversification. They can lead to a 'domino effect where some people are appointed and then this gives people a sense of belief that others can follow through ... lead[ing] to people coming forward and being willing to apply'.[137] An official Ministry of Justice target of at least 30 per cent of the full-time judiciary being

130 Lord Irvine, Oral evidence to the Home Affairs Select Committee, The Work of the Lord Chancellor's Department, 13 October 1997 [69].
131 Neuberger Report, Recommendation 5; McNally Report, p. 15. While the Constitution Committee Inquiry *did* distinguish between quotas and targets, it is disappointing that it appeared to take the Lord Chancellor's comment that they should 'try targets next', should the proposals currently being under consideration in the *Appointments and Diversity* consultation paper and those suggested by the Constitution Committee not work (Oral evidence, Constitution Committee Inquiry, 18 January 2012, Q379). It recommended that the setting of targets should be 'kept under review' and, should the numbers of women and BAME appointments have not increased in five years' time, then 'the Government should *consider* setting non-mandatory targets for the JAC to follow' (*Judicial Appointments* Report [105] my emphasis).
132 Malleson, 'The Case for Positive Action', pp. 396–397.
133 One recent example is the 30% Club, which is a group of chairmen (sic), including those from a number of City law firms, voluntarily committed to bringing more women onto UK corporate boards (http://www.30percentclub.org.uk/).
134 Judicial Appointments Commission, Written Evidence, Constitution Committee Inquiry, October 2011.
135 See, eg, discussion between Cordella Bart-Stewart, Nwabueze Nwokolo, Joy van Cooten and Frances Burton, Oral evidence, Constitution Committee Inquiry, 23 November 2011, Q264–268.
136 Baroness Falkner, Justice: Judicial Appointments, HL Hansard 726(127), 17 March 2011.
137 Seamus Taylor, HC Constitution Affairs, Minutes of Evidence, 18 November 2003, Q151.

women (as suggested by the UK Association of Women Judges[138]) by a certain date would also focus the JAC's attention. They would be required not only to take proactive steps to ensure sufficient applications from non-traditional candidates and that they are not then disadvantaged in the appointment process but also, should they fail to meet the target, to provide an explanation as to why this is together with a workable strategy as to how they will remedy this in the future.

Targets also have another important advantage over quotas. Unlike quotas, targets allow those charged with making judicial appointments to show leadership on diversity without altering the criteria on which appointments are made. Targets do not require the appointment of less-qualified people over those who are better-qualified for a particular post. All appointments continue to be made on merit. Rather they direct those charged with finding the best would-be judges to look harder and wider than they might do otherwise, to find merit in those who have traditionally been missing from the Bench. Indeed, a larger, more diverse pool and a more exhaustive scrutiny of those candidates will improve our chances of ensuring that only the most meritorious are appointed. In this way targets may well work to *increase* the quality of the appointees. As Lord Clarke has noted:

> It is in everyone's interest to have the widest possible pool of talent from which appointments can be drawn. To borrow a phrase it is better to be first in a field of many, than first in a field of one.[139]

Greater competition in an appointments process assessed on merit can only improve the quality of the appointments made. In short, as Lady Justice Hallett argues: '[g]reater diversity thus breeds greater merit'.[140] Of course, this may well simply prompt further questions as to what we mean by, and how we might go about identifying 'merit', which we will return to in detail in Chapter 6.

Another option which has gained prominence during the House of Lords Constitution Committee's inquiry, and which was subsequently proposed by the Ministry of Justice in its *Appointments and Diversity* consultation paper, is the use of the tie-break provision, under section 159 of the Equality Act 2010. This would allow those making appointments to favour disadvantaged or under-represented candidates where there are two or more candidates of equal merit. If we have no way of distinguishing candidates on merit – the accepted primary criterion by which appointments should be made – then, in such case, we have no option but

---

138 UK Association of Women Judges, Written evidence, Constitution Committee Inquiry.

139 Lord Clarke, 'Selecting Judges: Merit, Moral Courage, Judgment and Diversity', Speech, 22 September 2009.

140 Lady Justice Hallett, 'How the Judiciary is Changing' in *Judicial Appointments: Balancing Independence, Accountability and Legitimacy*, London: Judicial Appointments Commission, 2010, 89, p. 90.

to look to other considerations to guide appointment, and it is here that diversity might come in to provide a basis for picking one candidate over another. However, although the use of this measure in judicial appointments has garnered some high profile supporters including the Advisory Panel on Judicial Diversity, the Master of the Rolls, Lord Neuberger, Lady Justice Hallett and the members of the House of Lords Select Committee on the Constitution,[141] we might doubt whether it will make any practical difference. In order for the measure to bite, those making the appointments must come to the conclusion that the candidates are indistinguishable in terms of merit. The chances of this happening are slim. In fact, the JAC is on record saying that:

> The JAC will always select on merit and has to date been able to distinguish between the relevant merits of different candidates based on a careful assessment of an applicant's entire profile and background. The JAC therefore does not anticipate that this provision of the Equality Act will be relevant in practice.[142]

We seem then to be left with limited avenues for achieving greater judicial diversity other than to encourage people to apply and to sit and wait. One way out of this apparent dead-end would be if we could show that greater judicial diversity and appointment on merit could be seen to go hand in hand, such that the pursuit of merit *requires* us to secure greater diversity. We see an example of this in the statutory requirement that those selecting appointees to the Supreme Court must, at the same time as appointing on merit, 'ensure that between them the judges will have knowledge of, and experience of practice in, the law of each part of the United Kingdom'.[143] This typically manifests itself in the appointment of two Supreme Court justices from Scotland and one from Northern Ireland. This requirement of diversity is not seen as antagonistic to appointment on merit precisely because we recognise the value of having Scottish or Northern Irish experts on the Supreme Court bench when determining points of law from those jurisdictions. We appreciate that the Supreme Court is stronger for having this sort of jurisdictional diversity. This in itself tells us that at least some requirements of diversity are not just compatible with the pursuit of merit, but

---

141 Neuberger Report, Recommendation 21 [99–100]; Lord Neuberger and Lady Justice Hallett, Oral evidence, Constitution Committee Inquiry, 16 November 2011, Q240–242; Frances Gibb, 'Give women priority for top posts, judge urges', *The Times*, 14 November 2011; Judicial Appointments Report (98–101).

142 McNally Report, p. 33. The JAC repeated this in its response to the Ministry of Justice's *Appointments and Diversity* consultation paper (JAC Ministry of Justice, Appointments and Diversity: 'A Judiciary for the 21st Century': Response from the Judicial Appointments Commission (13 February 2012)).

143 CRA s 27(8).

demanded by it.[144] If we could make the same argument for women (and other under-represented groups) then we would have a solution to the diversity problem without running against appointment on merit. Of course, quite how having more women and other presently under-represented groups on the Bench might be seen to improve the quality of judicial decision-making and so make for a stronger, better informed judiciary still has to be addressed. But assuming that, as with jurisdictional diversity, this argument can be made and that there is no necessary clash between appointment on merit and the promotion of diversity, then we might look to amending the Constitutional Reform Act 2005 so that when selecting candidates for judicial appointment, consideration is given to 'the need for the judiciary broadly to reflect the diversity of the UK population, including traditionally un- or under-represented groups'.[145]

In the meantime, however, even the relatively uncontroversial changes to the judicial appointments process aimed at encouraging diversity are failing to make much headway. One example is the recommendation of the advisory panel that, given the concern that those making appointments have a tendency to select in their own image, there should 'always [be] a gender and, wherever possible, an ethnic mix' on the JAC and Supreme Court selection panels.[146] Given the relative ease with which this could be achieved, it is disappointing that one year on the Judicial Diversity Taskforce found that this standard was not being met.[147] In fact, it is yet another aspect of judicial diversity that is going into reverse: the Supreme Court selection panel established in autumn 2011 was, for the first time, comprised of five white men.

Getting off on the wrong foot

As we saw in the last chapter, on one view, the real cause of the lack of diversity in our judiciary is not deficiencies in the appointments process but rather the make-up of the pool from which appointments are made. If so (or to this extent), getting to a more diverse judiciary has less to do with *how* judges are appointed

144 As Baroness Hale acknowledged in her written evidence to the Constitution Committee Inquiry. It is, of course, also politically essential for there to be Scottish and Northern Irish representation in the UK Supreme Court. A political argument may also be made for women's representation.
145 Variations of this argument were made during the Constitution Committee Inquiry. See, eg, Lord Phillips's proposal of a new test (which he immediately rejected) requiring the appointments commission to 'select that candidate who will best meet the needs of the court, having regarded to the judicial qualities required of a Supreme Court justice and to the current composition of the court' (Frances Gibb, 'Judges call for rethink on top appointments: Is it in the interests of democracy for the Lord Chancellor to have more say over who gets judicial posts?', *The Times*, 20 October 2011); Erika Rackley, Oral evidence, Constitution Committee Inquiry, 6 July 2011, Q39; Thomas Legg, Written evidence, Constitution Committee Inquiry; Baroness Hale, Written evidence, Constitution Committee Inquiry.
146 Neuberger Report, Recommendations 31, 41 and 43.
147 McNally Report, p. 42.

than with the diversity of those entering the process.[148] Indeed, the fact progress towards a diverse judiciary continues to be slow despite such widespread reforms to the appointments process, has breathed new life into old and discredited 'trickle-up' arguments. On this view, given all the efforts we have made to improve how we appoint our judges, the continuing lack of judicial diversity can only reflect a lack of suitably-qualified women (and other non-traditional candidates) making their way through the legal profession. And so we are taken back to thinking that gender parity is simply a matter of time, of waiting for women to trickle-up onto the Bench. In the meantime, so long as the appointments process is fair and transparent, and diverse applications are positively encouraged, there is little more to be done. As Baroness Prashar, former chair of the JAC, has remarked on a number of occasions:

> It is futile to concentrate just on the diversity of the judiciary when the prob-
> lems are linked so intrinsically with the diversity of the legal profession as a
> whole ... As the legal profession remains unrepresentative, our ability to
> change the diversity profile of the judiciary overnight will be limited.[149]

Clearly, without greater diversity in the pool of potential judges, the JAC's ability to alter the make-up of the Bench is limited. And, as we saw in Chapter 2, the legal profession can – and should – do more to stem the flow of women and other non-traditional candidates out of the legal profession and to afford them the same opportunities for progression as their male counterparts. But, as we have also seen, this is not always the case.[150]

However, this reworked version of the trickle-up argument only goes so far. It is also clear that the JAC can and should do more to improve the representation of non-traditional groups on the Bench. We should resist the temptation to shift our primary focus back onto what women, and other under-represented groups, are doing (whether they are able or willing to apply and so on). Rather, we should continue to concentrate on the institutions and processes through which appointments are made. Five years on, while it is difficult to over-state the changes introduced to the judicial appointments process by the Constitutional Reform Act, the JAC has yet to make a noticeable difference to the make-up of the Bench.

---

148 See, eg, Interview with Lord Phillips (Supreme Court: does it deliver justice? – video), *The Guardian*, 25 October 2011 (5.40–6.24 minutes); Jonathan Sumption, Justice Committee 'Judicial Appointments Commission', Minutes of Evidence, HC 449-i, 7 September 2010, Q24; Lord Chancellor, House of Lords Select Committee on the Constitution, Annual Meeting with the Lord Chancellor, 19 January 2011.

149 Prashar, 'A New System for a New Century', [61], [64].

150 In fact, the Constitution Committee concluded that they were 'not convinced that either the Law Society or the partners of most of the large firms are sufficiently committed to the encouragement of solicitors applying to become judges' (*Judicial Appointments* Report, [125]).

And, while it may have very subtly laid the foundations for future diversity,[151] in the absence of visible results, the Lord Chancellor's more candid assessment of the JAC (that while it has done no harm, it has done little good either) seems closer to the mark.

So, how did the JAC get in this position? As we have seen, by the time the JAC started work the process of appointing judges had been the subject of debate for a number of years. It is clear that the lack of transparency in the old system of judicial appointment by invitation could not continue. It was no longer fit for purpose. However, while the lack of transparency opened up the judiciary to allegations of cronyism, for many members of the legal profession and judiciary the problem was not that the existing procedures were selecting the wrong people, but rather that the opaqueness of the process looked bad. It prevented them from being able to prove definitively that the right people *were* being appointed. In other words, the problem was not with the candidates who were (not) being appointed; not with how things *were* but with how things *looked*. Jonathan Sumption's summary of the situation is typical:

> The system of appointment by the executive in practice produced a judiciary which was both independent-minded and of the highest calibre. But the old maxim that 'if it ain't broke don't fix it' has its limits. The old system of appointments had been under attack for many years. Its defects were more apparent to the public than its pragmatic merits.[152]

Notwithstanding the quality of the appointments made, the 'defects' in the appointments process, most notably its lack of openness, left it – and crucially the judges appointed under it – vulnerable to attack. If this situation continued, the concern was that public confidence in the judiciary as a whole would be undermined. In Lord Phillips's words:

> The system demonstrably ensured that those who were appointed were very good; it did not, however, demonstrably ensure that those who were good were appointed. It was criticised as being a system in under which white Oxbridge males selected white Oxbridge males.[153]

And, to modify Sumption's point, if the main thing that is seen to be broken, by those who are in a position to effect change, is the transparency of the process

151 Baroness Prashar, Justice Committee 'Judicial Appointments Commission', Minutes of Evidence, HC 449-i, 7 September 2010, Q4.

152 Jonathan Sumption, 'The Constitutional Reform Act 2005' in *Judicial Appointments: Balancing Independence, Accountability and Legitimacy*, London: Judicial Appointments Commission, 2010, p. 31, 42.

153 Lord Phillips, 'Constitutional Reform – One Year On', Judicial Studies Board Annual Lecture, Inner Temple, London, 22 March 2007.

(rather than its results), then all that needs fixing – and all that will be fixed – is the transparency of the process. So, while it may be that the potential of reform to the appointments process to change the make-up of the judiciary was played up (for good or ill), it should be no surprise that strategies adopted to date have not made any real difference to this. If the desire to reform the appointments process stems primarily from a concern about a lack of transparency rather than deficiencies in the appointments that are actually made, then it should not be surprising if the effects of the reform are limited to opening up the process to more scrutiny but without any noticeable shift in the sorts of people appointed. Nor, given that the primary motivation for many of the reforms was this lack of transparency rather than concerns about the quality of judges appointed, should it be surprising that there has been little desire to deploy radical inventions, such as positive action in the form of quotas or targets, specifically focused on delivering judicial diversity. It is simply unrealistic to expect reforms intended to do one thing in fact to do something else. So, while it may be that the lack of diversity among those chosen through a particular appointments process may have been one contributing factor to that process coming under greater scrutiny, it does not follow that changes to that process will or should be expected to increase diversity on the Bench. The effectiveness of any remedy is likely to be limited to the problem it is seeking to cure.

Thus, from the outset, while most agreed that the appointments system was in need of repair, there has been less agreement as to the motivation, extent and desired impact of the renovations. While some view the changes as tantamount to positive discrimination – 'It's a standing joke, well I'm not female from an ethnic minority so they won't be interested in me. That's certainly something that's said flippantly in the bar'[154] – others are less convinced that changes to the process of appointing judges would make any difference to the actual appointments made:

> . . . it was very obvious . . . that [some members of the judiciary] were rather sceptical about what they saw as this politically correct approach of having an independent judicial appointments commission and how terrible it was that the idea of tapping people on the shoulder was frowned upon, because you get better candidates that way. Well it ain't broke we'd much rather continue in our own sweet way and we'll find a way of continuing in our own sweet way. We'd like to keep tapping people on the shoulder and if we can't, well, we'll find other ways of perpetuating a group of people who look and sound and smell like us.[155]

Suspicion and scepticism are rife. While few would now argue against the ideal of a diverse judiciary, lines continue to be drawn both as what this might mean and

154 White male barrister quoted in Opinion Leader Research, 'Final Report', p. 17.
155 ibid., p. 16.

how to achieve it. As battles rage over definitions of merit, what it means to be 'the best' candidate and how to ensure that they are appointed, the JAC appears to be caught in the middle: faced with the task of ensuring greater diversity in judicial appointments, while avoiding any real change to the nature of the judiciary itself.

Without doubt, the JAC started from a difficult position. Born out of compromise, it operates according to what Cheryl Thomas has described as a 'peculiar' process; 'a unique set of rules not used by any other appointments commission'.[156] However, in response, it has adopted what Lizzie Barmes and Kate Malleson describe as a position of 'tempered passivity'.[157] That is, while the JAC's ability to deliver 'meaningful change' to the make-up of the Bench was always going to be curtailed by the demographic and agenda of the legal profession, as well as by the restrictions of equality law and under the Constitutional Reform Act, the JAC has *further* restricted its ability to effect change though the choices it has made in relation to its internal decision-making processes and its relationship with the Ministry of Justice and the legal profession. In other words, it has failed to make the most of the flexibility it *does* have to put in place structural measures and procedures aimed at removing the barriers faced by non-traditional candidates and loosening the grip of the legal professions on the appointments process.

To use Barmes and Malleson's examples, the JAC might have responded to well established concerns of self-replication and the invisibility of non-traditional candidates by limiting its reliance on judicial references, particularly those obtained through direct consultation with sitting judges (rather than introducing its own category of 'nominated referees'). Similarly, it might have downplayed the importance of fee-paid judicial experience in selection decisions to allow for the appointment of practitioners from typically more diverse groups who are currently systematically excluded.[158] It could have developed a strong system of internal promotion to allow for easier progression from the (more diverse) tribunal and district Benches to the senior judiciary.[159] It might also have challenged the focus on entry-level positions and the indirect reliance on the discredited notion of a 'trickle-up' the judicial hierarchy by ensuring, particularly for senior appointments, that the pool of potential candidates is drawn from as wide a field as possible, rather than exclusively from the court below. At the very least, it might have agitated for stronger political leadership on judicial diversity from the Lord

---

156 Cheryl Thomas, Oral evidence, Constitution Committee Inquiry, 6 July 2011, Q1.

157 Barmes and Malleson, 'The Legal Profession as Gatekeeper', p. 261.

158 As Lord Falconer stressed to the Constitution Committee: 'We have been incredibly timid about going to government lawyers, prosecution lawyers, in-house counsel, academics, people who work in law centres – there is a whole group of places you could reach. We tell these people that they can apply, but you are never going to convince people that they will be appointed unless you start making appointments from this diverse group. By and large, most people would assume that they would not get through the process, and they are right' (Oral evidence, Constitution Committee Inquiry, 12 October 2011, Q157).

159 ibid.

Chancellor and Ministry of Justice in the form of targets or other guidance under section 65 of the Constitutional Reform Act 2005, rather than setting its face against any form of positive action. After all, none of these options is particularly radical. They are not novel. They have been suggested before. And so, while they all would have required the JAC to adopt a different position, and some may have raised a few eyebrows, none falls outside the JAC's remit or would have caused long-term difficulties. Instead, by retreating into a position of passivity, the JAC has lost the advantage of unfamiliarity and the goodwill that comes with novelty. In accepting the status quo, it has underplayed its hand. As we are seeing, efforts to increase judicial diversity are likely to be harder than ever. Without positive steps on the part of the JAC, or a level of political leadership from the Lord Chancellor and Ministry of Justice not seen to date, it is likely it will, remain in Baroness Prashar's words, a 'fig leaf' for the cultural and structural changes necessary to bring about judicial diversity.[160] In the meantime, diversity will, remain at most a welcome but desultory side-effect of the changes to the appointments process.

Without doubt the establishment of the JAC represented a turning point in the process of appointing judges. Yet despite the Law Society's wry observation that 'the fact that the complaints against the [changes to the process] are in the main coming from white male Oxbridge educated barristers (who are no longer guaranteed appointment) would suggest the JAC has succeeded'[161] in its main aim of making the process open and fair to all, it is clear that, to the extent that success is measured by diversity, there is still some way to go. After all, as Lady Hale notes: 'no system of appointments which produces only one woman [at the highest level] in the 92 years since the Sex Disqualification Removal Act 1919 can be considered remotely satisfactory'.[162] Changing the make-up of the Bench is proving to be a task even greater than had been thought. And so, while it continues to be important to make every effort to ensure that women are able to reach the upper levels of the legal profession and the fairness of the appointments process, it may be that the solution to judicial diversity lies elsewhere.

160 Baroness Prashar, Oral evidence, Constitution Committee Inquiry, 30 November 2011, Q332.
161 Law Society, Written evidence, Constitution Committee Inquiry, October 2011.
162 Baroness Hale, Written evidence, Constitution Committee Inquiry, October 2011.

Chapter 4

Representations of the woman judge

Revisiting the little mermaid

'But if you take my voice' said the little mermaid 'what shall I have left?'[1]

As we have seen, efforts to secure a diverse judiciary have typically focused on the appointments process and how we select our judges. However, as we have also seen, this has not taken us very far. Changes to the judicial appointments process are yet to have any significant effect on judicial diversity, at least in the upper echelons of the judiciary. One conclusion is that the appointments process requires further reform, that we need to do more to diversify the pool of potential judges or to ensure the fairness of the selection process. However, this assumes that the problem of judicial diversity only lies at – or before – the appointments stage of the process. In fact, there are reasons to believe that women continue to be disadvantaged even when they are appointed to the Bench. And so, if we want to achieve judicial diversity and to ensure that our women judges are equal not only in number but also in standing to their male counterparts, we need also to focus our attention on the experiences of women who have made it onto the Bench and on what it means to be a woman judge.[2]

1 Hans Christian Andersen, 'The Little Mermaid' in Naomi Lewis (trans) *Hans Andersen's Fairy Tales*, London: Penguin, 1981, p. 41, 61. *The Little Mermaid* is the story of a young mermaid who falls in love with a prince after she saves him from drowning. In order to join his world and win his love, she enters into a dangerous bargain. She sells her voice in exchange for legs to allow her to walk on land. To live, for she is now mortal, the prince must fall in love with her. Yet, although the silent mermaid intrigues the prince, he does not love her. On the morning of his wedding to a neighbouring princess, the little mermaid's sisters rise from the sea offering her an escape from her imminent death – a knife that she must plunge into the prince's heart. Unable to kill her prince, the little mermaid's heart breaks. She throws herself into the sea where she dissolves into the foam. As the story ends, she is transformed into a spirit of the air – neither mermaid nor human.

2 This chapter draws on and develops arguments previously published in Erika Rackley, 'Representations of the (woman) judge: Hercules, the little mermaid, and the vain and naked Emperor', *Legal Studies*, 22(4), 2002, 602 and Erika Rackley, 'Judicial diversity, the woman judge and fairy tale endings', *Legal Studies*, 27(1), 2007, 74.

Setting the scene

Psst! Did you hear about the law student who, unlike her male peers, was not allowed to sit and read the books in the Supreme Court library?[3] *Or about the magistrate whose judgment was challenged on the grounds that she was not a 'person'?*[4] *Surely, you must have heard about the US Supreme Court judge who graduated third in her class and was offered a job in a top US law firm – as a legal secretary?*[5] *And what about the plot by a pro-father pressure group to kidnap the dog belonging to the (former) President of the Family Division in order to show their displeasure with her perceived anti-father stance?*[6]

In 1869, the faculty of Columbia College refused Belva Lockwood's application to study law on the grounds that her 'admission would not be expedient as it would be likely to distract the attention of the young men'.[7] Fearing her siren call would lure the young men of the academy away from their set course like fated sailors, the selectors excluded her from their midst. As we shall see, Lockwood's story is far from unique. The experience of the woman lawyer and judge is typified by isolation and exclusion with the possibility of acceptance only at the price of the very attributes that set her apart – just like Hans Christian Andersen's little mermaid who sold her voice to walk on land with her prince. The tales where once upon a time feisty judicial heroines took on misogynistic villains and kindly guardians intent on thwarting their entrance to, and determining their adventures in, law's empire have been well documented. At once unnerving and reassuring, these stories of women lawyers and judges have become the stuff of folklore told from one generation to the next. The struggles and triumphs of the pioneer heroines, like the plots and characters of childhood fairy tales, although familiar, seem to belong to a different time: a time before equality was won, when difference was synonymous with danger and an 'outsider' was immediately suspicious. After all, nowadays, women law students not only outnumber and outperform their male counterparts at university, but the legal professions – intent on meeting their diversity targets – are increasingly keen to recruit women and members of other non-traditional groups.[8] And, of course, a diverse judiciary is increasingly seen as not simply desirable, but essential. Even Belva Lockwood's story had a happy

---

3 Lady Hale, 'Dignity', Ethel Benjamin Commemorative Address, Dunedin Art Gallery, New Zealand, 7 May 2010.

4 David Bright, 'The Other Woman: Lizzie Cyr and the Origins of the "Persons Case"', *Canadian Journal of Law & Society*, 13, 1998, 99, p. 112.

5 Rebecca M Salokar and Michael Wilson, 'Sandra Day O'Connor' in Rebecca M Salokar and Mary L Volcansek (eds), *Women in Law: A Bio-Bibliographical Sourcebook*, Westport, Connecticut: Greenwood Press, 1996, 210, p. 211.

6 John Elliot, 'Justice father talked of "suicide in front of Blair"', *The Sunday Times*, 22 January 2006.

7 Lorraine Dusky, *Still Unequal – The Shameful Truth about Women and Justice in America* (New York: Crown Publishers, 1996), 16 in Clare McGlynn, *The Woman Lawyer – Making the Difference*, London: Butterworths, 1998, p. 7.

8 See, eg, Richard Collier, *Men, Law and Gender: Essays on the 'Men' of Law*, London: Routledge, 2010, ch 4.

ending: she went on to become the first woman to be admitted to practice before the US Supreme Court. In short, Disney when it re-worked Hans Christian Andersen's tale got it right: the woman lawyer, like the little mermaid, is living happily ever after with her prince.[9] Isn't she?

Well, no. Not really. In fact, there is growing evidence that more often than not the woman lawyer is still waiting for that elusive happy ending – especially if she is a judge. Nevertheless, the fairy tale analogy is apposite; the stories of the woman judge have more in common with fairy tales than we might at first expect. Like these tales, the characters and plots are familiar enough to get our attention and unusual enough to retain it. In some the woman judge is a lone beacon, a pioneer in a hostile environment, ready, if able, to make a difference. In others, the arrival of sister companions serves merely to heighten tensions and emphasise the silence and suspicion that pervades the stories. Despite the significant differences in time zones, cultures, jurisdictions and generations that form the backdrop to these tales, the themes of isolation, antagonism and mistrust remain constant. And, in the same way that the talking wolves and gingerbread houses have led to common-place understandings of fairy tales as foolish stories or childhood fantasies reliant on improbabilities and lacking integrity or foundation,[10] the experiences of women judges in these tales often defy belief; they seem too incredible to be true. Hence we dismiss or downplay them as, at best, exaggerations and, at worst, exceptions. And yet, although individually the tales may have an air of the apocryphal, together they make for sobering reading.

This chapter explores these representations of the women judges and their role in arguments for judicial diversity. Using stories of women judges as 'representative cameos',[11] it frees the tales of female judges from their usual role as whispered anecdotes or intriguing opening gambits and establishes them as fairy tales, harnessing their power and ability to 'disrupt the apprehensible world . . . [and] open spaces for dreaming alternatives'.[12] At the same time the woman judge is cast as Hans Christian Andersen's little mermaid. It is suggested that the woman judge is *so* deviant that she is inevitably subject to irresistible pressure to conform. Like Andersen's mermaid, she is induced to deny herself and sell her voice; her siren call is silenced, her difference lost. This is not, of course, to suggest that the little mermaid's story mirrors that of *all* women judges or the entirety of an individual judge's experience, or that it in some way establishes, articulates or represents the woman judge's *essential* difference or the possibility of a different voice. Rather,

---

9 *The Little Mermaid* (1990) animation directed by M Henn, G Keane, D Marjoribanks, R Aquino, A Deja and M O'Callaghan, USA, Walt Disney Home Video.

10 Angela Carter, 'Introduction' in Angela Carter (ed), *Angela Carter's Book of Fairy Tales*, London: Virago Press, 2005, p. xiii–xiv.

11 Margaret Thornton, '"Otherness" on the Bench: How Merit is Gendered', *Sydney Law Review*, 29, 2007, 391, p. 411.

12 Marina Warner, *From the Beast to the Blonde: On Fairy Tales and their Tellers*, London: Vintage, 1995, p. xvi.

Andersen's tale is used to challenge the hold of attractive yet limiting understandings of the judge, of the judge as we picture him in our imagination, and the personality and characteristics we see him as possessing – our default judge, if you like. It is this image of the judge which encourages a construction of the woman judge as dangerous, other-worldly, different, and which in turn affects both women's desire to *become* judges and their ability to make a difference *as* judges.

The characters and methods of fairy tales are then deployed as catalysts to provoke debate about the judge, diversity and the judiciary; to expose stories, narrative and imagination as not only tools through which to develop understandings of the judge and judging, but as integral components of them. So that in seeking to loosen the grip of the default judge on our collective imagination, flushing out understandings of the judge and judging that deter or prevent women from joining the judiciary and constrain their potential within it, we might begin to fashion a fuller understanding of the judge and judging, informed by and reflecting the insights of these mermaids, in the hope that in time the Bench may become a place which women (and members of other non-traditional groups) can comfortably and constructively occupy.

Once upon a time – telling stories of the woman judge

In her introduction to *From the Beast to the Blonde*, Marina Warner begins her consideration of fairy tales and their tellers with a Kenyan fairy tale from Angela Carter's first anthology.[13] The story is about two wives: one is married to the sultan, the other to a poor villager. While the villager's wife thrives, the sultana gradually wastes away. The sultan summons the poor wife's husband and demands to know the secret of his wife's happiness. 'Very simple' the villager replies, 'I feed her the meat of the tongue'. When, after lavishing his wife with all the many varieties of tongue money can buy she still does not flourish, the sultan orders the wives to change places. Once in the village the sultan's wife immediately thrives, while her replacement languishes in the palace. Of course, the tongue meat the poor husband feeds the women is not material, but rather that of 'fairy tales, stories, jokes, songs: he nourishes them on talk . . . he banishes melancholy by refusing silence. Storytelling makes women thrive – and not exclusively women, the Kenyan fable implies, but other sorts of people, too, even sultans'.[14] Even, perhaps, lawyers?

Without the meat of the tongue, the tale suggests, we are destined to wither and fade. Storytelling is good for the soul. It not only nourishes us as individuals, but also brings people together. Consider, for example, bedtime stories, campfire

13 Anon, 'Tongue Meat' in Angela Carter (ed), *The Virago Book of Fairy Tales*, London: Virago Press, 1990, p. 215.
14 Warner, *From the Beast to the Blonde*, p. i.

tales, news reports, judgments, conference papers and so on. Stories invite people in, offering explanations as to how things are and opening avenues onto how things might be. Put simply, we tell stories in order to belong, to nurture connections and establish relationships; when we tell a story we become part of that tale as it becomes, at least for a time, our story.

> When we tell stories, we not only convey information, but we share a piece of history; we expand not only our knowledge of what happened, of what someone did, but also of why and how they did it, of how it felt, why it seemed necessary, how it fits into a worldview ... We learn what it is to walk in another's shoes, to experience another's pain, to anticipate another's pleasures, and by so learning we enlarge our own individual humanity and our society's sense of inclusion.[15]

The same is true of the stories told here. Passed down from generation to generation, as women lawyers and judges tell these stories, they share and identify common experiences about how it was – and still is – to be a woman in the legal profession and judiciary. However, stories and storytelling also have political effects. More than simply tales to idle away the hours, they are mechanisms for and of change. And so, the stories of the woman judge are more than simply educative tools, in the sense of being merely descriptive of what has happened, they become part of the story and, as such, catalysts for change.

The experience of being a woman judge is still often one marked by isolation, hostility and mistrust. Although the judiciary no longer performs 'intellectual somersaults'[16] to keep women out, a growing collection of tales or anecdotes suggests the judicial climate remains somewhat 'chilly' toward them:[17]

> By their anatomy, their skin pigmentation, or their accent, these outsiders are brandished as biased, not to be trusted as judges and not to be accepted as members of the judicial community.[18]

---

15 Robin West, *Narrative, Authority, and Law*, Ann Arbor: University of Michigan Press, 1993, p. 425.
16 Helena Kennedy, *Eve was Framed – Women and British Justice*, London: Chatto & Windus, 1992, p. 56.
17 Constance Backhouse, 'The Chilly Climate for Women Judges: Reflections on the Backlash from the *Ewanchuk Case*', *Canadian Journal of Women and Law*, 15, 2003, 167. In fact, it is not just *women* judges that experience this 'chilly' climate. The decisions of any 'outsider' judge, that is a judge who is *other than* white, heterosexual, male and so on, is liable to attack in a way that those of 'insider' judges are not. (See further, Regina Graycar, 'Gender, Race, Bias and Perspective: OR, How Otherness Colours Your Judgment', *International Journal of the Legal Profession*, 15(1–2), 2008, 73.) Nor are such experiences limited to women *judges*. They are a common feature of working life of many women in positions of authority (see, eg, Catherine Redfern and Kristin Aune, *Reclaiming the F Word: The New Feminist Movement*, London: Zed Books, 2010, pp. 144–146).
18 Claire L'Heureux-Dubé, 'Outsiders on the Bench: The Continuing Struggle for Equality', *Wisconsin Women's Law Journal*, 2001, 15, p. 28.

While some stories focus explicitly on the debilitating effect the woman judge's sex has on her ability to judge – such as the challenge to a planning tribunal's decision on the grounds that the 'tribunal was pregnant' (a tribunal member's five-month pregnancy, it was argued, meant that she no longer had the same 'clarity of mind and precision of thought' she had before pregnancy[19]) or the attempt to overrule a woman magistrate's decision on the grounds that, as a woman, she could not also be a 'person'[20] – others couch the same concern in terms of 'bias'. On some occasions the allegations of bias seem to be little more than a way of questioning or challenging the authority of the woman judge. Consider, for example, the allegation of judicial misconduct brought against a Madam Justice Southin, a judge in the British Columbia Court of Appeal, whose heavy smoking habit, it was suggested, gave rise to a reasonable apprehension of bias were she to be involved in cases in which the provisional government was a party as she would be 'beholden' to the Attorney General who had organised the installation of a ventilation system in her chambers.[21] Or the readers' comments to a newspaper article in which Lady Justice Hallett, who is widely tipped to be the next (and first woman) Lord Chief Justice, spoke of being propositioned, when a junior judge, by a senior male colleague, suggesting that her 'embittered' attitude and 'big chip on her shoulder' impeded *her* ability to judge.[22]

On other occasions, however, these allegations are directly linked to the woman judge's ability to judge fairly and impartially *because she is a woman*. The maleness of the judiciary means that the woman judge is not only atypical but 'presumptively partisan'.[23] Her identity as a woman immediately gives rise to a presumption of 'incompetency, inadequacy and unsuitability'.[24] And, while it may be tempting to think that attitudes have moved on, this does not appear to be the case. Compare, for example, the attempt in 1975 by a New York law firm to disqualify an African-American judge from adjudicating in a sex discrimination trial because she 'strongly identified with those who suffered discrimination in employment because of race and sex',[25] with the appeal some 30 years later against an international tribunal's decision on the grounds that the judge's former

19 Bronwyn Naylor, 'Pregnant Tribunals', *Legal Service Bulletin*, 14(1), 1989, 41 discussed in Regina Graycar, 'The Gender of Judgments: Some Reflections on "Bias"', *University of British Columbia Law Review*, 32, 1998, 1, p. 4.
20 Bright, 'The Other Woman', p. 112.
21 Canadian Judicial Council News Release, 'Judicial Council closes file in complaint against BC Madam Justice Southin', 21 March 2003.
22 Jessica Satherley, 'I was propositioned by the judge who promoted me: Top female Appeal Court justice's battle against sexism', *Daily Mail*, 8 November 2011.
23 Richard Devlin, 'We Can't Go On Together with Suspicious Minds: Judicial Bias and Racialized Perspective in *R v RDS*', *Dalhousie Law Journal*, 18, 1995, 408, p. 443.
24 Judge O'Sullivan quoted in Margaret Thornton, *Dissonance and Distrust: Women in the Legal Profession*, Oxford: Oxford University Press, 1996, p. 208.
25 *Blank v Sullivan & Cromwell*, 418 F Supp 1, 4 (SDNY 1975) discussed in L'Heureux-Dubé, 'Outsiders on the Bench' pp. 22–23.

membership of a UN expert group on gender and, more specifically, her stated belief that rape should be considered a war crime should have disqualified her from hearing a case on exactly that issue.[26]

Although the formal barriers barring women from entering the legal professions have largely been removed – a student graduating third in her class from a top law school today would be unlikely to find her employment options limited to being a legal secretary,[27] nor is it likely that a woman applicant to law school would be told to go home and take up crocheting,[28] or that a woman student would be refused pupillage on the basis that there was no toilet for her[29] – women judges continue to be excluded in more subtle, but no less invidious ways. Stories telling of her isolation and exclusion from the overt masculinity of the legal culture abound.

Consider, for example, the story about a woman judge expected to retire to another room with her guest after dinner whilst staying at the official judicial lodgings so that her male colleagues could enjoy their port and conversation unencumbered.[30] Or the judge who on her appointment to the Queensland Bench received the traditional honorary membership of the Tattersall's Club, Australia's self-proclaimed premier private members club, only to find this hastily withdrawn once they released she was a woman.[31] In fact, private members clubs are a common theme in the stories of the woman judge. Lady Hale has identified her colleagues' membership of the Garrick Club (which admits only men as members) in London as an example of the culture of informal networks and personal relationships as a systematic barrier restricting the progression of women and other non-traditional candidates: 'I regard it as quite shocking that so many of my colleagues belong to the Garrick Club, but they can't see what all the fuss is about'.[32] Lord Neuberger MR's response to Hale's comment is a case in point:

> Being the only woman in the Supreme Court is not an enviable position. [Lady Hale] carries it off with great dignity. But the idea that at the end of a heavy day, when for instance my wife is away, I go to the Garrick to discuss law or cases or to network is ridiculous. I go there to talk to people and relax, often with women there too.[33]

26 *Prosecutor v Furundzija*, Case No. IT-95-17/1A discussed in Graycar, 'Gender, Race, Bias and Perspective', pp. 80–81.
27 Salokar and Wilson, 'Sandra Day O'Connor', p. 211.
28 Ellen Anderson, *Judging Bertha Wilson – Law as Large as Life*, Toronto: University of Toronto Press, 2002, p. 38.
29 Anon, 'Hannah Wright: Obituary', *The Times*, 25 February 2008.
30 Brenda Hale interviewed in Elizabeth Cruickshank (ed), *Women in the Law: Strategic Career Management*, London: Law Society, 2003, p. 135.
31 Thornton, *Dissonance and Distrust*, p. 167.
32 It is estimated that around 25% of the senior judiciary are members of the Garrick Club, including four members of the Supreme Court (Frances Gibb, 'Men-only mentality puts the Garrick in contempt of a Supreme Court judge', *The Times*, 15 October 2011).
33 Frances Gibb, 'Give women priority for top posts, judge urges', *The Times*, 14 November 2011.

Nor do proficiency or strength in numbers provide much respite for the woman judge. In fact, it can sometimes make things worse. Another collection of stories coalesces around what has been described as a 'backlash' against women judges, particularly those who have reached the upper echelons of the judiciary. The treatment of Diane Fingleton, the first woman Chief Magistrate in Queensland, Australia, who was jailed for what was essentially a hastily written, and angry, email to a male colleague about what she viewed as 'disloyal' and 'disruptive' behaviour is a case in point.[34] Her conviction (for retaliation against a witness) and 12-month sentence were the culmination of a chain of events which, Rosemary Hunter concludes, 'could only have happened to a woman'.[35] The controversy following the *Ewanchuk*[36] case in Canada is another example. *Ewanchuk* involved an alleged sexual assault on a 17-year-old woman job applicant by a 49-year-old male (Ewanchuk) during a job interview. Justice McClung in the Alberta Court of Appeal upheld Ewanchuk's acquittal on the basis that the defence of implied consent had been made out. During the course of his judgment, McClung JA made a number of inappropriate comments about the behaviour of the claimant including the fact that she 'did not present herself to Ewanchuk . . . in a bonnet and crinolines' before concluding that the defendant's behaviour was 'less criminal than hormonal'.[37] The Supreme Court unanimously overturned the Court of Appeal. In a concurring opinion (with which Justice Gonthier agreed) Madam Justice L'Heureux-Dubé strongly criticised McClung JA's judgment which, she suggested, rested on and promoted 'archaic myths and stereotypes'[38] about sexual assaults. Over the course of 10 paragraphs she offered a step-by-step rebuttal of his reasoning in which the senior judge made it clear that she thought McClung JA had acted inappropriately:

> Even though McClung JA asserted that he had no intention of denigrating the complainant, one might wonder why he felt necessary to point out these aspects of the trial record [he had noted that the claimant was a mother of a six-month-old baby and her living arrangements]. Could it be to express that the complainant is not a virgin? Or that she is a person of questionable moral character because she is not married and lives with her boyfriend and another couple? These comments made by an appellate judge help reinforce the myth

---

34 Rosemary Hunter, 'Fear and Loathing in the Sunshine State', *Australian Feminist Studies*, 19(44), 2004, 145; Alan Ramsey, 'Swimming Upstream and Against Spite', *Sydney Morning Herald*, 2 February 2005; Anon, 'Everything to do with justice: former Qld Chief Magistrate Diane Fingleton', *Lawyers Weekly*, 29 September 2010.

35 Rosemary Hunter, 'The High Price of Success: The Backlash Against Women Judges in Australia' in Elizabeth Sheehy and Shelia McIntyre (eds), *Calling for Change: Women, Law, and the Legal Profession*, Ottawa: Ottawa University Press, 2006, p. 281. Her sentence was reduced to six months on appeal and was later quashed.

36 *R v Ewanchuk* [1999] 1 SCR 330.

37 ibid., [92].

38 ibid., [95].

that under such circumstances, either the complainant is less worthy of belief, she invited the sexual assault, or her sexual experience signals probable consent to further sexual activity.[39]

Had it ended there the case would simply have been another example of a male judge relying on inappropriate sexual stereotypes in his decision-making. However, rather than accepting this admittedly public dressing down with good grace, McClung JA launched a vitriolic and highly personal attack on L'Heureux-Dubé in the Canadian press.[40] At one point he appeared to blame L'Heureux-Dubé for the increasing rate of male suicides in Quebec – an unfortunate comment in any event, made worse in light of the fact that L'Heureux-Dubé's husband had committed suicide (although McClung subsequently denied any knowledge of this[41]).

In the UK, the backlash against women judges started early. Having survived early challenges to her appointment in 1945 (another common feature of these stories[42]), Sybil Campbell, England's first woman judge, was rarely out of the newspapers. Her tough line in the Police Court at Tower Bridge dealing mainly with petty thieves earned her the epithet the 'beast of Belsen' (just two months after the liberation of the Bergen-Belsen concentration camp), as well as the suggestion that the Home Secretary, Herbert Morrison, who was responsible for her appointment, should throw her into the river Thames.[43] And lest we think the press has moved on from such attacks, compare the *Sunday Pictorial*'s description of Sybil Campbell as someone who 'looks like Auntie. Your Auntie. My Auntie . . . [who] softly pushes open the dungeon door, smiles sweetly and another wrongdoer begins his penance',[44] with that of Lady Hale over 50 years later, soon after her appointment to the judicial committee of the House of Lords:

39 ibid., [89].
40 Janice Tibbetts and Shawn Ohler, 'Judges clash over landmark sex-assault ruling', *National Post*, 26 February 1999; Ted Morton, 'When judges square off: judicial mud-wrestling could end if McClung's apology was accepted', *Calgary Herald*, 6 March 1999.
41 CBC News, Canada Alberta judge apologizes for part of his letter, 10 November 2000.
42 See, eg, the attempts by the right-wing women's group 'REAL Women of Canada' to remove Madam Justice Wilson from the Canadian Supreme Court (Anderson, *Judging Bertha Wilson*, pp. xiii–xvii) and the criticism of Sonia Sotomayor's now famous 'wise Latina' comment prior to her appointment to the US Supreme Court (Editorial, 'Judging Sonia Sotomayor', *New York Times*, 30 May 2009).
43 Patrick Polden, 'The Lady of Tower Bridge: Sybil Campbell, England's first woman judge', *Women's History Review*, 8(3), 1999, 505, pp. 514–516. In fact, it is possible that there was more to the challenge in relation to Campbell's appointment. Before her appointment Campbell had been working in the Ministry of Food. This, her opponents claimed, meant that she did not meet the requirement for appointment of being a 'practising barrister'. This fuelled speculation among members of the Bar that her appointment was the result of positive discrimination (Herbert Morrison was a well-known supporter of women's rights who, apparently, 'loved to appoint women to positions which they had never held before'), prompting letters in *The Times* as well as questions in parliament. Although Morrison never fully addressed these concerns, the appointment stood (ibid., pp. 508, 511–513).
44 ibid., p. 515.

Lady Hale (Girton, Cambridge) is the English lady lawyer at her most singular Miss Marple crossed with Rumpole ... [who after explaining a particular point to the House of Commons Constitution Committee] licked her lips, looked away, and smiled disdainfully at some other poor wretch.[45]

Of course, Lady Hale's groundbreaking elevation to the House of Lords was always going to be greeted with dismay by certain elements of the press. They did not disappoint. As one commentator noted:

Case for the prosecution: she married her second husband nine days after divorcing her first; she wore thick glasses at school and 'was never very comfortable at dances'; worst of all, she has argued for gay civil partnerships and no-fault divorces.[46]

Cast by the *Daily Mail* as a 'ferocious feminist' intent on destroying the institution of marriage and other family values,[47] and which had been highly critical of Lady Hale during her time at the Law Commission some years earlier,[48] her appointment was seen to 'epitomise the moral vacuum within our judiciary and wider establishment':[49]

... despite the fact that she denied she was a hard-line feminist – 'a soft-line feminist' is the most she would admit to – the fact is that she is the most ideological, politically correct judge ever to have been appointed to the highest court in the jurisdiction. As such, she will be bringing this destructive perspective to bear upon binding legal decisions over some of the most difficult and contentious issues around.[50]

---

45 Quentin Letts, 'She smiled disdainfully at some other poor wretch', *The Daily Mail*, 19 November 2003.

46 Esther Addley, 'The women of the year', *The Guardian*, 19 December 2003.

47 Steve Doughty, 'The first lady of the Law Lords (and she wants to abolish marriage)', *The Daily Mail*, 24 October 2003; Geoffrey Levy, 'Nine days after her divorce, she wed husband Number Two', *The Daily Mail*, 13 November 2003.

48 Geoffrey Levy, 'Architect of a marriage wrecking measure', *The Daily Mail*, 26 April 1996.

49 Melanie Phillips, 'I deplore his actions but actually his cause is just', *The Daily Mail*, 5 November 2003.

50 Melanie Phillips, 'The Marriage Wrecker', *The Daily Mail*, 13 November 2003. Of course, the suggestion that the courts, particularly the family courts, are in the thrall of an 'extreme feminist agenda' and 'institutionally biased against men and marriage' is nothing new. (Phillips, 'I deplore his actions'). Nor is it limited to the UK. In Canada the right-wing, self-styled 'alternative women's group', REAL Women of Canada, has been campaigning for years against what they describe the 'feminist take-over' of the Canadian judicial system (REAL Women of Canada, 'The Feminist Canaries are Singing Again', *REALity*, XIX (3), 2000; REAL Women of Canada, 'The Risks to Society Caused by Fatherless Children', *REALity*, XXIX (g), 2010). Indeed, in Australia one particular disgruntled father likened his experience before an 'anti-father' and 'anti-man' woman judge to 'sending the Ku Klux Klan to judge a black man' (discussed in Graycar, 'Some Reflections on "Bias"', p. 6).

More recently, Lady Hale's insightful leading judgment in the unanimous Supreme Court decision in *Yemshaw v London Borough of Hounslow* [2011],[51] which extended the meaning of domestic violence in housing cases to include threatening or intimidating behaviour and abuse provoked another round of hyperbolic headlines,[52] inaccurate reporting and name calling:

> Thank goodness Lady Hale has never set foot in our home, or I'd be sleeping under Blackfriars Bridge tonight. I am, you see, guilty of domestic violence: I shout at my husband on a regular basis, with everything from accusations ('You slob!') to threats ('I'm going to throw that Blackberry out of the window!') . . . This judge is an ass! (And I'm not afraid to shout it, at the top of my lungs!)[53]

Nor are such outbursts confined to newspaper columnists and their ilk. In *R (McDonald) v Royal Borough of Kensington and Chelsea* [2011] the majority of the Supreme Court held that a local authority had acted lawfully in seeking to alter the appellant's care provision by providing her with incontinence pads or absorbent sheeting, rather than an overnight carer, despite the fact she was not incontinent. Lady Hale, taking a broader view of the appellant's needs, dissented:

> As Lord Lloyd put it in *Barry* 'in every case, simple or complex, the need of the individual will be assessed against the standards of civilised society as we know them in the United Kingdom' (p. 598F). In the United Kingdom we do not oblige people who can control their bodily functions to behave as if they cannot do so, unless they themselves find this the more convenient course. We are, I still believe, a civilised society.[54]

Of course, there is nothing unusual about judges disagreeing. Nor is it particularly surprising that Lady Hale took a different view from that of her male colleagues in this case. As Lady Hale has commented: 'it could just be that the physical differences between men and women mean that women have a different view of what human dignity entails in this particular context than do men'.[55] Nor is it surprising, given Lady Hale's significant expertise in this area, that two of the three majority judgments went to greater lengths than usual to distinguish their own approach and

51 [2011] UKSC 3.
52 Anon, 'Shout at your spouse and risk losing your home: It's just the same as domestic violence warns woman judge', *The Daily Mail*, 27 January 2011.
53 Christina Odone, 'I'm always shouting at my husband but no, Lady Hale, I don't think I ought to lose my home because of it', *The Telegraph*, 24 November 2011.
54 [2011] UKSC 33 [79].
55 Speaking at an InterLaw Diversity Forum event on the 'Feminist Judgments Project', Norton Rose, London, 13 October 2011 (transcript on file with author), although it should be noted here that the (woman) judge at first instance took a different view from that of Lady Hale.

criticise hers. What is surprising, however, is the language the majority use in their attack on Lady Hale's judgment. While Lord Brown finds Lady Hale's characterisation of the council's decision as 'nothing short of remarkable',[56] Lord Walker goes even further in his criticism of Hale's presentation of the majority's view:

> I find it rather regrettable that Lady Hale's judgment makes so many references to defecation. She says . . . the consequences (of what she describes as the logical implications of the majority decision) do not bear thinking about . . . I totally disagree with, and I deplore, Lady Hale's suggestion that the decision of the majority would logically entitle a local authority to withdraw help from a client so that she might be left lying in her faeces day and night, relieved only by periodic changes of absorbent pads or sheets.[57]

While one might note that Lady Hale refers to defecation just three times in her 3,512 word judgment and just once more than Lord Brown (and, since we are counting, she refers to faeces just once, compared to Lord Walker's six times), it is Lord Walker's use of the word 'deplore' which is most striking. As Robert George notes, this word is rarely used in judgments.[58] In fact, in his survey of judgments over the last 25 years, George found just one example of it being used in relation to another judge, in a case where the judge's actions amounted to serious professional misconduct.[59] Even in everyday life this description of the views of one's colleague would be considered not just strong but exceptional; its use in the context of the restrained and measured world of judgment-writing, in which profound disagreements are prefaced with expressions of respect or regret, truly is nothing short of remarkable.

Of course, the criticisms made of Lady Hale here are not explicitly tied to her sex – the objection is to her reasoning which appears independent of her status as a woman. However, in the context of a case in which Lady Hale herself has suggested that her sex may have shaped her approach, it becomes harder to disentangle criticism of her reasoning from her status as a woman judge. More broadly, the response to Lady Hale's judgments in both *Yemshaw* and *McDonald* fit into the broader pattern we have seen of women judges being more likely to be subjected to criticism than their male counterparts. As Regina Graycar comments in the course of her discussion of the use of adjectives of colour or gender or sexuality as 'markers of otherness' – 'I am still waiting to see a headline that says "White male heterosexual judge grants convicted rapist a hearing"'.[60] Of course, none of this

---

56 [2011] UKSC 33 [27].

57 ibid., [32].

58 Robert George, 'In Defence of Dissent: *R (McDonald) v Royal Borough of Kensington and Chelsea*', *Family Law*, October 2011, 1097, p. 1101.

59 *R v Wiggan* (unreported) 4 February 1999, Court of Appeal, in George, 'In Defence of Dissent', p. 1101.

60 Graycar, 'Gender, Race, Bias and Perspective', p. 79.

means that *all* criticisms of women judges are criticisms based on their sex. Women judges can get things wrong just as much as men. It may be that any number of the objections and criticisms detailed here may be explained and, perhaps, defended on grounds entirely independent of the fact that the judge was a woman. Yet, when viewed not in isolation but in the round, the picture they paint is clear: women judges encounter greater hostility and greater opposition than their male counterparts.

And this hostility is not limited to views on the performance of their judicial role or the quality of their judgments. Many women judges have had their personal lives subject to inappropriate levels of scrutiny and speculation.[61] US Supreme Court Justice Sonia Sotomayor has spoken publicly about the fact that women judicial candidates are held to different standards and judged more harshly than their male counterparts – to the extent that during the Supreme Court nomination process she was asked for the names of everyone she had ever dated.[62] Other women judges have suffered the ignominy of inane and/or pointed comments about their physicality, their sartorial choices or hairstyle. Consider, for example, the comment by one Yale Law School alumnus who suggested that the study and practice of law should be limited to women who were 'ugly'[63] or the 'Elena Kagan Isn't Lesbian – But Is Her Hair?'[64]-type newspaper and blog headlines that accompanied coverage of Justice Kagan's appointment to the US Supreme Court.

Allegations of bias, fraternal traditions and unsolicited style advice are all, it seems, in a day's work for the woman judge. She remains on the fringes of the masculine legal culture,[65] neither quite within nor outside, her sex clearly visible throughout. While the male judge may allow a few favoured women – 'queen bees' and such like[66] – to wear his robes, he retains ownership. Thus, although it may allow more women to join the Bench (though whether they want to is a different question), this rental arrangement is not enough. However often she wears his clothes, the *woman* judge can never shake off her prefix; she is never mistaken for the judge (although she may occasionally attract his attention).

---

61 See, eg, John Lisners, 'Cleveland Judge Sex Scandal', *The News of the World*, 17 July 1988; Janice Tibbetts, 'Alberta judge's remarks shake legal community: suggests Supreme Court Justice to blame for male suicide rate', *The Gazette*, 27 February 1999; Geoffrey Levy, 'Nine days after her divorce, she wed husband Number Two', *The Daily Mail*, 13 November 2003; Anon, 'What reduced a top woman judge to tears?', *The Daily Mail*, 22 June 2004; Peter Orvetti, 'Won't Ask, Won't Tell', *The Moderate Voice*, 18 May 2010; Satherley, 'I was propositioned by the judge who promoted me'.

62 Stephanie Francis Ward, 'Female Judicial Candidates are Held to Different Standards, Sotomayor Tells Students', *American Bar Association Journal*, 8 March 2011.

63 In McGlynn, *The Woman Lawyer*, p. 7.

64 Dana Rudolph, 'Elena Kagan Isn't Lesbian — But Is Her Hair?', *Change.Org*, 12 May 2010. Online. Available: http://gayrights.change.org/blog/view/elena_kagan_isnt_lesbian_but_is_her_hair (accessed 24 November 2011).

65 Thornton, *Dissonance and Distrust*, p. 3.

66 ibid., pp. 106–129.

Turning the page

So how should we respond to these tales about the woman judge? One obvious response is a sense of frustration or outrage at the way women judges have been – and continue to be – treated. We tell these stories because we want to shock the audience. We want to incite feelings of anger and disappointment in order to garner political support for change. Whether the immediate focus is on the slow rate of progress, or the crudely concealed misogyny that simmers beneath the surface, the bottom line is that it is wrong that women judges have a harder time on the Bench than their male counterparts.

And yet, especially among women judges themselves, there is a strong temptation to downplay or dismiss especially the more fanciful tales about the women judges as *non*-stories, as evidence of the banality that clutters up much of the media and internet, or as a rite of passage – something all women judges experience – and as such too familiar to be noteworthy or cause for concern. After all, as Lady Hale remarked in a public conversation with US Supreme Court Justice Ruth Bader Ginsburg, every woman has a bathroom story.[67] Lady Hale's concerned the construction of a new toilet just for her when she joined the Privy Council in 2004 and Justice Ginsburg's the opening times of the women's public toilet at the US Supreme Court.[68] Helena Kennedy's tale is slightly more graphic:

> I laughed out loud in the early 1990s when I found a letter from Inner Temple in my pigeonhole telling me that women's personal hygiene was causing a problem for the ancient sewage system of the Inn, which had never been designed to deal with women. Could we legal women desist, or insist on suitable bins being introduced into the lavatories. I saw it as a victory for women that we were here in sufficient numbers now to block the drains, but pitied the isolated female souls who would have to be very brave indeed to raise the issue at a chambers meeting.[69]

Although one might wonder why the women had to *ask* for such bins, the humour with which Kennedy tells her bathroom story underlines the point. Like the narratives of fairy tales, many of the tales seem almost too incredible to be true; at best the unique combination of extreme circumstances and volatile personalities and, at worst, unfortunate exceptions. Hence we downplay them. We dismiss them as outdated or exceptions, curiosities left over from another time and place. Their characters and narratives, akin to glass slippers and giant beanstalks, lend the

67 Lady Hale and Justice Ginsburg, 'The British and United States Legal Systems', Georgetown University Law Center webcast, 24 January 2008. Online. Available: http://www.law.georgetown. edu/webcast/eventDetail.cfm?eventID=473 (accessed 24 November 2011).

68 Phil Schatz, 'Judicial Profile: Hon. Ruth Bader Ginsburg, Associate Justice, Supreme Court of the United States', *The Federal Lawyer*, May 2010, pp. 27–28.

69 Kennedy, *Eve was Framed*, p. 45.

stories an air of unreality, subverting their authority. Their plots, as predictable and as malleable as those of fairy tales, vary according to (among other things) the political preferences and historical, geographical or cultural location of teller and/ or listener.

And yet, to stay with the *story* of a fairy tale is to misunderstand its purpose. The relative triviality of much of the subject matter of these stories – blocked toilets, club membership, heavy nicotine habits – belies their importance, not only as part of the oral history of the woman judge, but also in relation to understandings of the judge. Just like traditional fairy tales, where the story is less important than where it takes us, they offer a 'possibility of change, far beyond the boundaries of their improbable plots or fantastically illustrated pages'.[70] The tales women lawyers and judges tell about their experiences are not simply engaging tales or amusing anecdotes. Rather, they are revelatory of deeper truths about the position and status of women judges in particular and our understandings of the judge more generally. Told well these stories not only allow us to walk in the shoes of women in the legal professions – to acknowledge 'the real battles that took place to get women where they are today'[71] – but also to challenge the complacency 'that just because some things have changed, the struggle for equality is over'.[72]

Opting out – non-fiction accounts of women judges

So far the evidence of women judges' experience of being a judge has been largely anecdotal. As a result, the stories risk being dismissed as one-offs, or the result of an unfortunate combination of extreme circumstances or volatile personalities. However, in fact, a number of empirical research projects have found that these stories, or more specifically the judicial culture that underpins or fuels them, features heavily in women lawyers' decisions as to whether to seek judicial appointment. Many highly qualified women lawyers are put off from joining the judiciary and/or do not even consider the possibility of a judicial career because of concerns as to what it will actually be like to be a judge. There continues to be significant concern among women lawyers about the predominantly male atmosphere and environment of the senior judiciary.[73] As a result they are simply choosing to stay where they are. They simply do not want to join the judicial ranks.

Research for the Judicial Appointments Commission in 2009 found that women and BME respondents were more likely to be deterred from applying for judicial office because they found judicial establishment and culture more 'unappealing'

70 Warner, *From the Beast to the Blonde*, p. xii.
71 Sandra Day O'Connor, 'The Majesty of the Law', Interview for Online News Hour, 9 June 2003.
72 Brenda Hale quoted in Cruickshank, *Women in the Law*, p. 135.
73 Hazel Genn, *The Attractiveness of Senior Judicial Appointment to Highly Qualified Practitioners – Report to the Judicial Executive Board*, London: Directorate of Judicial Office for England and Wales, 2008, p. 16. See also Lord Lester, House of Commons Select Committee on Constitutional Affairs, Minutes of Evidence, 27 November 2003, Q268 (unrevised transcript).

than their white and/or male counterparts.[74] A similar study of lesbian, gay, bisexual and transgender (LGBT) experiences and views of the judiciary, published in 2011, found that just over half of BME LGBT respondents gave the 'judicial establishment' as a reason for never applying for judicial appointment, compared with just under a quarter of white LGBT respondents and 17 per cent of JAC respondents.[75] Overall, LGBT lawyers were also slightly more likely than those interviewed by the JAC to find the judicial culture 'unappealing', ranking it second behind the isolated nature of the role as the most unappealing aspect of being a Judge.[76] The survey also found a marked 'double whammy' effect among gay women/lesbians and BME LGBT lawyers. Both groups were significantly more likely to describe judicial culture to be 'unappealing' (77 and 71 per cent respectively) than white (46 per cent) or male (45 per cent) LGBT respondents.[77] BME LGBT lawyers were also more likely to identify potential gender/sexual hostility as a deterrent to applying for judicial office (61 per cent).[78]

It is clear then that judicial appointment is *less attractive* to women and other non-traditional candidates.[79] Concerns that the environment of the upper eche-lons of the judiciary will be 'hostile' toward them continue.[80] Indeed, for some women barristers interviewed by Hazel Genn in 2008 the High Court bench is nothing more than 'an extension of a male-dominated and conservative Bar, with the same culture of male self-confidence and intellectual posturing but with no respite'.[81] She also found that women solicitors in the same survey were reluctant, having made it to partnership, to 're-establish their credibility in a world they perceived to be even more antediluvian than city commercial practice'.[82] And as

---

74 Anthony Allen, *Barriers to Application for Judicial Appointment Research*, London: BMRB Social, 2009, p. 29.
75 Leslie J Moran and Daniel K Winterfeldt, *Barriers to Applications for Judicial Appointment Research: Lesbian, Gay, Bisexual, and Transgender Experiences*, London: InterLaw Diversity Forum, 2010, p. 16.
76 ibid., p. 22.
77 ibid.
78 ibid.
79 Of course, the unwelcome atmosphere is not the only reason why women choose not to apply for judicial appointment. Genn's research also found that despite the traditional attractions of judicial office – its appeal to an individual's sense of public service and ability to do justice, the prestige and financial security, change of pace and intellectual challenge – the most common reason given by both women and men for not applying was that they were happy in their current position. As one woman silk notes: 'I have no interest in full-time appointment. It is the conditions of service. Five-fold reduction in income. Less control over professional life and I would feel bound to go on Circuit . . . I have young children and I am not willing to do that. I'm married and I like to have dinner with my husband and friends rather than talking to a load of High Court judges. And also the social milieu . . . The idea of spending the next 15 years of my life being a High Court judge doing rubbish work is frankly too depressing to contemplate' (Genn, 'The attractiveness of senior judicial appointment', p. 21).
80 ibid., p. 22.
81 ibid., p. 23.
82 ibid.

Genn and others acknowledge, until a critical mass of women are appointed these views are difficult to rebut. Just as one respondent commented to Kate Malleson and Fareda Banda over a decade ago that 'the more women [are] appointed, the more women are likely to apply because they will see the role models and they may think that it is not a hopeless sexist institution',[83] the *absence* of women judges for many simply *confirms* the judiciary's hopelessly sexist status. Until the 'look' of the judiciary and judicial culture changes, the lack of women role models and support networks to provide advice and encouragement simply reinforces the perception of the judicial establishment and culture as one in which maleness dominates.

As with the anecdotal tales of women judges, there is a temptation to downplay these concerns, to suggest that they are grounded in 'misapprehensions about life as a High Court judge, which may once have been but are no longer true'.[84] Hence Lord Judge, in his Foreword to Genn's research, identifies the current High Court bench as one populated by a sprightly bunch of warm, independently-minded individuals ready to do their best to make any new arrivals as welcome and comfortable as possible. The subtext is that women are (at least in part) to blame for the lack of diversity. They are *excluding themselves* on the basis of assumptions about the judiciary and being a judge that are dated and simply inaccurate, that the only inequality in the judiciary is in 'their own bad dreams'.[85] The explanation, and indeed the blame, for the ongoing lack of diversity lies with these women *choosing not to apply*, rather than with the judiciary itself.

The stories of the woman judge caution against this view – of diminishing 'women's experiences, in deference to men's way of knowing'.[86] We tell the stories of the woman judge because they *are* true. They serve as a reminder that, however often we are told that they do not, women often *do* have a harder time as judges than their male counterparts. Whether we like it or not, the judicial bench *is* often a lonely place for the woman judge to be. US Supreme Court Justice Ruth Bader Ginsburg has spoken (before the appointments of Justices Sotomayor and Kagan) of how she missed the presence of former Supreme Court Justice Sandra Day O'Connor, particularly in the conferences where the justices discuss the cone privately:

83 Kate Malleson and Fareda Banda, *Factors affecting the decision to apply for Silk and Judicial Office* (Lord Chancellor's Department Research Programme 2/00), London: Lord Chancellor's Department, 2000, p. 24.
84 Lord Judge, 'Foreword' to Hazel Genn, *The Attractiveness of Senior Judicial Appointment to Highly Qualified Practitioners – Report to the Judicial Executive Board*, London: Directorate of Judicial Office for England and Wales, 2008, p. 4.
85 Patricia Williams, *Alchemy of Race and Rights: Diary of a Law Professor*, Cambridge, Mass.: Harvard University Press, 1991, p. 13.
86 ibid.

I don't know how many meetings I attended in the '60s and the '70s, where I would say something, and I thought it was a pretty good idea. . . . Then somebody else would say exactly what I said. Then people would become alert to it, respond to it . . . It can happen even in the conferences in the court. When I will say something – and I don't think I'm a confused speaker – and it isn't until somebody else says it that everyone will focus on the point.[87]

At best it seems, in Lady Hale's words, the woman judge inhabits a 'world where the natives are mainly friendly but often quite discernibly from another tribe':[88]

They mean well. Few, if any, of its members are actively misogynist or racist: but they have a lamentable lack of experience of having female or ethnic minority colleagues of equal status. They often simply do not know what to do with us or how to interpret what we say.[89]

And, at worst, it is a world in which her person and decision-making are more likely to be subject to intense scrutiny and her judgments are *more likely* to be criticised or challenged as biased. And, although these challenges are usually dismissed, they 'serve a kind of disciplinary constraining function . . . remind[ing] those whole racial or gender identities are indicated by adjectives [woman, African-American, BME, gay and so on] . . . of the tenuousness of their hold on their position'.[90]

Of course, this is not to say that *all* women judges have these experiences, or that those who do face a constant and unrelenting barrage of criticism and hostility. Clearly, there are women judges who have never felt that their sex (and the gender implications that derive from it) has made a difference to how they have been treated. The experience of Roslyn Higgins, the first woman appointed to, and later President of, the International Court of Justice, is a case in point:

I have never felt that my gender makes the remotest difference . . . I have felt, all my professional life, that I was simply working with colleagues, where gender was irrelevant (as was religion and colour). I appreciate that this experience may be exceptionally fortunate.[91]

Nevertheless the stories told here illustrate the possibility of 'a collective perspective'.[92] They stand against attempts to recast 'the general group experience as a fragmented series of specific, isolated events rather than a pervasive social

87 Joan Biskupiz, 'Ginsburg: Court needs another woman', *USA Today*, 10 May 2009.
88 Brenda Hale, 'Judging Women and Women Judging', *Counsel*, 10–12 August 2002, 10.
89 Brenda Hale, 'Equality in the Judiciary: A Tale of Two Continents', 10th Pilgrim Fathers' Lecture, 24 October 2003.
90 Graycar, 'Gender, race, bias and perspective', p. 80.
91 Quoted in McGlynn, *The Woman Lawyer*, p. 190.
92 Williams, *Alchemy of Race and Rights*, p. 13.

phenomenon' – of using the experience of the one woman judge who has never experienced *any* discrimination or hostility 'to attack the validity of there ever being any generalizable' woman judge's experience.[93] They shift the responsibility for change from the individual and back on to the institution. And they warn that until women judges are *in fact* treated in the same way as their male counterparts, and until this becomes an accepted part of judicial culture, then, as we are seeing, we are going to have a harder time persuading women to join the Bench.

Undressing the judge

So where does this leave us? What can we learn from the stories about the experiences of the woman judge? One thing is clear: the simple fact that women judges *are seen to have* a harder time on the Bench is *itself* a barrier to diversity. We know that women continue to *under*-apply for judicial appointment, particularly to the senior judiciary. By way of example, in the most recent competition for appointment to the High Court, women made up just 17 per cent of applicants despite making up 20 per cent of the pool of potential judges, an increase of just three per cent since 2006–2007.[94] And, of course, if fewer women apply, then fewer women are likely to be appointed; in 2010, the appointments of men outnumbered those of women by just over five to one. The stories provide an explanation as to *why* women are not applying for judicial office and for the lack of progress in increasing the diversity of our judiciary. They highlight the inability of the 'add women and stir'[95] approach to judicial diversity, adopted by the Ministry of Justice and JAC to date, to address the deeper structural and cultural disadvantages experienced by the woman judge. They show why, as we are seeing, changes to the appointments process alone will not lead to a diverse Bench, that simply opening the door to women is not enough. The message is that if we really want women to want to *be* judges and for them to make a difference *as* judges, there needs to be structural and institutional change not only to the culture and environment of the legal profession and judiciary and the appointments process, but also, as we shall see in the next chapter, to understandings of the judge and judging.

---

93 ibid.
94 This translates into just 15 women compared to 75 men. On this occasion women were also slightly less likely than men to be short-listed, although those who were had a slightly higher chance of being recommended for appointment. Two women and 11 men were recommended for appointment in this round (Judicial Appointments Commission, *Judicial Selection and Recommendations for Appointment Statistics, England and Wales, April 2010 to September 2010*, December 2010, Table: 4.1 and 4.2; Ministry of Justice and Judicial Appointments Commission, Statistical Digest of Judicial Appointments of Women and BME Candidates from 1998–99 to 2008–09, July 2010). BME and professional background statistics are not broken down by sex.
95 Regina Graycar, 'The Gender of Judgments: An Introduction' in Margaret Thornton (ed), *Public and Private – Feminist Legal Debates*, Oxford: Oxford University Press, 1995, p. 262, 268.

In the meantime, the best the woman judge can do is to keep her head down. Like Andersen's little mermaid, she faces a stark and brutal choice: being a woman or becoming a judge. She cannot be both:

> To speak as a judge is to speak in a way that cannot be bracketed . . . One cannot speak as a woman (judge) or even as (woman) judge. Judge must stand alone if judgment is to carry weight.[96]

In Andersen's fairy tale, the little mermaid sells her voice for long legs enabling her to walk alongside her prince. The temptation for women judges to do the same, to repress all signs of difference, is for many overwhelming. She repeats the mantra that she is a 'lawyer first, woman second',[97] and that a 'wise old man and a wise old woman reach the same conclusion',[98] so that she can take her place in a world where sex and gender are deemed 'irrelevant'.[99]

In fact, what the stories of the woman judge tell us is that *even if she does this* she remains likely to be given a harder time than her male colleagues. The woman judge is unavoidably marked by difference, and as such is a target for criticism, for promoting a particular agenda or simply exercising bad judgment. As Sandra Berns notes '[t]he silencing inherent in such claims is . . . a casting out, a sense of thrownness, an absolute exclusion from even the possibility of being authoritative'.[100] Uncomfortable echoes of the little mermaid's self-mutilation pervade the story of the woman judge: '[w]e are still expected to take our place on the Bench, suppress out experiences, sit quietly and talk softly and politely'.[101] As in *The Little Mermaid*, the moral of the stories of the women judges seems to be that 'cutting out your tongue is still not enough. To be saved more is required: self-obliteration, dissolution'.[102]

But why is it that women judges have a harder time than their male colleagues? Again the stories of the women judges are helpful here. Like the traditional tales of mermaids, fairy godmothers and frogs that turn into princes, the stories of the woman judge reveal truths which we might otherwise find hard to express. The nature of the criticisms they involve together with the fact that they are *more likely* to be made against judges from non-traditional groups suggests that, whether we know or acknowledge it or not, there is a perception of who the judge is and how judges should operate that women judges simply don't 'fit'. The stories reveal a

---

96 Sandra Berns and Paula Baron, 'Bloody Bones: A Legal Ghost Story and Entertainment in Two Voices – To Speak as a Judge', *Australian Feminist Law Journal*, 2, 1994, 125, p. 127.

97 Hale, 'A Tale of Two Continents'.

98 Attributed to Justice Jeanne Coyne of the Supreme Court of Oklahoma quoted in Sandra Day O'Connor, 'Portia's Progress', *New York University Law Review*, 66, 1991, 1546, p. 1558.

99 Dame Rosalyn Higgins QC quoted in McGlynn, *The Woman* Lawyer, p. 190.

100 Sandra Berns, *To Speak as a Judge – Difference, Voice and Power*, Dartmouth: Ashgate, 1999, p. 18, n 20.

101 L'Heureux-Dubé, 'Outsiders on the Bench', p. 30.

102 Warner, *From the Beast to the Blonde*, pp. 398–399.

deep, instinctive commitment to a particular image of the judge and judging. This 'default' judge – a judge who is 'anonymous, dehumanised, impartial, authoritative [and] . . . intrinsically male'[103] – retains a tenacious grip on the legal imagination. The fact that our judiciary has, since its origins, been monopolised by men, indeed by white men with very similar social and educational backgrounds, lends these physical and cultural attributes a normality, which encourages us to associate judges with those who possess these attributes. In this way, we become attuned to the judge in this particular form, providing our default mental image when contemplating the judge and the judicial role. This physical image of the judge is in turn associated with those characteristics which we see as typical of (good) judging: impartiality, fairness, authority, objectivity. Not only that: the physical and social homogeneity of our judges lends itself to a uniformity of judicial method and approach, which encourages us to believe in the neutrality of judging, in the possibility of adjudication without reference to any particular moral, social or political values. In this way, the physical image of the judge as a man is mirrored by and reinforces the view that good judges possess a particular closed set of characteristics which leads in turn to an understanding of judging as uniform and value-neutral.

This comes to a head when a woman dons judicial robes. The woman judge challenges both the physical appearance and professional attributes of the default judge:

> [H]er very otherness . . . enables her to understand that the realm of the universal and objective to which she has aspired is a fake . . . a mirror in which [her] brothers see themselves reflected, not as they are, but as they believe themselves to be.[104]

Her sex is immediately and constantly apparent. Although she is dressed as a judge, as the stories show, what we in fact see is a *woman*. As such she not only gets our attention but also acts as an irritant, troubling our understanding of what judges do. Her lack of physical 'fit' feeds substantive concerns about her professional attributes, that is *how* she will judge. Her status as a *woman* judge challenges traditional understandings of the judge as someone *without* identity, without race, class, sexuality, religion, sex and so on. The fear is that she will bring her experiences *as a woman* to her judicial role and that *in so doing* she will step outside the judge's traditional remit and use her judgments to develop a distinct – possibly feminist and almost certainly woman-centred – agenda; hence, the frequent pre-emptive and false accusations of bias made against her.

What the stories show us is that it is this image of the judge – and not women judges themselves – that needs to be changed, not least because the default

---

103 Brenda Hale, 'Equality and the Judiciary: Why Should We Want More Women Judges?', *Public Law*, 2001, 489, p. 497.
104 Berns, *To Speak as a Judge*, p. 34.

image of the judge is premised on a fundamental misinterpretation of what judges do. The pursuit of judicial diversity is being hampered by misguided assumptions about the nature of the judicial role. Our default image of the judge – what *he* is and what *he* does – leaves women judges marginalised and atypical. This atypicality means that women judges face greater obstacles to their acceptance *as judges* precisely because they are seen to fall outside and to threaten our (intuitive) understanding of what judges – the judges we are used to – look like and do. And so, while it might be tempting to dismiss the challenges to women judges as petty, as foolish stories of continuing prejudice or small minded-ness, we ought not overlook the extent to which, like all myths and fairy tales, they are grounded in a deeper truth:[105] women judges *are* different from their male counterparts. They *do* bring something different to the process of judging. And once we acknowledge this, not only might the judiciary become a better place for women to be, but we also have a stronger positive reason for wanting a more diverse judiciary.

Coda

Psst! Remember the top-ranking student offered the job of legal secretary? That was Sandra Day O'Connor, the first woman judge to sit in the US Supreme Court. And the woman student who was told to go home and take up crocheting – that was Bertha Wilson, the first woman judge to sit in the Canadian Supreme Court. You will not have forgotten about the woman judge asked to leave the room after dinner so that her male colleagues could enjoy their port and wine unencumbered – that was Brenda Hale – and she refused to go. Nor about the woman who was refused pupillage because there was no women's toilet; that was Hannah Wright who went on to become the first woman member of the Bar Council (after she promised to use the local public toilets). And the woman who was prevented from using the library? That was Ethel Benjamin, New Zealand's first woman lawyer and the first woman in the British Empire to appear as counsel in court. As for the endings of the other stories told here, Diane Fingleton returned to the legal profession as a magistrate in Caloundra, Queensland before retiring in June 2010, and all of the various attempts to disqualify women judges – because they were pregnant, heavy smokers, African-American, or because they spoke out against rape – they all eventually failed. And finally, remember Tattersall's, the male members-only club that withdrew its invitation to a newly appointed judge on learning she was a woman . . . well, some things never change.[106]

105 Richard Cavendish (ed), *Mythology: An Illustrated Encyclopedia of the Principal Myths and Religions of the World*, London: Little, Brown & Company, 1992, p. 8.
106 S Parnell and C Mathewson, 'Beatie Sticks with Tatt's Despite No-Women Vote', *Courier Mail*, 27 March 2003.

Chapter 5

Difference and the default judge

Haply a woman's voice may do some good,
When articles too nicely urged be stood on.[1]

The experiences of women judges detailed in the previous chapter go some way to telling us why progress towards a judiciary in which women are equal in both number and status to their male counterparts is so slow. And yet, while we must confront and reject the prejudices and misunderstandings which lie behind many of the obstacles women judges face, it would be wrong to conclude that the criticisms levelled at women judges are in all respects mistaken. Our default image of who the judge is and what he does leads us to treat women judges with suspicion, as a threat to the homogeneous neutrality of the (male) Bench. However, the problem here is not in seeing women as upsetting the status quo, but with the understanding of judges and the judicial role which they are seen to threaten. For, in one important sense, the criticisms directed at women judges are correct: women judges *are* different. The mistake is to conclude from this that women judges and the difference they might make to the judiciary and judicial decision-making are to be regretted or avoided. To see why this is mistaken, we need to be clear about what our judges really do and how they do it. Once we do this, not only does this objection to women judges fall away but we begin to see the real value women can bring to the judiciary.

The default judge: superhero, every-judge or fiction?

The stories in the previous chapter suggest that one of the obstacles to the acceptance of women judges is that there exists an understanding of the judge which women do not fit. As Lord Neuberger MR has recently acknowledged: '[m]ost of

1 Queen Isabel, *Henry V*, Act 5 sc 2.

us think of a judge as a white, probably public school, man'.[2] The consequence of this default understanding of the judge is that those who fall outside it are seen to threaten not just the physical and social homogeneity of the judiciary, but also the professional attributes we tend to associate with it: objectivity, impartiality, authority and so on. It is for this reason that women judges are more likely to be seen as radical and face claims of bias.

This image of the judge as objective, neutral, and detached from any particular moral or political leaning reflects a popular understanding of the judicial role. The judge must find and apply the law, understood as a system of rules with correct and incorrect outcomes, to the facts at hand. Moreover, he must do so without reference to what Lord Bingham has described as 'extraneous considerations', that is 'the prejudice or predilection of the judge, or worse . . . any personal agenda . . . whether conservative, liberal, feminist, libertarian or whatever'.[3] His primary purpose is to uphold the rule of law, and to this end he adopts a position somewhere between that of a 'demigod to whom objective truth has been revealed' and a 'legal pharmacist, dispensing the correct rule prescribed for the legal problem presented'.[4] This understanding of the judge has plenty of appeal. For one thing, given that our judges are not elected and so are neither representatives of, nor accountable to, those who come before them, it is understandable that we might prefer the job of law-making to be left exclusively to those democratically elected to make such determinations and whom we can eject if we dislike the decisions they have made. This approach sees parliament as solely charged with setting the rules, which it is then the courts' responsibility to apply and enforce.[5] Alongside this separation of powers argument is the simple concern of litigants to see that the rules that will be applied in the resolution of their cases will not vary with the identity of the judge who happens to be assigned to them. Justice should not be a lottery; like cases should be treated alike. Yet this is possible only if our judges are not making determinations of social policy or morality – issues on which different judges may reasonably differ – but are instead limited to the neutral application of a body of pre-set rules and principles.

The problem is that this conception of judging, however attractive it may be, is not – and cannot be – true. If we did not know it before, by the time Lord Reid rejected the declaratory theory of common law as a 'fairy tale' in the 1970s this understanding of what judges do had been exposed as fiction. Lord Reid put it thus:

2 Oral evidence to the House of Lords Select Committee on the Constitution Inquiry into Judicial Appointments Process, 16 November 2011, Q248.

3 Lord Bingham, 'The Judges: Active or Passive', 139, 2006, *Proceedings of the British Academy* 55, p. 70.

4 William J Brennan Jr, 'Reason, Passion, and "The Progress of the Law"', *Cardozo Law Review*, 10, 1998, 3, 4–5.

5 'The function of the legislature is to make the law, the function of the administration is to administer the law and the function of the judiciary is to interpret and enforce the law' (Lord Greene, 'Law and Progress', *Law Journal*, 94, 1944, 349).

There was a time when it was thought almost indecent to suggest that judges make law – they only declare it. Those with a taste for fairy tales seem to have thought that in some Aladdin's cave there is hidden the Common Law in all its splendour and that on a judge's appointment there descends on him knowledge of the magic words Open Sesame . . . But we do not believe in fairytales any more.[6]

Whatever one's view of the judicial role, it is clear that there are times when all judges must do more than simply follow the rules, when the rules run out or the authorities leave the matter in doubt or at least call for the exercise of some discretion, where judges of the highest ability and knowledge reach different conclusions and either outcome could be regarded as consistent with existing legal practice and precedent – what legal philosophers call 'hard cases'.[7] In all such cases, the authorities alone cannot give us an answer and the judge must turn to his or her sense of justice, to an understanding of the judicial function and the purpose of law and the like for a solution.

This point has been made by judges and legal theorists alike. As Joseph Raz notes:

Because of the vagueness, open texture and incompleteness of all legal systems there are many disputes for which the system does not provide a correct answer. Even if it rules out certain solutions as wrong, it may have others which are neither wrong nor right in law. If the system requires with respect to some such cases, as all legal systems in fact do, that the courts should not refuse to settle the dispute but should render judgment in it, then they are thereby required to determine the case in accordance with their own conception of what is right. Needless to say, even in such cases their discretion can be limited by general legal principles, but these will not eliminate the element of personal judgement of the merits.[8]

Whether the law is presented as made up of a fixed set of rules which in novel cases run out, at which point the judge must exercise a discretion in setting down

---

6 Lord Reid, 'The Judge as Law Maker', *Journal of the Society of Public Teachers of Law*, 12, 1972, 22.

7 See, eg, Ronald Dworkin, *Taking Rights Seriously*, London: Duckworth, 1977; Richard Posner, *How Judges Think*, Cambridge, Mass.: Harvard University Press, 2010.

8 Joseph Raz, *Practical Reason and Norms*, 1st edn, 1975, Oxford: Oxford University Press, 1999, pp. 139–140. See also, Benjamin N Cardozo, *The Nature of the Judicial Process*, New Haven: Yale University Press, 1921, p. 12; Baroness Hale, 'A Minority Opinion?', *Proceedings of the British Academy*, 154, 2008, 319; Terence Etherton, 'Liberty, the Archetype and Diversity: A Philosophy of Judging', *Public Law*, 2010, 727, pp. 740–742; Posner, *How Judges Think*, p. 8; Lady Justice Arden, 'Magna Carta and the Judges – Realising the Vision', Royal Holloway, University of London, June 2011.

a new rule,[9] or as a 'seamless web'[10] with its content determined only by reference to political morality, on which the views of individual judges will inevitably differ, in neither case is the judge's role limited to a neutral application of a predetermined set of rules. As Lord Mustill noted in *Airedale NHS Trust v Bland*,

> when the intellectual part of the task is complete and the decision-maker has to choose the factors which he will take into account, attach relevant weights to them and then strike a balance the judge is no better equipped, though no worse, than anyone else. In the end it is a matter of personal choice, dictated by his or her background, upbringing, education, convictions and temperament. Legal expertise gives no special advantage here.[11]

Lord Hoffmann put it simply: '[s]ince all judges are also people, this means that some degree of diversity in their applications of values is inevitable'.[12] It does not follow from this that judges are simply legislators or that judges are not subject to greater constraints in their decision-making than parliament and other legislative bodies. Judicial law-making is importantly different from legislative law-making, and the duty and role of the judge differs from that of the legislator.[13] The point is simply that, even acknowledging these constraints, judges have to do more than simply apply a set of predetermined rules and must instead make decisions involving matters of justice, of moral or social principle, on which, as a matter of practical inevitability, different individuals will differ.

And yet, while most would agree with Lord Reid that a judge must, sometimes, turn to her or his own sense of justice, of what is right or wrong, when deciding cases, its corollary – that *who* the judge is matters – remains contentious. The extent to which a judge's *personal* values and perspectives impact on his or her consideration of what the law should be, how the law should respond to the case at hand, what justice demands, and how her or his judicial responsibilities may best be performed and so on and the significance of this on the make up of the Bench, have been left largely untouched in accounts of adjudication. However, once one acknowledges that the law does not exist as a preformed set of rules which judges simply discover and apply to the facts at hand, and that on occasions the judge must form her or his own view as to what should happen, it follows that *who* the judge is matters. As Lady Justice Arden notes:

---

9 HLA Hart, *The Concept of Law*, Oxford: Oxford University Press, 1961.

10 Ronald Dworkin, *Law's Empire*, Oxford: Hart Publishing, 1986.

11 [1993] 789, pp. 887–888.

12 *Piglowska v Piglowski* [1999] 3 All ER 632, p. 644.

13 On judicial law-making see John Finnis, 'Natural Law: The Classical Tradition' in Jules Coleman and Scott Shapiro (eds), *The Oxford Handbook of Jurisprudence and Philosophy of Law*, Oxford: Oxford University Press, 2002, 1, pp. 10–11; John Gardner, 'Legal Positivism: 5½ Myths', *American Journal of Jurisprudence*, 46, 2001, 199, 215–218.

It is a reality in the twenty-first century that judges are called upon to make judgments of this kind in different cases and in different circumstances. They must do so with such assistance as they can find in existing decided cases. If (as often happens) there are no decided cases, they must decide questions involving value judgments within four corners of the statutory framework and with the benefit of their own awareness and experience of society and social issues, and their own considered view of how such matters ought fairly to be decided in the society in which we live.[14]

Different judges, different people, will answer these questions differently. We do not all share the same values and priorities and, even where we do, we prioritise and balance them differently. Insofar as judges must, at least on occasion, bring their own values to bear when deciding cases, and turn to their own understanding of what the law should be, how it should respond to particular problems, what values it should promote, it makes a difference which judge is making the decision.

Clearly none of this is to suggest that judges can or should incorporate *all* their values and preferences (or prejudices) into their judging. It is not to suggest that judges do – or should – have an agenda. As mentioned already, there are, rightly, significant constraints on judicial decision-making and on the considerations which ought to shape those decisions. It is simply to say that there will be times where the judge has to consider what, in her or his view, the law *should be*, how the law *should* respond to the case at hand, what justice demands, how her or his judicial responsibilities may best be performed, and *in such cases* the answer the judge gives will be determined, at least in part, by that judge's own values and perspectives: '[e]very decision-maker who walks into a courtroom . . . is armed not only with the relevant legal texts, but with a set of . . . experiences that are thoroughly embedded'.[15] *All* judges, whether or not they admit it and whether or not they think about it in these terms, have a philosophy, an understanding of their judicial role and the role of the law which shapes and informs their decision-making.[16] Indeed, if this were not the case, we should be amazed to see judges disagreeing so often. That they do reflects how much a judge's outlook or personal philosophy shapes their judging. Lady Hale puts it thus:

[T]he business of judging, especially in the hard cases, often involves a choice between different conclusions, any of which it may be possible to reach by respectable legal reasoning. The choice is likely to be motivated at a far

14 *Ilott v Mitson* [2011] 2 FLR 1 [68].
15 Rosalie Arbella quoted in Bertha Wilson, 'Will Women Judges Really Make a Difference?', *Osgoode Hall Law Journal*, 28(3), 1990, 507, p. 510. See also *R v S (RD)* [1997] 3 SCR 484 [38] (L'Heureux-Dubé and McLachlin JJ).
16 Etherton, 'Liberty, the Archetype and Diversity', pp. 729 and 740. See further, Hale, 'A Minority Opinion?', p. 322.

deeper level by the judge's own approach to the law, to the problem under discussion and to ideas of what makes a just result.[17]

And yet, as we saw in the previous chapter, the merest whiff that the outcome of any given case rests – *to any extent* – on the personality, preferences or characteristics of the judge that hears it causes considerable consternation and upset among litigants and the general public. The slightest indication that judges may be political actors with substantial power and opportunity to exercise their own preferences and persuasions threatens to introduce unsavoury elements of arbitrariness and partiality into a system which rests for its legitimacy on its distance from such contingencies. We rightly want to hold on to the principles of impartiality and democracy that are intrinsic to our traditional notion of judging. And so, while we may on occasion recognise that judges are not – and nor would we want them to be – 'computers in robes',[18] we *also* want to believe that when we stand before a judge that who that judge is does *not* matter, that like *cases will be* treated alike and that the justice dispensed by Mrs Justice A will be the same as that meted out by Mr Justice B. And, even though we know we cannot have it both ways, this does not stop us trying.

And so we hold tight to the fairy tale, to the default image of the judge. We point to his struggle against, and ability to overcome, the obstacles of prejudice and desire as evidence both of his capacity to judge and a reason for 'believ[ing] in' him.[19] We tell ourselves, and others, that who the judge is – his background and personality – are 'irrelevant' to his ability to perform his judicial role, that the outcome of the case will be unaffected by preference or interest because, as the default judge, he has none.[20] We even make him dress in his own cape and mask, well, gown and (sometimes) wig – his own superhero outfit. And even though we might, when pressed, admit that on occasion this disguise slips – and it becomes apparent who the judge is – we respond to this much like the husbands and fathers in Marie-Jeanne L'Héritier's fairy tale *La Robe de Sincérité*, who lie and say they can see the invisible embroidery that evidences the wearer's fidelity on their wives' and daughters' clothes in order to save their blushes.[21] We too keep quiet; we deny the reality of the judge and carry on just as before, hoping no one will notice. We operate *as if* the personality of the judge does not matter, as if a judge's personal preferences do *not* affect their understanding of their judicial role, as if justice is not

17 Hale, 'A Minority Opinion?', p. 320.
18 Martha Minow and Elizabeth Spelman, 'Passion for Justice' in JT Noonan Jr and KI Winston, *The Responsible Judge: Readings in Judicial Ethics*, Westport: Praeger, 1993, 257, pp. 259–260.
19 Duncan Kennedy, *A Critique of Adjudication {fin de siècle}*, Cambridge, Mass.: Harvard University Press, 1997, pp. 3–4.
20 Lord Judge, 'Equality in Justice Day', Royal Courts of Justice, London, 24 October 2008.
21 Marie-Jeanne L'Héritier's precursor to Hans Christian Andersen's more familiar tale, *The Emperor's New Clothes*, is discussed by Marina Warner in *From the Beast to the Blonde: On Fairy Tales and their Tellers* (London: Vintage, 1995, pp. 177–179).

dependent on the judge who dispenses it, while all the time knowing – like the men in L'Héritier's tale – that what we are denying is true:

> ... everyone wants it to be true that it is not only possible but common for judges to judge nonideologically. But everyone is aware of the critique, and everyone knows that the naïve theory of the rule of law is a fairy tale.[22]

And for the most part this strategy of denial works.[23] The point is this: we recognise that the image of the judge and his superhero powers are not real, that he is, if you like, a creature of our imagination – a relic left behind when Lord Reid exposed the fairy tale. Hence, we can dismiss him as a fiction. However, what we fail to recognise is that his status as fiction does not prevent him from having operative effects. This default image of the judge is not as benign as we might wish to believe. Caught in our collective state of denial, we fail to acknowledge the extent to which the default image constrains counter-images of the judge, including, as we have seen, that of the woman judge. We overlook the power of the imagination to clothe and elevate the judge, and the grip this attractive, yet ultimately suffocating, image of the default judge has on our understandings both of *who* the judge is and *how* they should judge.

It may be that the suggestion that there is a general 'strategy' of denial goes too far. It may well be that the default judge is the result of an instinctive understanding of how a judge *should* be rather than conspiracy. However, superhero, every-judge or fiction, it is clear that something has to give. For a start, accepting that *all* judges must, sometimes, fall back on their own sense of what is just, what ought to be done, means that any blanket criticism of judges for relying, on occasion, on their own values and perspectives is mistaken. Next, and more importantly, there is no ground for levelling such criticisms primarily at *women* judges. The claim that women judges will (sometimes) decide cases by reference to their own individual perspectives is misplaced, not because they will not do this – they will – but because this is no less true of their male counterparts. The most we might say is that a woman's perspectives will (sometimes) differ from a man's and so that having women judges will lead to different viewpoints finding their way into judicial decisions and into the law. But then, as we shall see, far from being a cause for complaint and criticism, this provides one of the strongest arguments in favour of judicial diversity.

But what of the suggestion that women (as a class) might differ from their male counterparts? Even once we acknowledge the role that values and perspectives play in judging, is there any reason to think women generally will judge differently from men?

---

22 Kennedy, *A Critique of Adjudication*, p. 192.
23 A stance of denial in relation to a range of aspects of the adjudicative process introduced and developed by Kennedy in *A Critique of Adjudication* is discussed by Gary Minda, 'Denial: Not Just a River in Egypt', *Cardozo Law Review*, 22, 2001, 901.

Excluding difference

The claim that women lawyers are different from their male counterparts, and in particular, that women judges might make a difference to the cases they decide has a chequered history. Assumptions about their difference – whether it exists, what it is, what impact it might have and so on – have dogged women law students, lawyers and judges for years. Questions as to whether the woman lawyer or judge can or will 'make a difference', is already 'making the difference' or, less optimistically, whether it is time to 'move beyond' difference or that difference 'won't do', litter the titles of numerous books and articles.[24] While the emphasis varies, reflecting the fluctuation in mood and agenda of the authors, the central theme – the difference of women in the legal professions – has remained constant. There is clearly *something* to say about women lawyers, judges and difference, although quite what this is is a matter of debate.

What *is* clear is that traditionally many women lawyers and judges have been wary of staking their claim to being 'different'. Given its long association with women's exclusion from, and marginalisation within, the study and practice of law, their reticence is unsurprising. For years women were excluded from the legal and other professions on the basis that they were too different.[25] As late as 1964 women were excluded from circuit meetings and mess on the Midland circuit for fear that their presence would 'inhibit the atmosphere' and 'completely alter the character and nature' of the mess, and that they might use the occasion 'in order to advance their professional chances'.[26] Well into the late 1970s the Inns of Court continued to be run with 'echo[es] of the public school, the military mess and the gentlemen's clubs'.[27] Even today, while the view that '[w]omen are just not chaps'[28]

24 See, eg Wilson, 'Will Women Judges Really Make a Difference?'; Clare McGlynn, *The Woman Lawyer – Making the Difference*, London: Butterworths, 1998; Hilary Sommerlad, 'Can Women Lawyer Differently? A Perspective from the UK' in Ulrike Schultz and Gisela Shaw (eds), *Women in the World's Legal Professions*, Oxford: Hart Publishing, 2003, p. 191; Kate Malleson, 'Justifying Gender Equality on the Bench: Why Difference Won't Do', *Feminist Legal Studies*, 11, 2003, 1; Lady Hale, 'Making a Difference? Why we Need a More Diverse Judiciary', *Northern Ireland Legal Quarterly*, 56(3), 2005, 281; Sally Kenney, 'Moving Beyond Difference: A New Scholarly Agenda for Gender and Judging', paper presented at the Law and Society annual meeting, Baltimore, 6–9 July 2006.

25 See, eg, Albie Sachs and Joan Hoff Wilson, *Sexism and the Law: A Study of Male Beliefs and Judicial Bias*, Oxford: Martin Robertson,1978; Michael Beloff, 'Sisters-in-Law: The Irresistible Rise of Women in Wigs', The Gray's Inn Reading 2009; Rosemary Auchmuty, 'Whatever happened to Miss Bebb? *Bebb v The Law Society* and women's legal history', *Legal Studies*, 31(2), 2011, 199 and, for a comparative perspective see Mary Jane Mossman, *The First Women Lawyers: A Comparative Study of Gender, Law and the Professions*, Oxford: Hart Publishing, 2006.

26 Brian Abel-Smith and Robert Stevens, *Lawyers and the Courts: A Sociological Study of the English Legal System 1750–1965*, London: Heinemann 1967, pp. 431–432.

27 Helena Kennedy, 'Women at the Bar' in Robert Hazell (ed), *The Bar on Trial*, London: Quartet Books, 1978, 148, p. 157.

28 ibid.

is unlikely to be openly expressed, the endless conversations over lunch in the judges' lodges about football and Bar gossip does little to make them feel welcome.[29]

The woman judge has two broad responses to this. Either she can dismiss claims of her difference as 'dangerous and unanswerable', as recollecting old myths women lawyers have 'struggled to put behind them',[30] and argue instead for inclusion on the basis of her *similarity* to her male colleagues. Or she can embrace and exploit the potential value of her 'difference'. (Attempts to negotiate some middle ground which secures her position as a lawyer first and woman second, while recognising that in reality things are not quite 'as simple as that',[31] are best seen as a restrained version of the second option.) Traditionally, most women lawyers and judges, particularly those who entered the legal profession before women started to do so in greater numbers in the 1970s, have opted for the first response – not least because, in Helena Kennedy's words, they have 'been taught to believe that their acceptance is conditional on conformity to the predominant male ethos'.[32] Moreover, given that any suggestion that women judges are 'different' from their male colleagues goes to the heart of our understandings of the judge and judging, women judges have been reluctant to 'claim that they look at things differently from men, partly because this would be manifestly inaccurate in many cases and partly because *it would make them less well qualified to be judges*'.[33] In order to head off confrontation, they adopt the guise of the default judge, presenting themselves as *exactly the same* as their male counterparts: a lawyer first *and* second, neither man nor woman. Or, as the former President of the Family Division, Lady Butler-Sloss, would have it, as 'unisex' judges.[34] And who can blame them? There's a sense in which the woman judge is *so* deviant that she is inevitably subject to an irrepressible urge to conform, to obliterate the 'stigmata of difference'.[35] As strategies for survival go, denying the effect of gender (and all the assumptions and insights that go with it) is not without cost, both for the woman judge and the judiciary more generally. Indeed, for some women, such is the extent of the denial, the feminine prefix is not simply 'dangerous' but inaccurate: the woman judge becomes a contradiction in terms. Like Andersen's mermaid, she is induced to sell

---

29 Penny Darbyshire, *Sitting in Judgment: The Working Lives of Judges*, Oxford: Hart Publishing, 2011, p. 423.

30 Sandra Day O'Connor, 'Portia's Progress', *New York University Law Review*, 66, 1991, 1546, p. 1557.

31 Brenda Hale, 'Equality in the Judiciary: A Tale of Two Continents', 10th Pilgrim Fathers' Lecture, 24 October 2003.

32 Kennedy, 'Women at the Bar', p. 158.

33 Brenda Hale, 'Equality and the Judiciary: Why Should We Want More Women Judges?', *Public Law*, 2001, 489, p. 499 (my emphasis).

34 Although, to be fair, this may also have something to do with the fact that, given the novelty of her appointment to the Court of Appeal, and until a Practice Direction seven years later, she was referred to in court as 'My Lady, Lord Justice Butler-Sloss' (Anon, 'Butler-Sloss is content to be a unisex judge', *The Times*, 21 November 2000; Mode of Address: Dame Elizabeth Butler-Sloss [1994] EW Misc 1 (Practice Note)).

35 Sandra Berns, *To Speak as a Judge – Difference, Voice and Power*, Dartmouth: Ashgate, 1999, p. 33.

her voice in order to walk on land (or enter the court room) with her prince; her dangerous siren call is silenced and, in the silence, difference is lost.[36]

But what of the second option: where the woman judge acknowledges her difference? Could this offer an alternative to a response that seeks to excise difference? What if the little mermaid refused to sell her voice? Could her difference make a difference to the style and substance of judicial decision-making?

Embracing difference

If it were the case that women judges *did*, at least on occasion, judge differently from their male colleagues, then an increase in the number of women judges would have a significant impact on the adjudicative process. And, if it could be shown that the difference women judges might make to decision-making was a *positive* difference, and that the greater diversity of views and perspectives a diverse Bench would bring would *enrich* the decision-making process, this would prove to be an almost unassailable argument for more women judges. However, the legacy of what Kate Malleson has described as the 'over-enthusiastic adoption of the argument that women judges will inevitably improve the quality of justice because of the difference they will bring to the Bench'[37] continues to cast a long shadow over difference-based arguments for judicial diversity. Claims suggesting that gender influences a judge's decision-making have proven to be controversial. Scholarly opinion is divided as to the extent to which differences between men and women judges are identifiable, or if the search for women's (or women judges') 'different voice' is an essentialising myth with problematic connotations for women who do not conform to its features.

Lawyering and judging in a different voice

The suggestion that women judge 'differently' to their male colleagues is typically tied to the work of Carol Gilligan.[38] In her book, *In a Different Voice*, Gilligan sought

---

36 This is not to suggest that *all* women will experience being a judge in this way. Indeed, Lady Hale has suggested that while this description may 'strike a chord' in relation to the first woman to sit on the High Court bench, Mrs Justice Lane, it would not do in relation to the second, Mrs Justice Heilbron ('Making a Difference?', p. 288). She also stated that she has 'absolutely no intention of turning into the little mermaid' (ibid., p. 292).

37 Malleson, 'Justifying Gender Equality on the Bench', p. 13.

38 Although political scholars, such as Beverley Blair Cook, were pioneering the research on the relationship between sex, gender and judging before this (Sally J Kenney, 'Thinking About Gender and Judging', *International Journal of the Legal Profession*, 1–2, 2008, 87). Indeed, as early as 1872, the argument was being made (although not accepted) that '[t]here are many cases in which the silver voice of a woman would accomplish more than the severity and sternness of men could achieve', Matthew Hale Carpenter (counsel for Ms Bradwell) in *Bradwell v Illinois*, 83 US 130, 137 (1872).

to highlight the absence and devaluing in traditional psychological theory of ways of moral reasoning and decision-making typically associated with women:[39]

> My questions are about voice and relationship. And my questions are about psychological theories and processes and theory, particularly theories in which men's experience stands for all of human experience – theories which eclipse the lives of women and shut out women's voices.[40]

Through a series of research studies, Gilligan identified two distinct 'voices' or reasoning processes corresponding (at least in terms of her research subjects) with men and women. Gilligan suggested that while men tended to reason from an 'ethic of justice', prioritising abstraction, separation, rights, hierarchy, autonomy and impartiality, women typically reasoned from an 'ethic of care', which prioritised responsibility, relationships, connection, partiality and focused on concrete circumstances. From here she argued that the 'women's voice' was not deficient (as was assumed by dominant psychological theories) but rather was *different to* the traditional (masculine) voice.[41] Gilligan's purpose was to establish the values of the ethic of care – community, connection, relationships – *as equal to* those underlying the dominant ethic of justice – abstraction, rights, autonomy and so on – so that a more complete understanding of moral reasoning might develop which was no longer 'simply about justice or simply about caring . . . [but] about bringing them together to transform the domain'.[42]

Love it or hate it (and people do in equal measure[43]), there is little doubt that Gilligan's articulation of a deliberately and distinctively 'different' way of thinking about the world that promoted relationships and responsibility struck a strong chord with women who had a vague sense of not being heard. It coincided with and contributed to a general 'shift in feminist thinking towards the celebration, rather than mere toleration or compensation, of women's difference from men'.[44]

39 Carol Gilligan, *In a Different Voice: Psychological Theory and Women's Development*, Cambridge, Mass.: Harvard University Press, 1982; repr 1993.
40 Carol Gilligan, 'Letter to Readers' in Carol Gilligan, *In a Different Voice: Psychological Theory and Women's Development*, Cambridge, Mass.: Harvard University Press, 1982; repr 1993, ix, p. xiii.
41 Vanessa Munro, *Law and Politics at the Perimeter: Re-Evaluating Key Debates in Feminist Theory*, Oxford: Hart Publishing, 2007, p. 23.
42 Carol Gilligan quoted in Isabel Marcus and Paul Spiegelman, 'The 1984 James McCormick Mitchell Lecture – Feminist Discourse, Moral Values, and the Law – A Conversation', *Buffalo Law Review*, 34, 1985, 11, p. 45 – an edited transcript of a discussion between Ellen DuBois, Mary Dunlap, Carol Gilligan, Catharine MacKinnon, and Carrie Menkel-Meadow, moderated by Isabel Marcus and Paul Spiegelman.
43 See, eg, Judy Auerbach, Linda Blum, Vicki Smith and Christine Williams, 'On Gilligan's "In a Different Voice"', *Feminist Studies*, 11(1), 1985, 149 and papers by Linda K Kerber, Catherine G Greeno, Eleanor E Maccoby, Zella Luria, Carol B Stack and Carol Gilligan, 'On "In a Different Voice": An Interdisciplinary Forum', *Signs*, 11(2), 1986, 304.
44 Munro, *Law and Politics at the Perimeter*, p. 23.

It was becoming clear that arguments grounded in equality, which emphasised the *similarity* between men and women, 'would not cure the substantive inequality that beset most women's lives';[45] more was needed than 'merely open[ing the] doors to institutions designed with men in mind'.[46] As Vanessa Munro notes:

> Feminist reform, if it [was] to bring about equality, must concentrate not only on affording the opportunity for women's inclusion in the institutions of public life, but also on radically re-imagining those institutions and the values that underpin them.[47]

The law and legal professions were no exception. CP Hawkes's warning in 1930 that the position of women lawyers would 'for sometime . . . necessarily be uncertain and fraught with embarrassments' had proven apposite.[48] Almost half a century later, sexism in the legal profession continued to be rife. Discrimination 'flourished', but went 'unchecked'.[49] Although, as Rose Pearson and Albie Sachs note, quite why 'being equipped with male sexual organs or an extra chromosome should make a person particularly suited to conveying a house or pleading in court or sending someone to prison has yet to be explained',[50] the qualities of the archetypal professional lawyer – 'an easy superficial politeness and amenability, but underneath an ability to compete, attack with verbal acumen, and come out on top' – were 'almost synonymous with the idealised image of middle-class masculinity'.[51] Moreover, it was thought that these were qualities which women lawyers were unable or unwilling to adopt: 'their socialisation, which stresses neither competitiveness nor the suppression of feelings, . . . [was] too "caring", . . . dilut[ing] the detached, scrupulously unindividualised nature of interaction with clients'.[52] The assumption that women barristers were 'over-emotional' was widespread. In the view of the Bar Council:

45 Martha Chamallas, *Introduction to Feminist Legal Theory*, 2nd edn, New York: Aspen Publishing, 2003, p. 17.
46 Martha Fineman, 'Feminist Theory and Law', *Harvard Journal of Law and Public Policy*, 18, 1995, 349, 352.
47 Munro, *Law and Politics*, p. 24.
48 CP Hawkes, *Chambers in the Temple: Comments and Conceits 'in Camera'*, London: Methuen & Co, 1930, p. 73.
49 Kennedy, 'Women at the Bar', p. 161.
50 Rose Pearson and Albie Sachs, 'Barristers and Gentlemen: A Critical Look at Sexism in the Legal Profession', *Modern Law Review*, 43, 1980, 400, pp. 407–408.
51 ibid., 410.
52 ibid., 411. This is not to suggest that these views have been extinguished from the legal profession; typically 'male' characteristics continue to be more professionally desirable than those associated with women. See further Chapter 2, fn 127–164 and accompanying text.

[t]he fact has to be faced ... that the profession of barrister requires the masculine approach (however fallacious it may be) to reasoning and argument, and women only succeed in such activities if they have a masculine disposition.[53]

Against this backdrop it was unsurprising that women lawyers were keen to emphasise the qualities they could bring, and contribution they could make, *as women* to the legal profession. Helena Kennedy, writing in the late 1970s argued:

If there is only one thing in which this writer does believe strongly, it is that women barristers can make a separate contribution, and the Bar will be the loser if women are forced to behave just like men ... the sort of qualities which women can bring to their work (and which need not exclude the power to reason) are a greater awareness of people's feelings, a sense of humility and a genuine desire to help clients rather than to impress them.[54]

Inevitably many of these arguments were permeated with claims about the 'maleness' of the legal system and profession.[55] The expectation was that once more women joined the legal profession, assuming that at least some of them spoke, at least some of the time, with something akin to Gilligan's different voice, a radically different legal system and profession would follow.[56] Women lawyers, drawing on an ethic of care, would, it was suggested, search for ways around abstract, adversarial rules,[57] with the result that the courtroom battle might be replaced with a more caring and inclusive process in which the opposing side is understood, not as an enemy to be defeated but as someone to be 'cared for, thought about and dealt with'.[58] And, in time, the legal system might come to resemble something more like a 'conversation'; 'a more co-operative, less war-like system of communication

---

53 Bar Council, Response to the Monopolies Commission (1969) in Kennedy, 'Women at the Bar', p. 158.
54 Kennedy, 'Women at the Bar', p. 158.
55 Although they were carefully distanced from invoking notions of one single woman's voice (Carrie Menkel-Meadow, 'Portia in a Different Voice: Speculations on a Women's Lawyering Process', *Berkeley Women's Law Journal*, 1(1), 1985, 39, p. 62; Carrie Menkel-Meadow, 'Excluded Voices: New Voices in the Legal Profession Making New Voices in the Law', *University of Miami Law Review*, 42, 1987, 29, p. 30).
56 Menkel-Meadow, 'Portia in a Different Voice', pp. 55–88; Naomi Cahn, 'Styles of Lawyering', *Hastings Law Journal*, 43, 1992, 1039; Carrie Menkel-Meadow, 'Portia Redux: Another Look at Gender, Feminism, and Legal Ethics', *Virginia Journal of Social Policy and Law*, 2, 1994, 75, p. 87.
57 Menkel-Meadow, 'Portia in a Different Voice', p. 55.
58 Carrie Menkel-Meadow, 'The Comparative Sociology of Women Lawyers: The "Feminization" of the Legal Profession', *Osgoode Hall Law Journal*, 24(4), 1986, 897, 915.

between disputants in which solutions are mutually agreed upon rather than dictated by an outsider, won by the victor, and imposed on the loser'.[59] From here it was a short step to arguments that the women lawyers appointed to the Bench might bring the same values and concerns with them. After all, it was argued that '[i]f the male judge emphasises justice, might the female judge pay attention to mercy, seeking that resolution "in which no one is hurt"?' The hunt for the woman judge's 'different voice' was well and truly on.

Searching for judicial difference

Although perhaps 'intuitively obvious',[60] and despite a long and widespread search, strong evidence supporting the claim that women judges have a 'different voice' has proved elusive. Studies supporting differences between male and female judges are, at best, equivocal.[61] In 2010 a comprehensive review of over 30 quantitative studies from the US into the relationship between sex[62] and judging found that while around one-third pointed to clear differences between men and women judges, another third found no sex-based differences at all, with the remainder

59 Menkel-Meadow, 'Portia in a Different Voice', pp. 54–56.
60 Jilda M Aliotta, 'Justice O'Connor and the Equal Protection Clause: A Feminine Voice?', *Judicature*, 78, 1995, 232.
61 See, eg, from the extensive and varied US literature, Susan L Miller and Shana L Maier, 'Moving Beyond Numbers: What Female Judges Say About Different Judicial Voices', *Journal of Women, Politics and Policy*, 29(4), (2008), 527, pp. 529–534; Christina L Boyd, Lee Epstein and Andrew D Martin, 'Untangling the Causal Effects of Sex on Judging', *American Journal of Political Science*, 54(2), (2010), 389 and 'Web Appendix to Untangling the Causal Effects of Sex on Judging'. Online. Available: http://epstein.law.northwestern.edu/research/genderjudging.html (accessed 11 July 2010); Rosalind Dixon, 'Female Justices, Feminism and the Politics of Judicial Appointment: A Re-Examination', *Yale Journal of Law and Feminism*, 21(2), 2010, 297. Non-US research includes: Bryna Bogoch, 'Judging in a "Different Voice": Gender and the Sentencing of Violent Offenders', *International Journal of Sociology and Law*, 27, 1999, 51 (Israel); H Barwick, J Burns and A Gray, *Gender Equality in the New Zealand Judicial System: Judges' Perceptions of Gender Issues*, Wellington: Joint Working Group on Gender Equality, 1996 (New Zealand); Sean Rehaag, 'Do Women Refugee Judges Really Make a Difference? An Empirical Analysis of Gender and Outcomes in Canadian Refugee Decisions', *Canadian Journal of Women and Law*, 23, 2011, 627 and Marie-Claire Belleau and Rebecca Johnson, 'Judging Gender: Difference and Dissent at the Supreme Court of Canada', *International Journal of the Legal Profession*, 15(1–2), 2008, 57 (Canada); Kimi L King and Megan Greening, 'Gender Justice or Just Gender? The Role of Gender in Sexual Assault Decisions in the International Criminal Tribunal for the Former Yugoslavia', *Social Science Quarterly*, 88(5), 2007, 1049 (ICTY).
62 There are difficulties with terminology here. Studies in this area typically use sex (rather than gender) as a variable because it gives a firmer base to the qualitative empirical assessments; the category gender is harder to pin down and distinguish. However, what they are usually interested in, and what they typically refer to, is the impact of *gender*, that is the experiences of the woman judge *as a woman*, on a judge's decision-making. There is also a danger that these studies fall into the trap of gender essentialism, of assuming that women judge differently on the basis of characteristics intrinsic to their biological sex (see further, Kenney, 'Thinking About Gender and Judging', p. 88).

pointing in both directions.[63] Its overall conclusion that 'the presence of women in the federal appellate judiciary *rarely* has an appreciable empirical effect on judicial outcomes'[64] is unsurprising. However, as the authors point out, '[r]arely . . . is not never'.[65] In fact, in line with other surveys, they *did* observe consistent and statistically significant differences between male and female judges in cases involving sex discrimination. In such cases 'not only do males and females bring distinct approaches . . . but the presence of a female on the panel actually *causes* male judges to vote in a way they otherwise would not'.[66] The gender of the judge(s) makes a difference both *individually* (in that it causes judges to behave differently) and *collectively* (in that the presence of a judge of a different sex causes *the rest of the panel* to act differently). This is consistent with what is described as an 'informational' account of the impact of gender on judging, which suggests that in cases where women judges are assumed to possess particular experience or expertise, their male counterparts defer to the 'unique and valuable' perspectives and knowledge of their female colleagues.[67] Similarly, a study of sentencing practices at the International Criminal Tribunal for the Former Yugoslavia (ICTY) found that in cases of sexual violence against women, the sentence imposed was increased by just under four years when there was a woman judge on the panel. By way of contrast, *all* male panels gave significantly longer sentences, by up to almost nine years, in cases involving a male victim, which were reduced by just under three years when a woman judge was on the panel.[68] Nevertheless, the weight of academic opinion remains largely against the existences of a direct or positive correlation between a judge's gender and their decision-making. With some

63 Boyd et al, 'Untangling the Causal Effects of Sex on Judging', p. 392. There are a number of methodological difficulties with studies which may provide some explanation for these contradictory results. First, the inability of researchers to isolate gender from the many other aspects of a judge's identity and background that may *also* impact on their decision-making (race, sexual orientation, age, class, professional background and so on) makes it impossible to make any claim about the effect of *gender*, as a discrete characteristic, on judging. Second, their focus on results or outcomes (and in the US, on voting patterns) obscures differences in *process*, that is in judges' reasoning (Miller and Maier, 'Moving Beyond Numbers', p. 535; Sherrilyn A Ifill, 'Judicial Diversity', *Green Bag*, 13, 2D, 2009, 45, p. 52). Finally, differences in specificity and focus (the level of the court, jurisdiction, time-period, number of women judges, range of cases and such like) may well mean that we may not be comparing like with like. In fact, Miller and Maier conclude that research to date reveals more about the weakness in the methodology and data employed, than the effect of gender has (or not) on judicial decision-making (ibid., p. 534).
64 Boyd et al, 'Untangling the Causal Effects of Sex on Judging', p. 406.
65 ibid.
66 Boyd et al, 'Untangling the Causal Effects of Sex on Judging', p. 406. The chance of a male judge voting in favour of the claimant increases by 12–14% when a woman sits on the panel. See also Sue Davis, Susan Haire and Donald R Songer, 'Voting Behaviour and Gender on the US Court of Appeals', *Judicature*, 77(3), 1993, 129; Jennifer L Peresie, 'Female Judges Matter: Gender and Collegial Decision-making in the Federal Appellate Courts', *Yale Law Journal*, 114(7), 2005, 1759.
67 Boyd et al, 'Untangling the Causal Effects of Sex on Judging', p. 392.
68 King and Greening, 'Gender Justice or Just Gender?', p. 1066.

feminist legal scholars arguing that, given the inconsistent empirical evidence, flawed methodology and unsubstantiated claims, rather than searching for essential differences across the judiciary as a whole, we should instead focus our attention on specific cohorts of judges, on 'understanding how different groups of judges approach (and *ought* to approach) their tasks'.[69]

In any event, we should, of course, be cautious of attempts to invoke some shared women's experience or identity – to suggest, for example, that women judges judge *in the same way*, or that there is, and that women judges articulate, a single, distinctive 'female' perspective on key issues – for this risks falling foul of 'the favourite feminist sin': gender essentialism.[70] This typically takes one of two forms: false universalism and gender imperialism.[71] While the former claims the experiences of the most privileged group of women (white, middle-class, heterosexual) as that of *all* women, the latter falsely prioritises *gender* over other identity characteristics (race, sexual orientation, class and so on) which are also likely to contribute to one's attitudes and judgments. Anti-essentialist scholars argue that efforts to 'distil' a unitary women's experience risk replacing one unsatisfactory norm (the experiences of men) with another (those of white, middle-class, heterosexual women). As Joanne Conaghan notes,

> women-centredness is potentially as oppressive as the male-dominated discourse it seeks to displace in presupposing a female experience which is unitary rather than variegated – informed and shaped by a range of social, cultural and cognitive factors (race, class, sexuality, and so on).[72]

In the context of the judiciary, this concern is even more acute. Given the current lack of diversity among (women) judges, there is a danger that any articulation of a common judicial 'woman's' voice (assuming such a thing existed) would, in fact, reflect the experiences of a small, privileged group of women. Moreover, in light of the narrowness of their background (and the nature of the job) women judges are unlikely to have anything more in common, *other than their gender*, with the women litigants than they do with their male colleagues.[73] At the same time, the primacy accorded to efforts to identify the effects of *gender* on judging not only privileges gender over other identity characteristics which may also influence

---

69 Rehaag, 'Do Women Refugee Judges Really Make a Difference?', p. 635. See further Rosemary Hunter, 'Can *feminist* judges make a difference?', *International Journal of the Legal Profession*, 15(1–2), 2008, 7, p. 30; Kenney, 'Thinking About Gender and Judging', p. 105.

70 Dianne L Brooks, 'A Commentary on the Essence of Anti-Essentialism in Feminist Legal Theory', *Feminist Legal Studies*, 2(2), 1994, 115, 120. See also Diana Fuss, *Essentially Speaking: Feminism, Nature and Difference*, New York: Routledge, 1989; Gayatri Spivak, 'In a Word', *Differences*, 1989, 124.

71 Katharine T Bartlett, 'Gender Law', *Duke Journal of Gender Law and Policy* 1, 1994, 1.

72 Joanne Conaghan, 'Reassessing the Feminist Theoretical Project in Law', *Journal of Law and Society*, 27(3), 2000, 351, 367.

73 Malleson, 'Justifying Gender Equality on the Bench', p. 12.

the judge's decision-making, but also *reduces* the woman judge to a single aspect of identity.[74] It ignores the interaction *between* identity characteristics such as race, ethnicity, sexuality, class, age and religion. If only one qualifying adjective is allowed – if, for example, a judge is *either* a 'woman' *or* from a 'BME background', instead of being 'both' a woman 'and' from a BME background[75] – then her real and undifferentiated experience of being a *woman BME* judge, and the potential impact of this on her decision-making, is overlooked or erased. Moreover as Sally Kenney notes,

> [b]y stripping away class, race, sexual orientation, to drill down to the core of what constitutes sex differences, one inevitably approaches sex as a biological category (one that feminists reject) instead of gender as a social process, a process that is intersectional, not just something that happens to women who are otherwise privileged.[76]

So where does this leave arguments for women judges' difference? Insofar as the claim that women judge differently is dependent on being able to establish a shared experience of all women judges and the existence of a single, distinctive 'female' or 'feminine' approach to judicial decision-making, then we appear to have reached the end of the road. No unique and common perspective, no 'different voice', shared by all women judges has been, or is likely to be, found. Without doubt, the temptation to dismiss the search for the influence of gender on judging as empirically weak, theoretically suspect and strategically risky is strong.[77] The quest for the woman judge's 'different voice' is either futile (in which case the argument for more women judges on the basis of their difference from their male colleagues is undermined) or misguided (in that the pursuit of women judges' common difference comes at the cost of disregarding other important differences between women), or maybe both. The suggestion that, while male judges concentrate on 'justice', women judges might appeal to 'mercy' is both simplistic and erroneous. Indeed, this understanding of the influence of gender on judging was always implausible. The invocation of the woman judge's 'different voice' (whether or not akin to that articulated by Gilligan) is at best an unhelpful shorthand and, at worst, a dangerous distortion, pulling researchers towards the perils of essentialism. What we can say, however, is that gender is one of the things that influences women *and men* judges' decision-making and so may be *one* reason why

---

74 See, eg, Elizabeth V Spelman, *Inessential Woman: Problems of Exclusion in Feminist Thought*, Boston: Beacon Press, 1988; Angela P Harris, 'Race and Essentialism in Feminist Legal Theory', *Stanford Law Review*, 42, 1990, 581; Kimberlé Crenshaw, 'Mapping the Margins: Intersectionality, Identity Politics, and Violence Against Women of Color', *Stanford Law Review*, 43, 1991, 1241.

75 Chamallas, *Introduction to Feminist Legal Theory*, p. 20.

76 Kenney, 'Thinking About Gender and Judging', p. 89.

77 Malleson, 'Justifying Gender Equality on the Bench'.

judges sometimes differ. And, as we shall see, this far less ambitious and far more plausible claim is, in fact, all that we need: it leaves women judges with plenty of scope to be different and to bring these differences to their judicial decision-making, which means there is life still in the argument that the difference women judges can make gives us reason to value judicial diversity.

Reclaiming difference

Rejecting the suggestion that there is a unique difference shared by all women judges does not entail the rejection of *all* claims about the effect of gender on judging. It is possible to disentangle arguments for the importance of gender on judicial decision-making from a commitment to, and the criticisms of, Gilligan's different voice, to, as Sally Kenney argues, 'think about gender differences in ways that are theoretically sophisticated, empirically true and do not lead to women's disadvantage'.[78] And happily so. After all, there is a reason we are still talking about and looking for women judges' difference, and why something about claims to difference ring true.[79] Arguments about gender and difference do deliver, although not perhaps in the way we expected.

The default judge and the different voice

So why might we think that women judges might judge differently to their male colleagues? Or, more accurately, why might we think that being a woman might make a difference to how one judges? What reasons do we have for thinking that gender is one of the things that, at least on occasion, plays a part in judging?

One reason is our understanding of the role of the judge. Once we acknowledge that the law does not exist as a set of pre-determined rules which judges simply discover and apply to the facts at hand, it follows that judges must, at least on occasion, bring their own values to bear when deciding cases. As already noted, insofar as people have different values and viewpoints, the values applied will differ from judge to judge with the result that different judges will judge differently. Divergence in values leads to divergence in judging. This prompts a further question as to where these differences come from. What shapes and informs an individual's attitudes and values, one's moral and political viewpoints which, in turn determines how one judges?

The answer must be that they come from an individual's own reflections on such questions, which in turn are, at least in part, shaped by experiences. We know this, for example, by the fact that our views change as we are exposed to different perspectives. Our attitudes are shaped and develop over time as the things we go through cause us to think differently, to gain new insights and

---

78 Kenney, 'Thinking About Gender and Judging', p. 87.
79 Boyd et al, 'Untangling the Causal Effects of Sex on Judging', p. 390.

perspectives, sometimes revising views we had previously formed, sometimes confirming judgments we had already made, sometimes causing us to consider questions previously unconsidered. These experiences will vary from the relatively trivial (books we have read, conversations we have had) to the more fundamental (parenthood, serious illness, bereavement). And a constant backdrop to all these experiences, and a contributing factor to many, is one's gender. As such there is good reason to think that insofar as our views are shaped by personal experiences, that gender will be *a* contributing factor to one's general outlook and values. Indeed, it seems implausible that something so fundamental to our identities as our gender will not, on some occasions, make some difference to our attitude and viewpoints. And insofar as gender is one of the things that shapes our viewpoints, this will necessarily point toward differences in outlook between men and women.

Clearly this is not to say that men and women will differ on all issues all of the time. Or, that there will be issues on which they will always differ. Nor is it to suggest that all women by virtue of this single common characteristic will share a common value or outlook. The extent and ways in which our gender shapes our life experiences and how this then impacts on our outlook and values will vary from person to person. Thus insofar as women *do* share common experiences or outlooks, we should not assume that these will be reflected in a common approach or 'voice'. One reason for this is because, as noted already, gender does not operate in isolation. There are any number of additional factors (race, sexual orientation, class and so on) which also shape our lives and hence our values and outlook. Diversity of experiences as women are likely to be manifested in a diversity of perspectives and attitudes. Moreover, insofar as women *do* have shared experiences and needs,[80] this does not mean that women will experience them in the same way (due in large part to diverse experiences prior to this point). To claim that there are experiences that are specific to women and which they experience as women is not to claim that these are experiences that *all* women have, let alone to claim that those who have will respond to them in the same way. However, the fact that a particular experience is not shared by *all* women or in the same way does not mean that the experience cannot be said to be exclusive to women. Pregnancy and childbirth are obvious examples of exclusively female experiences. Moreover, they are experiences which, at the very least, have the capacity to affect a woman's outlook, values and perspectives. But, of course, not all women have these experiences. And those that do, will not experience them in the same way. (And, of course, none of this is to suggest that the only experience common to women is as (potential) mothers.) It is simply to say that there are certain things which are special about being a woman or unique to women, and that this is not the same as saying (and so not dependent on) this being common to *all* women.

---

80 Purna Sen, 'Difference is not all that counts' in Deborah Cameron and Joan Scanlon (eds), *The Trouble and Strife Reader*, London: Bloomsbury Academic, 1999, 78, p. 83.

With this in mind, it is simply unrealistic to think that women *judges* will speak – or judge – in the same way, that they will share a unified common perspective or viewpoint, any more than we should expect women generally to do so. So to think that gender *does* play a part in judging does not require one to think that it does this alone, that it is the *only* factor. Just as we expect gender to make a difference, so we should also expect other identity characteristics to make a difference as well.

However, it does not follow from an absence of a uniform voice that gender cannot and does not make a difference to judging, that women judges do not bring different voices and perspectives to their judging than their male counterparts. As Diana Bryant, Chief Justice Family Court of Australia, explains:

> The idea that women judges 'make a difference' does not necessarily have to rely on biologically determinist constructions of womanhood. Women and men, in general, have different life experiences . . . We do not expect the impossible of our male judges – that in the act of judging they are unaffected and uninfluenced by their upbringing, schooling, family life, work history and values – in short, their entire familial, social and economic environment. It is hardly consistent, or fair, to expect women judges to be a veritable blank slate.[81]

All one needs to establish is that gender is *a* factor which might, on occasions, shape a judge's views and preferences and in turn the way they judge. To suggest otherwise is to argue that of all the many factors and experiences that go to shaping a person's views, gender is *never* one of them. And, insofar as gender is *one* of the things, we should expect that at least sometimes the different lives and experiences of women and men, attributable to their differences in gender, will lead to differences in their attitudes, values and perspectives. And we should expect, in turn, that they will bring these experiences and these differences to their understanding and interpretation of law. It appears that difficulties with difference-based arguments, then, stem not from the notion of gender-based differences themselves, but rather from *how* we go about conceptualising and looking for them, and in particular, the expectation that they would result in some form of common or 'different' voice.

In fact, the most we might expect is a general, although by no means uniform trend of women judges being different from their male counterparts – albeit in different ways, and at different times, to each other. Research by Marie-Claire Belleau and Rebecca Johnson looking at patterns of dissent on the Canadian Supreme Court over a 15-year period supports this view. Although they found little evidence of a unified women's voice shared by all seven women judges who served on the court during this period, their study did reveal a single – crucial – commonality among women judges: an ability and willingness to disagree. And

81 Diana Bryant, 'Creating Justice', Australian Women Lawyers Second National Conference Melbourne, 13 June 2008.

so, while the women judges 'did not always share the same perspective', they 'shared a positioning that left them seeing something different, or having a different view about how a common result should be better understood'.[82] Their difference lay in a shared capacity and inclination for difference, revealed not in the *sameness* or particularity of a single voice, but rather in their collective willingness to see things differently and to offer alternative explanations or perspectives on decisions reached.

Women judges: making a difference

There is a further reason why we might think that gender has an impact on how women judge: women judges themselves tell us that this is the case. Typically this is in response to questions and concerns about the difference their gender might make to their decision-making, whether women judges *as women* will make a difference to the justice dispensed. And, although they are usually keen to distance themselves from stereotypically 'feminine' qualities – warmth, forgiveness, sensitivity and so on – and the existence of an unified 'female' or 'different' voice, most also admit that *all* their life experiences *including but not limited to being a woman* influence and inform their values and judgement. The result is that 'sometimes women just think differently from men'.[83] Consider, for example, Justice Abrahamson's (the first woman appointed to the Wisconsin Supreme Court) reply to the question of whether she thought women judges would 'make a difference in the administration of justice':

> I think that when people ask if 'being a woman' brings something special to the court, they are really asking whether there is a special sensitivity that a person's background might bring to the court. My gender – or, more properly, the experiences my gender has forced upon me – has, of course, made me sensitive to certain issues, both legal and nonlegal. So have other parts of my background. My point is that nobody is just a woman or a man. Each of us is a person with diverse experiences and each of us brings to the Bench experiences that affect our view of law and life and decision-making.[84]

Similarly, Madame Justice Wilson sparked calls for her resignation in the early 1990s with her tentative suggestion that:

> If . . . women judges through their differing perspectives on life can bring a new humanity to bear on the decision-making process, perhaps they *will*

82 Belleau and Johnson, 'Judging Gender', p. 63.
83 Margaret Dee McGarity, 'Diversity in the Judiciary', *Wisconsin Women's Law Journal*, 8, 1992–1993, 175, p. 177.
84 Shirley S Abrahamson, 'The Woman Has Robes: Four Questions', *Golden Gate University Law Review*, 14, 1984, 489, pp. 493–494.

make a difference. Perhaps they will succeed in infusing the law with an understanding of what it means to be fully human.[85]

As time has gone on, especially in jurisdictions where women have been appointed to the Bench in relatively large numbers, and to the senior judiciary, women judges have become somewhat more forthright in claiming their right to be different. By the time Madam Justice McLachlin was appointed Chief Justice of the Canadian Supreme Court in 2000, Wilson's 'if' and 'perhaps' had been replaced with 'can' and 'does':

> The presence of women on the Bench can and does make a substantive difference. In so far as women are possessed of special experiences, concerns, and interests, these inevitably affect the way that they address the problems that confront them.[86]

Women, Lady Justice Arden notes, 'bring new perspectives to bear as well as their intellectual skills and knowledge of the law. They have different life experiences. They have in some respects different approaches'.[87] Judge Judith Kaye put it even more concisely: 'I take my gender with me wherever I go'.[88]

We have, therefore, good reason to think that gender has an impact on how judges judge. This aligns with what we know about judicial decision-making – what sorts of decision judges have to make, what sorts of factors are likely to shape how those decisions are made – and it is what women judges themselves are telling us. So, while there is reasonable doubt as to where gender does and should make a difference, and so as to where women judges are likely to do things differently from their male colleagues, to doubt that gender has any influence on judicial decision-making requires us to deny *either* that judges never have recourse to their 'own' values and hence their own perspectives and insights when judging *or* that, of all the factors that might shape a judge's views on such occasions, gender is *never* one of them. It would require us too to say that the women judges who have themselves acknowledged the difference their gender makes are, to a woman, mistaken. Such denials have no plausibility.

However, although we have no reason to doubt that gender does indeed make a difference to judicial decision-making, identifying those differences will typically be far from straightforward. As mentioned previously, a judge's gender does not exist in isolation but rather lines up alongside an array of other attributes and experiences, all of which, by themselves or in combination, are likely to have some

85 Wilson, 'Will Women Judges Really Make a Difference?', p. 522.
86 Beverley McLachlin, 'Promoting Gender Equality in the Judiciary', Seminar to the Association of Women Barristers, House of Commons, 2 July 2003.
87 Lady Justice Arden, 'Diversity in the appointment of Queen's Counsel and judges: what does the future hold?' Address to the Chancery Bar Association, London, 12 January 2007.
88 In Theresa Beiner, 'Female Judging', *University of Toledo Law Review*, 36, 2005, 821, p. 837.

influence on the way she or he judges. Because of this, it will never be possible to detach fully gender from those other factors, marking out which judgments, or which passages from which judgments are specifically attributable to the judge's gender. This will rarely, if ever, be clear to the judge herself, let alone to the rest of us. Nonetheless, the argument so far suggests that there will be occasions where gender *is* a contributing factor and, even if our conclusions will be necessarily tentative, that we can identify cases where it is at least *plausible* to see the woman judge's gender as (in part) a factor in the decision she reached. So, in the following sections, I shall look at two judgments of Lady Hale (the first and only woman on the UK Supreme Court), her dissents in *R v J* [2004][89] and, more recently, in *Radmacher (formerly Granatino) v Granatino* [2010],[90] which I think can at least plausibly be understood (and have been understood by others) to be informed, in part, by her experiences and insights as a woman. At the very least, these will act as illustrations of how gender *could* make a difference to judicial decision-making and where those differences might be found.[91]

Radmacher (formerly Granatino) v Granatino

In *Radmacher* the UK Supreme Court was asked to determine the weight to be given to a pre-nuptial agreement (or 'ante-nuptial' agreement, as the Supreme Court preferred to call it[92]) between a German heiress and French investment banker (turned DPhil student and academic). The couple, who had made their home in London, had separated after eight years of marriage. They had two children. The husband, in contravention of a pre-nuptial agreement which stated that neither party would make a claim for ancillary relief against the other should the marriage fail, sought an order against his ex-wife for financial support in the form of a lump sum and periodic payments. He argued that the agreement was procedurally defective on the basis that he had not received independent legal advice and that he was not made aware of the full extent of his wife's wealth before

---

89 [2004] UKHL 42.
90 [2010] UKSC 42.
91 It might be argued that some cases are necessarily more receptive to, or inclined toward, the analysis and insights of women judges than others, that certain cases are 'cherry-picked' to point toward judicial similarity or sameness. However, this criticism only goes so far. The cases discussed in this chapter and in Chapter 6 cannot alone reveal or establish broad or more general truths in relation to Lady Hale's jurisprudence and difference – let alone that of the woman judge more generally. However, they do, nonetheless, reveal something about the processes of judgment in the particular case at hand. Difference, in this context, provides a point of departure rather than any fixed destination(s) (see further Erika Rackley, 'Detailing Judicial Difference', *Feminist Legal Studies*, 17(1), 2009, 11).
92 Little turns on this terminology (although cf Richard Todd, 'The Inevitable Triumph of the Ante-Nuptial Contract', *Family Law*, July, 2006, 539); however, in treating both pre-nuptial and post-nuptial agreements as 'nuptial agreements', the majority's reasoning in *Radmacher*, even though primarily addressing ante-nuptial agreements, has wider applicability.

signing the agreement, the agreement made no provision in the event of the couple having children and, in any event, it was manifestly unfair that the agreement allowed for no provision for either party should the marriage end.[93] The agreement at issue in *Radmacher* would have been recognised as binding in Germany and France; however, pre-nuptial agreements have had a troubled history in English law resulting in the 'worst of both worlds'[94] whereby marital agreements are, as Rix LJ noted, 'at one and the same time *both* unenforceable and invalid as being against public policy' *and* something which the court is, on occasions, prepared to take into account.[95] Although over the years many of the public policy objections (for instance, that the enforceability of such agreements posed a threat to the sanctity of marriage[96]) had fallen away, there continued to be disagreement about weight that should be given to these agreements in ancillary relief proceedings.

At its heart *Radmacher* involved a clash of values about the modern status of marriage and the freedom with which parties ought to be able to negotiate its terms.[97] On one view, the couple were competent adults who had freely entered into an agreement and the courts should respect their choices by holding the parties to the terms of the agreement. In the words of Lord Justice Thorpe in the Court of Appeal: '[d]ue respect for adult autonomy suggests that, subject of course to proper safeguards, a carefully fashioned contract should be available as an alternative to the stress, anxieties and expense of a submission to the width of the judicial discretion'.[98] On the other view, pre-nuptial agreements are *always* about giving one party less than that party is entitled to, they *always* work to deprive the weaker party of the protections of marriage, and so the courts should only hold the parties to their agreement where the circumstances are such that it is fair to do so. This was the view of Mrs Justice Baron at first instance (allowing Mr Granatino's claim and granting him a lump sum in excess of £5.5 million and a yearly allowance of around £35,000 for each of his two daughters while they continued in education):

> To my mind, independent scrutiny of these agreements remains as necessary in modern times as it was in the last century because of the vulnerability of parties involved at times of high emotion where inequality of bargaining

93 *NG v KR (Pre-Nuptial Contract)* [2008] EWHC 1532 (Fam) [8].

94 *Pounds v Pounds* [1994] WLR 1535, p. 1550 (Hoffmann LJ) cited by Rix LJ in *Radmacher* [2009] EWCA Civ 649 [64].

95 [2009] EWCA Civ 649 (Rix LJ). The Law Commission has consulted on the law relating to marital property agreements (Law Commission, *Marital Property Agreements*, CP198, London: Law Commission, 2011). Its report and a draft bill are expected in late 2012.

96 See, eg, *M v M* [2002] 1 FLR 654, p. 661.

97 [2010] UKSC 42 [135] (Lady Hale); Lady Hale speaking at an InterLaw Diversity Forum event on the 'Feminist Judgments Project', Norton Rose, London, 13 October 2011 (transcript on file with author).

98 [2009] EWCA Civ 649 [27].

power may exist between them. Although civilization has made much progress over the centuries and the roles of men and women have altered so that, in some cultures, equality has been achieved that does not mean that fundamental human nature has changed . . . [the court] should not be blind to human frailty and susceptibility when love and separation are involved. The need for careful safeguards to protect the weaker party and ensure fairness remains.[99]

Mr Granatino's success at first instance was short-lived. Although unable to treat the agreement as 'presumptively dispositive',[100] the Court of Appeal nevertheless sought to give it 'decisive weight',[101] reducing Mr Granatino's award to reflect the fact that he had freely entered into the agreement and understood its implications.[102]

In the Supreme Court, both values and views were expressed. The majority of the Supreme Court (8–1) was of the view that where the parties have freely entered into a pre-nuptial agreement and the circumstances are such that it is fair to hold the parties to it, the agreement can have compelling or decisive weight.[103] The case merits more detailed discussion than is possible here;[104] however, the Supreme Court effectively established a rebuttable presumption in favour of enforcing such agreements, providing a 'two-stage test of fairness' is satisfied, requiring that the agreement was fairly entered into and is fair to enforce.[105]

The majority's starting point was that pre-nuptial agreements should be given weight because 'there should be respect for individual autonomy':

The court should accord respect to the decision of a married couple as to the manner in which their financial affairs should be regulated. It would be

99 *NG v KR (Pre-Nuptial Contract)* [2008] EWHC 1532 (Fam) [129].
100 [2009] EWCA Civ 649 [122] (Wilson LJ).
101 ibid., [81] (Rix LJ); [146] (Wilson LJ).
102 Thorpe LJ explicitly stated that the 'major funds' were provided on the basis of Mr Granatino's role as a father rather than a former husband (ibid., [50]).
103 [2010] UKSC 42 [135], [75]. Unusually, and reflecting the importance of the case, the Supreme Court sat in a panel of nine. The leading judgment was given by Lord Phillips (President of the Supreme Court), with a concurrence from Lord Mance, who agreed with the conclusion of the majority but who, in common with Lady Hale, expressed no view on whether a pre-nuptial agreement is legally binding.
104 See further Joanna Miles, 'Marriage and Divorce in the Supreme Court and the Law Commission: for Love or Money?', *Modern Law Review*, 74(3), 2011, 430; Jens M Scherpe, 'Fairness, freedom and foreign elements – marital agreements in England and Wales after *Radmacher v Granatino*', *Child and Family Law Quarterly*, December, 2011, 4; Jonathan Herring, Peter G Harris and Robert H George, 'Ante-nuptial agreements: fairness, equality and presumptions', *Law Quarterly Review*, 127, 2011, 335.
105 Scherpe, 'Fairness, freedom and foreign elements'.

paternalistic and patronising to override their agreement simply on the basis that the court knows best.[106]

Although the court was reluctant to lay down rules which would fetter the judge's ability to reach a fair result, it did offer some, fairly extensive, guidance as to the factors a court might take into account, including the effect of the agreement on the reasonable requirements of any children of the family.[107] An agreement is also more likely to be considered fair when it relates to existing circumstances, rather than 'the contingencies of an uncertain future'.[108] Upholding the decision of the Court of Appeal, the majority agreed that the trial judge had paid insufficient attention to the terms of pre-nuptial agreement and that there was nothing to suggest that it was unfair to hold Mr Granatino to it (subject to making some provision for the needs of the couple's daughters).[109]

Lady Hale took a different view. Her starting point was the nature of modern marriage (and civil partnership) and the role of the courts in addressing these issues. Despite 'considerable freedom and flexibility within the marital package', in her view, marriage is a 'status' (as well as, of course, a contract) which includes an 'irreducible minimum', including 'a couple's mutual duty to support one another and their children'.[110] At issue then was the extent to which individuals should be able to contract out of the protections and obligations that stem from the status of marriage, 'how far individual couples should be free to re-write [this] essential feature of the marital relationship as they choose'.[111] Noting that the issue of marital agreements was something on which 'knowledgeable and thoughtful people may legitimately hold differing views',[112] her dissenting view begins with what appears to be a call for judicial restraint. The law concerning marital agreements is by all accounts in such a muddle that the only 'democratic way of achieving comprehensive and principled reform' is to wait (so far as is possible) for the results of the Law Commission's review and recommendations for legislative reform to be considered by parliament: 'There is some enthusiasm for reform within the judiciary and the profession, and in the media, and one can well understand why. But that does not mean that it is right'.[113] However, she goes on to outline six points of disagreement with the majority. These included the test to be applied when determining the weight to be attached to an pre-nuptial agreement in ancillary relief cases which, as set out by the majority, was, in her

---

106 [2010] UKSC 42 [78]. Although, of course, ancillary relief operates on the basis that 'the court knows best' and this is underlined in *Radmacher*. It is not the agreement that leads to the award but the order of the court using ancillary relief which accepts the terms of the pre-nuptial agreement.
107 ibid., [77] [79–83].
108 ibid., [80].
109 ibid., [114–123].
110 ibid., [132].
111 ibid.
112 ibid., [135].
113 ibid.

view, an 'impermissible judicial gloss' on the court's statutory duties.[114] While she agreed with the majority's approach insofar as it required the court to look at 'what is fair *now* and not what might have seemed fair *then*', she disagreed with where the majority placed the 'burden of persuasion'.[115] It should, she argued, be for the party seeking to enforce the agreement to show why it is fair to do so, rather than for the (usually) economically weaker party to establish why this would be unfair (as required by the majority's formulation of the test).[116] In any event, it was unfair for a pre-nuptial agreement to deprive the economically weaker spouse of the protection, such as ancillary relief, which stems from the status of marriage.[117] She believed that the Court of Appeal had therefore 'erred in principle . . . in equating married with unmarried parenthood'.[118] By treating the couple as if they *had never been married*, the lower court had, in her view, undermined the importance and status of marriage and the obligations *married* parents owe to each other (for example, in providing continuing financial support for a parent who has irredeemably compromised her position in the labour market, even after the children of the family have grown up).[119] She also took a rather different and more sympathetic view than the majority of Mr Granatino's behaviour, both in terms of his failure to take legal advice before signing the agreement and his decision to leave his career in banking, noting that the latter:

> was not as completely selfish as some may have thought it to be. The wife appears to have agreed with it at the time. And why should she not? The couple were rich enough each to be able to pursue their own dreams . . . If the decision was taken for the good of the family as a whole, this would

114 ibid., [138]. Lady Hale also disagreed with the majority's 'mercifully obiter' comments that pre-nuptial agreements are legally enforceable contracts and that it was open to them to decide this. Finally she disagreed with the majority's suggestion that there were no relevant differences, in policy terms, between agreements made before or after marriage.

115 Brenda Hale, 'Equality and autonomy in family law', *Journal of Social Welfare & Family Law*, 33(1), 2011, 3, p. 11.

116 Lord Mance believed that the wording was unlikely to be important in practice, although he preferred the majority's formulation ([2010] UKSC 42 [129]).

117 ibid., [191–193].

118 ibid., [195].

119 As was the case, eg, in *Miller v Miller; McFarlane v McFarlane* [2006] UKHL 24 [154]. Joanna Miles has suggested that Lady Hale's argument is difficult to follow here, in part because Lady Hale's hypothetical example does not apply in this case – it is unlikely that Mr Granatino would need continuing support, attributable to his parental status, after the children grew up. This being the case, Miles continues, the basis on which Lady Hale is making the continuing award can only be understood as a form of 'sharing' or 'compensation'. The latter stands in opposition to the majority's view that Mr Granatino's decision to leave his highly-paid job and move into academia was his own choice and was not motivated by his family's need (Miles, 'Marriage and Divorce', pp. 443–444).

have been for the benefit of the children as well as their parents. Happy parents make for happy children. Discontented parents make for discontented children.[120]

And so, while Lady Hale would have given more weight to the pre-nuptial agreement than the trial judge, she would have done more to recognise his status as the ex-husband of Ms Radmacher and father of their children, by granting Mr Granatino his English home, or a replacement for it, for life.[121]

Of course, that the judges in *Radmacher* had different views on the weight that should be accorded to pre-nuptial agreements is hardly surprising. As Lady Hale notes, not only is this something about which people may have different views, but both views (and the values underpinning them) have 'a perfectly sound grounding in legal principle'.[122] What is noticeable, however, is that the judges in the case were divided along gender lines.[123] *Both* and *only* the women judges who heard the case took the view that marriage is not a commercial contract, that the obligations it lays down are not only decided by the parties but also by the state, and that people should only be held to their pre-nuptial agreements where it is fair that they should do so. And so, it is at least plausible to suggest that this was no coincidence. As Lady Hale has herself noted,

> when you then look at it and you say well it's only . . . the two women in the case taking [this] view, maybe you ask yourself why might that be. But there we go. I would of course argue that [it] is closer to what family[law]'s always all about than is the former but then I would say that, wouldn't I.[124]

Radmacher is then a clear example of a case where judges, armed with the same materials and with the same knowledge of the law, differ and differ because they

120 [2010] UKSC 42 [194].
121 ibid., [194–195].
122 Lady Hale speaking at an InterLaw Diversity Forum event on the 'Feminist Judgments Project', Norton Rose, London, 13 October 2011 (transcript on file with author).
123 Hale, 'Equality and autonomy', p. 3.
124 Lady Hale speaking at an InterLaw Diversity Forum event on the 'Feminist Judgments Project', Norton Rose, London, 13 October 2011 (transcript on file with author). As well as sharing a gender, the trial judge (Mrs Justice Baron) and Lady Hale are both also experienced family lawyers. It may be better to see the case as a split between the family lawyers (seen in the drive toward fairness and Lady Hale's broader focus on marriage) and the commercial lawyers (who adopt a narrow, legalistic focus concerned with giving effect to individual bargains, rather than wider implications), although Wilson LJ in the of Appeal falls outside this categorisation. At the time, Lady Hale was the only family law specialist in the Supreme Court, while several of her male colleagues had a background in commercial law, where certainty and the sanctity of contract are paramount and two also hailed from Scotland where domestic law already gives legal status to pre-nuptial agreements (Peter G Harris, Robert H George and Jonathan Herring, 'With this ring I thee wed (terms and conditions apply)', *Family Law*, April, 2011, 367, p. 372).

have different understandings of what values the law *ought* to reflect and embody. It is also a case where men and women judges have differed. And, given the nature of the dispute and the issues it raises, it is possible to argue that these differences were at least in part attributable to the different experiences, and hence the different insights and perspectives men and women have on the role and effect of such agreements, and indeed of marriage more generally. After all, as Lady Hale observed, 'there is a gender dimension to the issue which some may think ill-suited to decision by a court consisting of eight men and one woman'.[125] In so doing, she brings to the fore the real 'winners' and 'losers' of the *Radmacher* decision, those most likely to benefit (primarily rich men) and lose out (primarily women) as a result of the majority's verdict:

> Would any self-respecting young woman sign up to an agreement which assumed that she would be the only one who might otherwise have a claim, thus placing no limit on the claims that might be made against her, and then limited her claim to a pre-determined sum for each year of marriage regardless of the circumstances, as if her wifely services were being bought by the year? Yet that is what these precedents do.[126]

Her judgment makes explicit the consequences of the majority's focus on autonomy and the importance of certainty, and the extent to which it allows a couple to 'bypass . . . the clear stance against discrimination and inequality which the previous case law has established' so that one person may 'engage in gender discrimination' simply on the basis that 'the other person has consented to the treatment'.[127] Her 'recontextualisation' (understood as revealing rather than introducing context) of the effects and impact of pre-nuptial agreements on the weaker party, (usually) the (often younger) wife, exposes the assumptions underlying the majority's approach and the interests this privileges.[128]

Extra-judicially, Lady Hale has suggested that it was 'unfortunate that the issues arose in the context of a very rich wife and a much less well-off husband, for there is little doubt that they are deeply gender related, but commentators – and even judges – are often slow to acknowledge this'.[129] Lord Justice Thorpe's explicit refusal to accept that 'the seekers [of pre-nuptial agreements] are the

---

125 [2010] UKSC 42 [137–138].

126 ibid., [137]. Andy Hayward has suggested that Lady Hale here explodes the majority's 'false feminism' by showing how that the majority's purportedly progressive intentions (upholding a pre-nuptial agreement in favour of a rich heiress and turning on its head the typical construction of such agreements as prejudicing women) is likely to *disadvantage* women generally, by opening the door to the pre-nuptial agreement in less extraordinary cases (comment to author).

127 Herring et al, 'Ante-nuptial agreements', pp. 338–339.

128 Nicola Lacey, *Unspeakable Subjects: Feminist Essays in Legal and Social Theory*, Oxford: Hart Publishing, 1998, pp. 6–7.

129 Hale, 'Equality and autonomy', p. 3.

predominantly male super-rich, anxious to ensure that the contemplated marriage will not prove too expensive on its future dissolution'[130] and Lord Justice Wilson's suggestion that women are 'patronised', rather than protected, by the unenforceability of pre-nuptial agreements are perhaps comments in point.[131] Lady Hale made the same point in her judgment:

> These difficult issues cannot be resolved in an individual case, in particular a case with such very unusual features as this one. Different people will naturally react to this particular human story in different ways, depending upon their values and experience of life . . . Above all, perhaps, the court hearing a particular case can all too easily lose sight of the fact that, unlike a separation agreement, the object of an ante-nuptial agreement is to deny the economically weaker spouse the provision to which she – it is usually although by no means invariably she – would otherwise be entitled.[132]

Over the course of a few sentences, Lady Hale makes the case for the inclusion of diverse experiences and insights on the Bench; her judgment in *Radmacher* manifests it.

R v J

J and C lived in the same village, their families were friends and J rented his business premises from C's father.[133] When C was 13, she started working for J, who was 22 years her senior, on Saturdays and during school holidays. J used this opportunity to cultivate a sexual relationship with C. Between July 1996 and September 1997 they had regular vaginal and oral sexual intercourse, which J video-taped. C did not tell anyone what had happened until three years later, when she was 17. J was charged and convicted of indecent assault (under section 14 of the Sexual Offences Act 1956 (SOA)) and indecency with a child, contrary to section 1(1) of the Indecency with Children Act 1960.

J appealed against his conviction for indecent assault (which related solely to his sexual intercourse with C). The substance of his appeal was that the Crown Prosecution Service's (CPS) motivation for prosecuting him for indecent assault, as opposed to unlawful sexual intercourse with a girl under 16 (under section 6(1)

---

130 [2009] EWCA Civ 649 [122], [27]. In fact, research by Emma Hitchings for the Law Commission on the experiences of practitioners in drafting and advising clients on marital property agreements found that – in contrast to Lord Justice Thorpe's belief – the practitioners interviewed were more likely to encounter this type of 'big money' case (Emma Hitchings, 'From Pre-Nups to Post-Nups: Dealing with Marital Property Agreements', *Family Law*, November, 2009, 1056, 1059).

131 [2009] EWCA Civ 649 [122], [127].

132 [2010] UKSC 42 [136–137].

133 An earlier version of this discussion of *R v J* was published in Erika Rackley, 'Difference in the House of Lords', *Social and Legal Studies*, 15(2), 2006, 163, 179–181.

of the SOA), was to avoid the 12-month time limit applying to the latter offence and which had expired. This, J argued, amounted to an abuse of process. The majority of the House of Lords agreed. In his leading opinion, Lord Bingham suggested that to find otherwise would require an 'impossible reading' of the 1956 Act, essentially depriving the time restriction from having any meaningful effect:

> . . . what possible purpose could Parliament have intended to serve by prohibiting prosecution under section 6 after the lapse of 12 months if exactly the same conduct could thereafter be prosecuted, with exposure to the same penalty, under section 14?[134]

It was not the court's role to facilitate what the majority agreed was an attempt by the CPS to circumvent the clear intent of parliament. Holding the CPS's decision to prosecute J for indecent assault to be ultra vires, Lord Steyn noted '[i]n our parliamentary democracy nobody is above the law. The powers of the CPS are extensive but not extensive enough to permit it to take decisions intended to evade the clear intent of parliament', and that it was as 'plain as a pikestaff' that this is what the CPS policy had intended to do.[135]

Just nine months into her appointment to the Appellate Committee of the House of Lords, Lady Hale saw things differently. She was of the view that the majority's decision amounted to 'a misuse of principle and language':[136]

> In my view, the appellant [J] was guilty of conduct which constituted the offences with which he was charged at the time when he committed them; there is no good reason why he should not have been charged with and convicted of them; and the only unfairness will be that done to his victim [C], and the many others in her situation, by your Lordships' decision.[137]

In weighing up the 'countervailing considerations of policy and justice', Lady Hale came down firmly in favour of a 'need to protect the young from sexual exploitation and abuse'.[138] The offender knew 'perfectly well' at the time that he was committing a criminal offence and to allow him to derive a fortuitous benefit from a time limit would be 'particularly undeserved'.[139] She continued:

> [w]e do not know why this complainant said nothing until she was 17, but sexual abusers commonly groom their victims by making them believe that their behaviour is normal. They make their victims fall in love with them.

134 [2004] UKHL 42 [18].
135 ibid., [38].
136 ibid., [81].
137 ibid., [69].
138 ibid., [72].
139 ibid., [80].

They often threaten or cajole them into silence. Delayed reporting is then the result of the abuser's own actions and merits no special protection.[140]

In short, the better the abuser executes their abuse, the *less* likely they are to be punished for their actions. Hence Lady Hale's conclusion that

> the 1956 Act was a mess when it was enacted and it became an even greater mess with later amendments. It is not possible to discern within it such coherent parliamentary intention as to require it to be construed so as to forbid prosecution for a 'mere' act of sexual intercourse after 12 months where that act properly falls within the definition of an indecent assault . . . we do not have to supply Parliament with the thinking it never did and the words that it never used.[141]

Described by Brice Dickson as 'the most startling example' of Lady Hale making it clear that 'she will not be cowed into falling into line with the traditional view of her male colleagues',[142] the striking thing about Lady Hale's dissent in *R v J* is not simply that she refused to fall into line with her new colleagues, but also the *way* in which she did so, *how* she articulated her disagreement. Her 'powerful and cogent criticism'[143] of the majority's reasoning and decision not only exposed their (mis) use of statutory interpretation and appeal to non-existent parliamentary intentions, but also raised important substantive questions about the nature and reality of sexual abuse. She locates the consequences of the majority's decision – that in cases of historic sex abuse falling within the scope of the SOA 1956, men who groom young teenage girls for sex may well escape prosecution because of the girl's (understandable) delay reporting the offence – against a backdrop of broader statements about the realities of abusive relationships and women's experience of sex more generally. This in turn works 'to expand and transform law's "common knowledge" of the world'.[144] Her response to Lord Bingham's suggestion that the CPS would have done better, in this instance, to focus on acts of *oral* intercourse possibly combined with other peripheral sex acts (which were not time barred),[145] in order to secure a conviction – that is, to prosecute the offender *for everything but* the unlawful sexual intercourse – reveals not only the practical and legal

---

140 ibid.

141 ibid., [89].

142 Brice Dickson, 'A Hard Act to Follow: The Bingham Court, 2000–8' in Louis Blom-Cooper, Brice Dickson and Gavin Drewry (eds), *The Judicial House of Lords 1876–2009*, Oxford: Oxford University Press, 2009, 255, pp. 273–274.

143 David Ormerod, 'Appeal: Change in law since conviction – Court of Appeal's approach to conviction under previous law', *Criminal Law Review*, 1, 2008, 50, 52.

144 Rosemary Hunter, 'Justice Marcia Neave: Case Study of a Feminist Judge' in Ulrike Schultz and Gisela Shaw (eds), *Gender and Judging*, Oxford: Hart Publishing, forthcoming.

145 [2004] UKHL 42 [25].

difficulties in such an approach, but also his (and the other Law Lords') failure to recognise fully the harm done to the victim in this case:

> [T]he integrity of the criminal justice system requires that it makes sense to victims and the general public as well as to the accused. How can it possibly be explained to the victim in this case that her abuser can be prosecuted for the oral sexual intercourse but not for the vaginal? Women vary in whether they see oral or vaginal intercourse as more serious and in their degrees of reluctance to comply with either. How can it be explained that he can be prosecuted for any peripheral and preparatory sexual acts but not for those which were part and parcel of committing or attempting to commit the act of vaginal intercourse? . . . This sort of irrational and incoherent distinction is exactly what brings the legal system into disrepute.[146]

Ultimately, of course, Lady Hale's arguments made no difference to the resolution of the case: J's conviction in relation to the charges for indecent assault was quashed. The full extent of the abuse C suffered was rendered legally harmless. A dissenting judgment can never alter the outcome of a case. Instead, its success lies in the extent to which it is able to challenge the majority's story and weaken its hold on our collective imagination, its ability to sow seeds of difference so that they might flourish in future cases and willingness to articulate alternative perspectives, and to develop new understandings of the issues at hand.[147] After all, as Lady Hale has noted on another occasion, 'it all depends on how you tell the story';[148] '[o]ut of today's minority opinion can sometimes come the orthodoxy of tomorrow'.[149]

For present purposes, what matters is that here too we see an example of judicial difference. Here, as in *Radmacher*, we have a case raising gendered issues – and so a case on which we might expect a judge's gender to be most likely to make a difference to the way she or he decides it – and where the woman judge not only decides differently to her male colleagues, but also provides insights and a narrative missing from their judgments. And, while as before, we may not be able to say for sure where these differences come from, and so how exactly it came to be that Lady Hale came to disagree with the reasoning and conclusion of the majority, *R v J* stands as a further example of where gender appears to have played at least *some* part in the decision a woman judge has reached and in grounding the differences between her and her male colleagues.

---

146 ibid., [79].
147 Berns, *To Speak as a Judge*, p. 8.
148 *Smith v Northants* [2009] UKHL 27 [32].
149 Hale, 'A Minority Opinion', p. 332. In fact, Lady Hale's dissent in *R v J* has since garnered support as the lower courts have sought to grapple with the fallout from the majority's decision (see, eg, *R v Cottrell; R v Fletcher* [2007] EWCA Crim 2016 [23–29]; Ormerod, 'Appeal: Change in Law', p. 52; Jonathan Rogers, 'Fundamentally Objectionable', *New Law Journal*, 157, 2007, 1252).

What difference?

So where does this leave arguments that being a woman might make a difference to how one judges? Two things are clear. First, arguments for women judges' difference do not stand and fall on an ability to identify a single, unified women's perspective and experience on a given issue or 'different voice'. While we have every reason to think that women will, by virtue of their distinctive experiences and the insights these provide, sometimes judge differently to men, any attempt to pin down the precise impact of gender on their judging is impossible. While being a woman is *one of the factors* that will affect one's judging, it will not *always* make a difference, nor is it the *only* factor to influence and inform judging. Although the gender of the woman judge gets our attention,[150] like all judges, the experiences and perspectives that inform the values a judge brings to judging extend beyond this. Thus while, in the examples above, Lady Hale's gender catches our eye, like *all* judges, her judging is informed by experiences that extend beyond this. After all, Lady Hale is not only different because she is a woman, but also because she is the only Supreme Court justice to have spent most of her professional life *away* from the Bar. Is then her judgment in *Radmacher* informed by her gender, or by her experiences promoting the reform and rationalisation of the common law as a Law Commissioner? Did she agree with Mrs Justice Baron at first instance because of their common experiences as women or as experts in family law? And what of her self-identification as a feminist? Can we see her evidence of her 'feminist mini-malist' philosophy of judging in her decision-making?[151] And if so, where does this leave arguments as to her difference grounded in her gender? Is her dissent in *R v J*, for example, informed by her experiences as a woman or by her politics as a feminist?[152]

The search for the woman Judge's 'different voice' is unhelpful. It assumes that one's views are informed by one's gender in isolation, rather than through the

---

150 In his Gray's Inn Lecture, Michael Beloff comments that: 'For my part I had always recognised that in the assessment of fact, or the exercise of discretion, a judge's gender might well be influential in a decision. What I had not appreciated, until we had our first female member of our highest tribunal is that gender could also influence the shape of legal principle and precedent' ('Sisters-in-Law: The Irresistible Rise of Women in Wigs', The Gray's Inn Reading, 2009).

151 Hale, 'A Minority Opinion', p. 336.

152 In fact, a number of Lady Hale's judgments can be seen to adhere to Rosemary Hunter's defini-tion of a 'feminist judgment' (Hunter, 'Can *feminist* judges make a difference?', p. 7). See, eg, drawing attention to the gender implications of purportedly neutral rules or legal practices and writing women's experiences into judgment (*K v Secretary of State for the Home Department; Fornah v Secretary of State for the Home Department* [2006] UKHL 46 (discussed in Chapter 6) and *R (Hoxha) v Special Adjudicator* [2005] UKHL 19 [27–39]), contextual decision-making (*R v J* [2004] UKHL 42; and *Stack v Dowden* [2007] UKHL 17; *ZH (Tanzania) (FC) (Appellant) v Secretary of State for the Home Department* [2011] UKSC 4), deploying feminist scholarship (*R (Begum) v Governors of Denbigh High School* [2006] UKHL 15) and remedying injustices and promoting substantive equality (*M v Secretary of State for Work and Pensions* [2006] 2 AC 91; *R (Kehoe) v Secretary of State for Work and Pensions* [2006] 1 AC 42).

cross-fertilisation of a variety of identity characteristics and experiences. It is likely, as Lady Hale notes, that these – and other – characteristics and experiences are 'at least as influential' as her gender on her decision-making and that they work together to inform and shape her judgments.[153] It is important to resist the temptation to promote one characteristic over others, to conflate multiple sites of difference. That she is a woman, while important, is not all-encompassing. Nor, in our rush to emphasise difference, should we seek to deny or downplay the ways in which many women judges (including Lady Hale) are similar to their male peers – most obviously in relation to her race, university educational background[154] and social class.

Secondly, although in the cases above the presence of Lady Hale was not decisive to the decision the courts reached, what they do support is the view that the woman judge has a distinct contribution to make, that a woman's particular perspectives, insights and experiences can impact on the way she judges. That Lady Hale is different from her male colleagues is clear. Her deliberate and strategic choice to highlight the gendered implications of the case at hand, to write the experiences of women into her judgment and the law, sets her apart.[155] It gets our attention. Her judgments in *Radmacher* and *J v C* stand out because – whether or not we endorse the view that a male judge, lacking these experiences and insights, *could not* have written them[156] – a male judge *has not* written them. So, what we also see in cases like this is the reality that our judges judge differently and hence that who our judges are matters.[157] Here lies the grain of truth in the challenges to women judges explored in Chapter 4. Women judges *will*, sometimes, do things differently; they *will*, sometimes, reach decisions male judges would not reach. But far from being a cause for concern, as the next chapter will show, this in fact provides the clearest argument for their value and for the value of a truly diverse judiciary.

The woman judge allows us to see better, to see more clearly, what has been true all along: judging is not mechanical, it is not computation; judges must, on occasion, fall back on their sense of justice, their conception of the values the law should uphold. And, where they do, they are likely to differ. So, while the distinctive perspectives women judges might offer, the different arguments they might endorse and the different conclusions they might reach catch our attention, their real significance lies in the extent to which they expose the myth of the default

153 Hale, 'Equality and the Judiciary', p. 500.
154 Though unlike her colleagues, Brenda Hale attended a non fee-paying school.
155 Compare, Hunter, 'Justice Marcia Neave'.
156 Although clearly the life experiences of a judge inform their judging and judgment, it does not follow that a judge *must* have had certain experiences *in order to be able to judge*. As Lady Hale has acknowledged in another context 'I would like to think that a wider experience of the world is helpful: knowing a little about bearing and bringing up children must make some difference . . . [to how one judges; however,] there have been some wonderful family judges who have never changed a nappy or cooked a fish finger in their lives' (Hale, 'Equality and the Judiciary', p. 501).
157 Berns, *To Speak as a Judge*, p. 8.

judge:[158] the judge without politics, without personality, without preference. Indeed, the fact that this myth has survived for so long only goes to show how deeply homogeneous our judiciary has been and still is: the similarity in background and experiences produces a similarity in attitude and values which is easily misread as *neutrality*.[159] The woman judge's gender puts us on notice. But what it puts us on notice of is not simply the difference of the woman judge, but the dependence of *all* judges on their background, values and experiences. The woman judge upsets this misleading and unhelpful image of the superhero or default judge. Her presence disrupts the *homo*geneity of the Bench, exposing unarticulated gendered assumptions embodied in our understanding of the judge and judging where difference is inescapably present yet denied. So understood, the search for the woman judge's difference, her 'different voice', is best viewed as a fiction or myth.[160] Its promise lies not in its literal truth – in our ability to identify a common and unified voice shared by *all* women (judges) – but rather in its ability to render contingent particular but dominant understandings of the judge and judging.[161] The introduction of different perspectives and experiences to the Bench enables us to fashion a fuller understanding of the role of the judge and judging, and with it one of the strongest arguments in favour of judicial diversity. After all, once we accept that who the judge is matters, then it matters who our judges are.

158 Hale, 'A Minority Opinion', p. 320.
159 Regina Graycar, 'The Gender of Judgments: An Introduction' in Margaret Thornton (ed), *Public and Private – Feminist Legal Debates*, Oxford: Oxford University Press, 1995, 262, p. 261.
160 Erika Rackley, 'From Arachne to Charlotte: An Imaginative Revisiting of Gilligan's *In a Different Voice*', *William & Mary Journal of Women and the Law*, 13(3), 2007, 751.
161 Maria Drakopoulou, 'The Ethic of Care, Female Subjectivity and Feminist Legal Scholarship', *Feminist Legal Studies*, 8(2), 2000, 199, p. 204; Belleau and Johnson, 'Judging Gender', p. 69.

Chapter 6

Making the argument for judicial diversity

> I would love the Supreme Court to be 50:50 men and women from the point of view of perception, but it is more important that the Supreme Court should consist of the 12 most outstanding candidates.
>
> (Lord Phillips)[1]

Once one acknowledges that judging is not the mechanical application of pre-determined rules, which judges must simply discover and apply to the facts at hand, it becomes clear that judges must, to this extent, make decisions guided by their own sense of what the law *should* be, the values and principles it should embody and promote. In such cases, *who* the judge is matters, since it will determine both the way the judge sets about deciding cases and the substantive conclusions they reach. Insofar as a judge's sense of what the law should be doing will be informed and shaped by their experiences, we should expect gender, as the inescapable backdrop to all our experiences and as a central contributor to many, to be one factor which influences how one judges. So, as we saw in the previous chapter, we should expect there to be times when women judges do 'make a difference' to judging and to how cases are decided.

Now, this does not in itself make the case for the appointment of more women judges. The recognition that a judge's decision-making is, on occasion, shaped and informed by *who* the judge is, by their experiences as men or women of a particular race, ethnicity, class, sexuality and so on, is not yet an argument *for* judicial diversity. At most, it identifies one consequence of a diverse judiciary – namely diversity in the style and substance of decision-making. But it *does* allow us to see how such an argument could be made. For if we can show that the difference women judges make to judicial decision-making is a *positive* one, and that the judiciary is stronger and the justice dispensed *better* the more diverse its decision-makers, then we have an argument for why judicial diversity is a good thing. Not

1 Lord Phillips, Oral evidence to the House of Lords Select Committee on the Constitution Inquiry into Judicial Appointments Process, 19 October 2011, Q187 (Constitution Committee Inquiry).

only that, but we also have an argument for judicial diversity which is immune to the traditional opponent to measures to increase diversity: the necessity of appointing on merit. For if a diverse judiciary really is a *better* judiciary, a judiciary *better* placed to apply and to develop the law fairly and reasonably, then the pursuit of diversity and appointment on merit go hand in hand with the common aim of ensuring that our judiciary is the best it can be.

Diversity in judging

To the extent that judging requires consideration not just of our legal practices – of what other judges and legal officials have said and done in the past – but also of what really are *good* reasons for deciding the case one way or another, what *is* just, fair, reasonable and so on, different judges will judge differently. Where judges must rely on their own sense of justice, of what the law is there to do and how it might best do it, judicial decision-making will inevitably be shaped by *who* the judge is, and so by the background and experiences which inform and shape one's views on these matters. Necessarily, the experiences and background of any one judge will be limited, and so too will the insights one's experiences and background might provide. The most we might say is that an individual with a greater variety of experiences is likely to have a greater armoury of perspectives and insights which they might profitably bring to bear on their judging. When surveying the judiciary as a whole, however, the knowledge and insights of its various members are combined. Although any one judge will only have lived one life, with one set of experiences, by which their judging may be informed, the judiciary as a group has lived many, with a combined set of experiences which no one person could match. And, to the extent that good judgment is informed by and so a product of such experiences and the insights and information they can provide, we can say that a judiciary with a greater wealth of expertise or insights to draw on is better equipped and better informed than one with a narrower background or range of knowledge. Conversely, a judiciary, and the justice it dispenses, is poorer for a *lack* of diversity, the more limited the experiences of its members. To be clear, none of this is to say that all insights and experiences are of equal value but it *is* to say that, all things being equal, a judge and a judiciary with a broader array of perspectives and expertise, with a diverse range of life experiences, is better positioned to assess the merits of competing arguments or alternative routes the law could take and to decide the case accordingly. It is to agree with Lord Justice Etherton that 'a judiciary with a diversity of experience . . . is more likely to achieve the most just decision and the best outcome for society',[2] that the judiciary is stronger, and the justice dispensed better, the more varied the perspectives and experiences that are involved in its decision-making.

2   Terence Etherton, 'Liberty, the Archetype and Diversity: A Philosophy of Judging', *Public Law*, 2010, 727, p. 728.

Why is this? Our sense of justice or of how things might best work may, in one sense, be intuitive, but that does not mean that it exists independently of our own experiences or that it is not affected and informed by our living and interacting in the world: '[i]t plainly helps a judge not only in finding facts but in formulating law to be able empathetically to understand the law's impact on people of different kinds'.[3] As we saw in the previous chapter, gender, as an ever-present feature in our lives and often a contributing factor to many of our experiences will be *at least one of the things* that, on occasion, informs our judgments on such questions. Because of this, there will be times when a woman judge will not only judge differently to her male colleagues but, to the extent that her experience as a woman gives her a *better*, fuller understanding of the issues at stake, she is in a position to reach a *better* decision than a judge without this understanding. This was, of course, US Supreme Court Justice Sonia Sotomayor's point in her widely cited adaptation of Minnesota Supreme Court Justice Coyne's comment that 'a wise Latina woman *with the richness of her experiences* would more often than not reach a better conclusion than a white male who hasn't lived that life'.[4] She continued:

> Personal experiences affect the facts that judges choose to see. My hope is that I will take the good from my experiences and extrapolate them further into areas with which I am unfamiliar. I simply do not know exactly what that difference will be in my judging. But I accept there will be some based on my gender and my Latina heritage.[5]

Other women judges have made much the same point. US Supreme Court Justice Ruth Bader Ginsburg, for example, has argued that being a woman helps a judge to have a better understanding of the issues at stake in cases of sex and pregnancy discrimination in the workplace, as well as of the humiliation of a 13-year-old girl who has been strip-searched:

> Maybe a 13-year-old boy in a locker room doesn't have that same feeling about his body. But a girl who's just at the age where she is developing,

---

3 Ronald Dworkin, 'Justice Sotomayor: The Unjust Hearings', *The New York Review of Books*, 24 September 2009.

4 Sonia Sotomayor, 'A Latina Judge's Voice', *Berkeley La Raza Law Journal*, 13, 2002, 87, p. 92.

5 ibid. During her appearances before the US Senate, Sotomayor sought to clarify her much-publicised comment. Her intention was not she argued – as her critics had suggested – to imply that judicial decisions are, or should be, dictated by the judge's background, irrespective of the confines of the law. Nor was it to suggest that either gender, or indeed any single racial or ethnic group, had an advantage when it came to good judging (although, interestingly, this seemed to be the implication of some of the Republican criticism). Rather, she argued it was a 'rhetorical flourish that fell flat' in a speech attempting to 'inspire young Hispanic, Latino students and lawyers to believe that their life experiences added value to the process' (14 July 2009). For an empirical analysis of Sotomayor's claim see Stephen J Choi, Mitu Gulati, Mirya Holman and Eric A Posner, 'Judging Women', *Journal of Empirical Studies*, 8(3), 2011, 504.

whether she has developed a lot . . . or . . . has not developed at all, (might be) embarrassed about that . . . It's a very sensitive age for a girl. I didn't think that my colleagues, some of them, quite understood.[6]

Similarly, Patricia Wald, a former judge on the International Criminal Tribunal for the former Yugoslavia, has suggested that women judges have 'unique perceptions' of the harms suffered by the victims of displacement and sexual violence in the context of war (predominantly women), noting that a woman judge was on the panel in *all* of the first five ground-breaking cases involving the recognition of gender crimes.[7]

However, even if one thinks that the addition of women judges' perspectives and insights, described above and in the previous chapter, are a valuable and useful addition to the judiciary – that the insights a woman might offer can, on occasion, lead to *better* judging – this also seems to admit that the outcome of such cases will come down to the personal experiences of the judge who happens to hear it. And if this is right, the delivery of justice then appears to be, to this extent, a lottery. Whether the judge in any given case is a man or a woman, or whether there is a woman judge on a panel, is a matter of chance. Accordingly, whose insights you get the benefit of (or, perhaps, whose prejudices you are on the receiving end of) seems to be luck of the draw: either you get a woman judge and so all the benefits (or disadvantages) of a woman judge's perspectives or you do not. Either way, the justice done seems to be random.

This appears to be a significant stumbling block. Insofar as diversity in the experiences and perspectives of judges leads to divergence of outcome – to like cases being treated differently – then this is, without doubt, a bad thing. It is one thing to recognise that at least some of the time judges have to rely on their own knowledge and experiences to decide cases, and that these necessarily vary from person to person. It is quite another to accept that the decision in any given case depends on the judge you happen to get on the day. On any view, justice requires that like cases be treated alike, and so a legal system which sees its decision-making vary with the identity of the judge is one which is failing to do justice.

One response is to say that this is already the case. Even amongst our relatively homogeneous body of judges we find differing views and values, which manifest themselves in differences in the decisions they reach.[8] Were this not the case, we

---

6 Joan Biskupiz, 'Ginsburg: Court needs another woman', *USA Today*, 10 May 2009; Bill Mears, 'Justice Ginsburg ready to welcome Sotomayor', *USA Today*, 16 June 2009; Emily Bazelon, 'The Place of Women on the Court', *New York Times Magazine*, 12 July 2009.

7 Patricia M Wald, 'Women on International Courts: Some Lessons Learned', *International Criminal Law Review*, 11, 2011, 401, pp. 403–404.

8 As Lord Phillips noted in a BBC documentary in 2011, '[i]f you sit five out of the twelve justices and you reach a decision 3:2, it's fairly obvious that if you'd had a different five you might have reached the decision 2:3 the other way' (in Alan Paterson and Chris Paterson, *Guarding the Guardians? Towards an independent, accountable and diverse senior judiciary* (London: CentreForum, 2012), p. 40).

would have no dissenting judgments, and few appeals would be allowed. For the reasons given in the previous chapter, *some* differences between judges and between the ways they judge are inevitable. But if it is true that women judges will bring with them *further* differences, even more diverse arguments and perspectives, then is this only going to lead to even greater divergences in approach between our judges? And, does this mean in turn that it will matter all the more which judges are assigned to which cases, and that, especially in hard cases, the decision will depend, even more than at present, on which judge you happen to get? And, if so, does increased judicial diversity effectively make justice even more of a lottery, only increasing the likelihood of like cases not being treated alike?

Presented with these options we might well opt for a *less* diverse judiciary in favour of consistency, uniformity and predictability of outcome. To be clear this gives us no reason for preferring any particular single social group and so this is not to suggest that the judiciary should continue to be monopolised (as, at its upper levels, it largely remains) by white, middle-class Oxbridge-educated male barristers. Rather it is to argue that one unintentional advantage of this status quo is that this narrower range of experiences and insights among the judges means they are more likely to produce a more coherent and consistent body of law (albeit one formed on the basis of understandings of women's experiences which bear 'little if any relation to the complex realities'[9] of women's lives). Representation and equality arguments for judicial diversity aside, if this is the case, it seems that there are good reasons, grounded in the substantive quality of decision-making, for thinking that when it comes to judicial diversity, *less* is more.

Improving the judicial product

Clearly, if our judiciary functioned simply as an assortment of individual judges, operating in isolation from one other and relying on their own individual experiences and perspectives, then we would have to admit that more diversity on the Bench would lead to broader variations, and hence inconsistencies, in the way cases were decided than there are at present. Like cases would be treated alike less often. On this basis, we would be hard pressed to argue that judicial diversity – whatever its other attractions and justifications – would lead to cases being decided *better*, to *improved* decision-making. However, this paints a misleading, and indeed unattractive, picture of how our judiciary – and how the law – works.

Judging is a collective enterprise. This is perhaps most apparent when judges sit in panels. Here a woman judge sitting with male judges may complement and so offer a counterbalance to the views and experiences of her (male) colleagues, providing a 'different' take on the issue at hand. While the scope for the woman

---

9 Regina Graycar, 'The Gender of Judgments: An Introduction' in Margaret Thornton (ed), *Public and Private – Feminist Legal Debates*, Oxford: Oxford University Press, 1995, p. 262, 268.

judge influencing the decision-making of her male colleagues will depend on the practices and dynamics of the court (as well as the relationship between the individual panel members), in all cases opportunities are there. During oral arguments, for example, a woman judge may, through her interjections and questions, draw out arguments and aspects of the case overlooked or downplayed by her colleagues, which may in turn influence the direction of the arguments made and conclusion reached.[10] In a case before the US Supreme Court in 2009 involving discrimination related to the impact of maternity leave on pension entitlements,[11] it was reported that Justice Ginsburg, at that time the only woman on the court, 'dominated' the oral arguments and displayed openly her frustration at what she saw as her male colleagues' 'certain lack of understanding' about the ongoing discrimination women face in the workplace.[12] Although she was unsuccessful in persuading the majority of her colleagues to agree with her as to the outcome of the case, her presence ensured that arguments about workplace equality were aired and addressed; she later commented that the oral arguments had been made 'just for her'.[13]

At other times, the woman judge may seek to inform or influence her colleagues' decision-making behind closed doors. Although practices differ from court to court as to the amount of (formal) discussion judges have about a case while it is being heard, judges will typically meet to discuss the case before beginning to draft their judgment(s).[14] In the UK Supreme Court, this follows a practice whereby the judges take it in turns to give their preliminary views and reasoning as to the outcome of the case, in order of seniority starting with the most junior judge on the panel. This initial discussion plays a vital role in the judges' decision-making

10 See, eg, Justice Pillay's interventions in the case against Jean Paul Akayesu in the International Criminal Tribunal for Rwanda (*Prosecutor v Akayesu* Case No ICTR-96-4-T (2 September 1998)). Akayesu was found guilty of ordering, instigating, aiding and abetting crimes against humanity (including rape and sexual violence) and acts of genocide against Tutsi people. The original indictment against Akayesu did not include charges of sexual violence; however, during the trial the witnesses, encouraged by Justice Pillay (the only woman judge present), began to talk of rape and other acts of sexual violence. The trial was adjourned. Following more detailed investigations the indictment against Akayesu was amended by Chief Prosecutor Louise Arbour, and when the trial resumed, a year later, extensive witness testimonies detailing the use of rape and sexual violence were introduced (Kelly Askin, 'Sexual Violence in Decisions and Indictments of the Yugoslav and Rwandan Tribunals: Current Status', *American Journal of International Law*, 93(1), 1999, 97; see also in Erika Rackley, 'Judicial diversity, the woman judge and fairy tale endings', *Legal Studies*, 27(1), 2007, 74, pp. 90–91).
11 *AT&T Corp. v Hulteen et al*, 556 US ___, 129 S Ct 1962 (2009).
12 Biskupiz, 'Ginsburg'.
13 ibid.
14 See generally, Alan Paterson, *The Law Lords*, London: Macmillan Press, 1982, pp. 89–109; Brenda Hale and Rosemary Hunter, 'A Conversation with Baroness Hale', *Feminist Legal Studies*, 16(2), 2008, 237, pp. 246–247; Penny Darbyshire, *Sitting in Judgment: The Working Lives of Judges*, Oxford: Hart Publishing, 2011, pp. 336–339; 384–386; Alan Paterson, *Lawyers and the Public Good: Democracy in Action?* Cambridge: Cambridge University Press, 2012, ch 4.

process, 'solidifying' the views of the panel members.[15] It is here that the woman judge can 'make her case', highlighting aspects of the case or the arguments made that she thinks are important and bringing her distinct insights and perspectives on the matter at hand to the other judges. We know too that judges sometimes circulate their draft judgments to other panel members, providing further opportunities for members of the panel to shape their colleagues' deliberations and final judgment(s) of the court, as well as to rethink – and even abandon – theirs. For instance, here is how Lord Walker prefaced his speech in *Stack v Dowden*:

> My Lords, I have had the advantage of reading in draft the opinion of my noble and learned friend, Baroness Hale of Richmond. Having done so I have set aside as redundant most of the opinion which I had prepared. I cannot usefully add to, still less improve upon, her account of the human and social issues involved, the practicalities of registered conveyancing, and the particular (and in some ways unusual) facts that have led to this appeal reaching your Lordships' House.[16]

This communal aspect to the process of coming to judgment should not be underestimated. Indeed, it has been suggested that a judge's interaction and discussions about the case with their colleagues is *the* principal influencing factor on the decision they reach.[17] Both in this initial discussion and in the exchanges which follow as the panel members draft their judgments, each judge will influence and be influenced by the arguments of his or her colleagues. Here then the woman judge can contribute not simply by providing her own judgment but by informing the judgments of her male counterparts, prompting them to think again about their own understanding of the case and, where necessary, to adjust their arguments and tailor the conclusions that will appear in their written judgments.[18]

Accordingly, even in cases such as *Radmacher (formerly Granatino) v Granatino*[19] and *R v J*[20] (discussed in Chapter 5) where Lady Hale's views did not win the day, her presence on the panel nonetheless meant that certain arguments were made and

---

15 Hale and Hunter, 'Conversation', p. 247.
16 *Stack v Dowden* [2007] UKHL 17 [14]. See also comment of Lord Phillips in *Edwards v Chesterfield Royal Hospital NHS Foundation Trust; Botham (FC) v Ministry of Defence* [2011] UKSC 58: 'When initially I saw in draft the judgment of Lord Dyson, my reaction was that it was so plainly right in the result that my inclination was simply to add my agreement to it. The judgments of Lady Hale and Lord Kerr have, however, caused me to give further consideration to this difficult area of the law. While I have not changed my mind as to the result, the route by which I have reached it is not on all fours with that of Lord Dyson. For that reason I am adding my judgment to those of Lord Dyson and Lord Mance' ([70]).
17 Paterson, *The Law Lords*, p. 34.
18 ibid., pp. 89–109; Biskupiz, 'Ginsburg'; Richard Posner, *How Judges Think*, Cambridge, Mass.: Harvard University Press, 2010, p. 33; Darbyshire, *Sitting in Judgment*, p. 352.
19 [2010] UKSC 42.
20 [2004] UKHL 42.

heard. It ensured that the majority judgments were written with at least an aware-ness of alternative viewpoints or significant 'points of difference' on issues at hand.[21] More significant, however, are cases in which the distinctive arguments of women judges are not just heard but taken up, where the insights and experiences of women judges prevail. This might most obviously take the form of a leading judgment,[22] but it can also be seen – and is perhaps most telling – in cases where the arguments offered by the woman judge are not only seen in her own judg-ment, but also in the reasoning of her colleagues. Of course, it is difficult to say for sure where and to what extent a particular judgment or line of argument was influenced by the presence of a woman judge on the panel. Nonetheless, we can identify what appear to be examples of women judges having this sort of influence. One example is the House of Lords' decision in *Secretary of State for the Home Department v K (FC); Fornah (FC) v Secretary of State for the Home Department*,[23] a case described as bearing 'all the hallmarks of Britain's first [and only] woman law lord'.[24]

Judging gender: K and Fornah in the House of Lords[25]

This twin appeal involved two women – 'Mrs K' and 'Miss Fornah' – seeking asylum in the UK. Mrs K, an Iranian national, fled to the UK in October 2001. She had been raped and persecuted by the Revolutionary Guards in Iran following, and as a result of, her husband's arrest six months earlier. Zainab (Esther) Fornah arrived in the UK from Sierra Leone in March 2003, aged 15. She had left her home country to avoid being forced to undergo female genital mutilation (FGM), which was performed on the overwhelming majority of girls in Sierra Leone. The question in both of the appeals was whether the appellant was a 'refugee', defined in article 1A(2) of the 1951 Geneva Convention Relating to the Status of Refugees and the 1967 Protocol, as any person who:

> owing to well-founded fear of being persecuted for reasons of race, religion, nationality, membership of a particular social group or political opinion, is outside the country of nationality and is unable or, owing to such fear, is unwilling to avail himself of the protection of that country.

21   Michael Kirby, 'Judicial Dissent: Common Law and Civil Law Traditions', *Law Quarterly Review*, 123, 2007 379, pp. 396–397.

22   See, eg, *In Re G (Children)* [2006] UKHL 43; *AL (Serbia) (FC) (Appellant) v Secretary of State for the Home Department; R (on the application of Rudi) (FC) (Appellant) v Secretary of State for the Home Department* [2008] UKHL 42; *Stack v Dowden* [2007] UKHL 17; *Yemshaw v London Borough of Hounslow* [2011] UKSC 3.

23   *K v Secretary of State for the Home Department; Fornah v Secretary of State for the Home Department* [2006] UKHL 46.

24   Leader, 'In Praise of . . . Lady Hale of Richmond', *The Guardian*, 20 October 2006.

25   This section draws on arguments in Erika Rackley, 'What a difference difference makes: gendered harms and judicial diversity', *International Journal of the Legal Profession*, 15(1–2), 2008, 37.

It was common ground that the harm the women feared was sufficiently serious so as to amount to persecution, and that their fear was well founded.[26] However, in both cases, the Court of Appeal had rejected the women's claims on the basis that they had been unable to establish that they feared persecution *for reasons of* their membership of a particular social group.[27] The House of Lords unanimously allowed both appeals, holding that Mrs K had a well founded fear of persecution as a member of her husband's family, and Miss Fornah either as a Sierra Leonean woman, or (more narrowly) as an uninitiated or intact indigenous woman in Sierra Leone.

Without a doubt, the House of Lords' decision in *K* and *Fornah* is important in establishing a gender-sensitive, gender-inclusive interpretation of the 1951 Refugee Convention. Its contextual and straightforward approach to the Convention and, in particular, the definition of a particular social group, widely acknowledged as the Convention ground with the least clarity, has won support from organisations and lawyers working with women in the fields of asylum and immigration.[28] It has been recognised as setting out a 'bracing new approach to women's rights',[29] with Lady Hale at its helm 'undertaking herself *and urging on others* a gender-sensitive approach to the interpretation of the law'.[30] Lady Hale's opinion begins, as one might expect, by up-fronting its gender-focus:

> My Lords, my noble and learned friend, Lord Bingham of Cornhill, has said everything that needs to be said about each of these appeals. The answer in each case is so blindingly obvious that it must be a mystery to some why either of them had to reach this House. I would like to add a few words only because each case, in its different way, raises issues of gender-related and gender-specific persecution.[31]

Over the course of her opinion she details the gender-specific nature of the harm feared by the women. Taking each appeal in turn she praises the adjudicator who

26 Although both women had been granted indefinite leave to remain in the UK under art 3 of the ECHR (prohibition of torture and inhuman and degrading treatment or punishment), the case continued to be of practical importance not only for the appellants who would enjoy stronger protection if recognised as refugees, but also in relation to the future use of UK jurisprudence in determining the application of the Refugee Convention in countries not party to the ECHR (*Fornah* [2006] [1], [121]).

27 *Fornah v Secretary of State for the Home Department* [2005] EWCA Civ 680; *K v Secretary of State for Home Department* [2004] EWCA Civ 986.

28 Mehvish Chaudhry, 'Particular Social Groups Post *Fornah*', *Journal of Immigration, Asylum and Nationality Law*, 2008, 21(2), 137; Refugee Women's Resource Project @ AsylumAid, *Women's Asylum News*, Issue 64, October 2006, pp. 1–4; Rights of Women, *Focus on Women*, Issue 6, 2007, p. 4; Linda Tsang, 'Lawyer of the Week', *The Times*, 28 November 2006.

29 Leader, 'In Praise of . . . Lady Hale of Richmond'.

30 Tsang, 'Lawyer of the Week' (emphasis added).

31 [2006] UKHL 46 [83].

allowed Mrs K's first appeal for his 'admirable' recognition of the full extent of Mrs K's situation in accepting not only the rape (which K had understandably not mentioned when first arriving in the UK) but also the risk to Mrs K's child as evidence, and as contributing to her fear of persecution,[32] before dismissing the 'sexist reasoning' embodied in the notion of 'primary' and 'secondary' members of a family,[33] which treats Mrs K as an 'adjunct' of her husband rather than having a claim to asylum in her own right.[34] After explaining, in some depth, the social context and physical realities of FGM,[35] Hale goes on to recognise the institutional gender-bias inherent in the 1951 Refugee Convention, and the extent to which women's refugee status has been refracted through 'a framework of male experiences'.[36] Her aim is to ensure that the many women across the world who flee because of fears similar to those of Mrs K and Miss Fornah are seen to be 'just as worthy' of its full protection as the men fleeing 'persecution because of their dissident political views',[37] who typically and more easily falling within its remit. In this way her opinion highlights, and contributes to, the world waking up

> to the fact that women as a sex may be persecuted in ways which are different from the ways in which men are persecuted and that they may be persecuted because of the inferior status accorded to their gender in their home society.[38]

However, the particular significance of *K* and *Fornah* for our purposes lies in the *similarity* between Lady Hale's opinion and those of her male colleagues. This is particularly notable in relation to Miss Fornah's claim.[39] Unusually, her claim was heard by a woman judge in each of the latter stages of its appeal – Lady Hale in

32 ibid.
33 As established in *Quijano v Secretary of State for the Home Department* [1997] Imm AR 227.
34 [2006] UKHL 46 [105].
35 ibid., [90–96]. It is important to note here postcolonial feminist criticism of the application of human rights framework in cases such as *Fornah*. These suggest that often gender and culture are prioritised over cultural racism and colonialism. However, as Harriet Samuels argues, noting Lady Hale's reference to the controversies surrounding FGM, in *Fornah* 'equality norms are used to de-exoticise FGM. It is seen as part of a global pattern of violence against women and this makes [FGM itself] seem less extraordinary' (Harriet Samuels, 'Women, Culture and Human Rights: Feminist Interventions in Human Rights Law?' in Reza Banakar (ed), *Rights in Context: Law and Justice in Late Modern Society*, Dartmouth: Ashgate, 2010, 317, p. 327).
36 UNHCR, *Guidelines on Gender-Related Persecution* (2002) [5] in [2006] UKHL 46 [85].
37 [2006] UKHL 46 [115] (Lady Hale).
38 ibid. See also Lady Hale's discussion of the gender dimension to the persecution suffered by Mrs B in *(Hoxha) v Special Adjudicator* [2005] UKHL 19 [30–40].
39 This is likely because the decision in relation to Mrs K's claim was relatively straightforward once the Court of Appeal decision in *Quijano* had been overruled ([2006] UKHL 46 [104–107] (Lady Hale)).

the House of Lords and Lady Justice Arden in the Court of Appeal – allowing for a comparison of two senior women judges, their reasoning and their influence on the outcome and decision-making processes in the case.

In the Court of Appeal, the judges split along gender lines: the male majority made, in Helena Kennedy's word's, 'all the right noises about how awful FGM is' before taking 'sanctuary in a mean and narrow interpretation of the law' to reject Miss Fornah's claim.[40] This view was underlined by Lady Justice Arden's dissent which, in contrast to her male colleagues' focus on an individualistic understanding of FGM and over-emphasis of its societal acceptance in Sierra Leone, drew attention to the broader, group-focused conception of harm required by the Convention and the effect of FGM in marking out uninitiated women in Sierra Leone *as a group* for persecution.[41] Her different perspective and lone position as the only woman on the court did not go unnoticed. 'Yet again', the legal support group Asylum Aid commented, 'women's rights remain in the realm of the minority opinion and that this minority opinion is a female one seems no coincidence'.[42]

The Court of Appeal decision, therefore, stands as an example – like *Radmacher* and *R v J* – of a case where the woman judge offers an alternative analysis, providing a mouthpiece for a different way of looking at the issues at hand, but which in the end comes to nothing as she is outvoted by her male colleagues. It is not hard to imagine that, had the case instead been heard by a panel of two women and one man, the result would have been different. On this basis, Kennedy suggested that the Court of Appeal's 'appalling' decision in *Fornah*

> argues for more women judges in our courts. It is cases like these which high-light problems of gender issues still continuing in our courtroom because the men involved do not realise that their own mindset is often what determines their approach to law.[43]

But this suggests that, although increased numbers of women on the Bench will even out some injustices of the kind we see in the Court of Appeal in *Fornah*, making them a rarer occurrence, we will, inevitably, be left in cases like this with splits along gender lines. And, if so, the decision the court reaches and hence the fate of the parties will turn on the luck of the draw and which judges they happen to get. This is not in and of itself a particularly strong argument for more women judges. However, when we turn to the House of Lords' decision we can see a different, brighter future.

40 Helena Kennedy, Debate on female genital mutilation, HL Hansard, 844–68, 856, 8 December 2005.
41 [2005] EWCA Civ 680 [63].
42 Refugee Women's Resource Project @ AsylumAid, *Women's Asylum News*, Issue 52, July/August 2005, p. 5.
43 Kennedy, 'Debate on female genital mutilation'. See also Rights of Women, *Focus on Women*.

Unlike their male colleagues in the Court of Appeal, the Law Lords had little problem agreeing with Lady Hale that Miss Fornah was deserving of refugee status under the Convention.[44] However, what is interesting about the opinions of the Law Lords, is not just that they reached the same *conclusion* as Lady Hale, but also that they appear to follow her lead in adopting a gender-aware and gender-informed approach to the issues at hand. As a result, they 'convincingly dispel the myth that FGM is simply a custom performed by women on women, and provide a powerful recognition that the practice constitutes a blatant breach of human rights in male-dominated societies'.[45] Lord Justice Auld's attempt to suggest that, although 'evil', FGM 'is not, in the circumstances in which it is practised in Sierra Leone, discriminatory in such a way as to set those who undergo it apart from society',[46] receives short shrift from Lord Bingham: 'FGM may ensure a young woman's acceptance in Sierra Leonean society, but she is accepted on the basis of institutionalised inferiority . . . FGM is an extreme expression and very cruel expression of male dominance . . . and of the discrimination to which all women in Sierra Leone are subject'.[47] To similar effect, Lord Hope held:

> There is a strong element of sexual discrimination in Sierra Leone where patriarchy is deeply entrenched which serves to identify females in that country as a particular social group . . . Discrimination involves making unfair or unjust distinctions to the disadvantage of one group or class of people as compared with others. Women in Sierra Leone are discriminated against because the law will not protect them from female genital mutilation.[48]

Indeed, read together it is, at times, difficult to distinguish Lady Hale's reasoning from those of her colleagues. Compare the following examples rebutting the weight given by the majority of the Court of Appeal to the fact that FGM is typically carried out by women:

> For various reasons – compulsion, or a desire to curry favour with the perse-cuting group, or an attempt to conceal membership of the persecuted group – members of the persecuted group may be involved in carrying out the

---

44   Sharon Pickering suggests that the law lords show a 'degree of contempt' toward the earlier judg-ments which adopt, in Pickering's words, 'unduly restrictive readings of the Convention' and in which 'legal platitudes concerning the "regrettable" nature and outcomes of gendered discrimina-tion and persecution have predominated over the difficult legal work necessary to include gender-based violence within the meaning of the Convention' (*Women, Boarders and Violence: Current Issues in Aslyum, Forced Migration, and Trafficking*, New York: Springer, 2010, p. 77).
45   Stephen Cragg, 'Legislation update', *The Times*, 24 October 2006.
46   ibid., [1] and [44].
47   [2006] UKHL 46 [31].
48   ibid., [54].

persecution. Here, for whatever misguided reasons, women inflict the mutilation on other women. The persecution is just as real and the need for protection in this country is just as compelling, irrespective of the sex of the person carrying out the mutilation.[49]

It is nothing to the point that FGM in Sierra Leone is carried out by women ... Most vicious initiatory rituals are in fact perpetuated by those who were themselves subject to the ritual as initiates and see no reason why others should not share the experience.[50]

It cannot make any difference that it is practised by women upon women and girls. Those who have already been persecuted are often expected to perpetuate the persecution of succeeding generations, as any reader of *Tom Brown's Schooldays* knows.[51]

What the House of Lords' opinions in *Fornah* show is how the presence of women judges and the distinctive perspectives and arguments they might bring need not exist in parallel and in contrast to the arguments and reasoning of their male counterparts. For here we see arguments first made by Lady Justice Arden and reaffirmed by Lady Hale also taken up by the other (male) judges in the House of Lords.[52] So, while the outcome of the Court of Appeal stands as a reminder that the insights women judges can offer will not always be endorsed – and that, to this extent, the possibility of women judges making a difference to judicial decision-making depends (at present) on their male counterparts being open to new arguments and alternative viewpoints – we can see in the House of Lords' decision a clear, positive example of the difference women judges can make. As *Fornah* shows, the promise of a diverse judiciary is not the promise of a multiplicity of approaches and values each fighting for recognition, but of a judiciary enriched by its openness to viewpoints previously marginalised and of decision-making which is better for being better-informed.[53]

Redressing judicial disadvantage

The argument that the insights and perspectives of women judges might usefully be combined with those of their male counterparts to produce better

---

49 ibid., [81] (Lord Rodger).
50 ibid., [31] (Lord Bingham).
51 ibid., [110] (Lady Hale).
52 In fact, three of Lady Hale's four colleagues were more persuaded by Arden LJ's dissenting formulation of the definition of the relevant social group for the purposes of the Convention (ibid., [56] (Lord Hope), [74] (Lord Rodger) and [119] (Lord Brown)).
53 Of course, a BME perspective was missing in both the Court of Appeal and House of Lords. Given the postcolonial feminist criticism of the human rights rhetoric underpinning cases such as *Fornah*, without doubt the decision-making process would have been improved further by the inclusion of perspectives and insights of women from these groups.

decision-making might seem to apply only or at least be most clear at appellate level, where men and women can decide cases side-by-side. However, even when judges work alone, there is no reason to think that they work in complete isolation from each other, or that the reasoning and insights of other judges do not influence their decisions. Although (strictly) past decisions are authoritative only for the particular legal rule they set down, judgments have a significance beyond this. The observations made by the judge, the arguments canvassed and referenced in the judgment are all reported, read and used by those wanting to understand the law and make legal arguments of their own. This means that the insights and arguments of women judges have a reach beyond the cases in which they sit and those questions where these arguments have prevailed. As more women judges write judgments, their reasoning and observations in these cases will become part of the broader catalogue of legal materials and judicial knowledge that judges draw on when reaching their decisions. So, a judge who has had the benefit of working in a judiciary with more women is more likely to be attuned to a wider range of perspectives than one who derives his knowledge from a single (male) source.

It is just this idea of a broader received judicial wisdom, which has been the target of feminist legal scholars, who have for some time sought to expose and challenge the extent to which judicial knowledge and decision-making is often grounded in (masculine) gendered assumptions or sexual stereotypes, with the result that there is sometimes a disjuncture between (some) judges' 'common sense' understanding of a particular event and how women experience it.[54] This is typically illustrated by examples where male judges have grounded their judgments in distorted understandings of the facts or issues at hand or have invoked particular, problematic gender stereotypes, such as the comments of a Manitoba Queen's Bench judge who described a convicted rapist as a 'clumsy Don Juan', suggesting that his victim's attire and the fact she was 'looking to party' meant that 'sex was in the air'.[55] The same goes for the suggestion of a county court judge in the UK, in a case involving workplace stress, that the employer ought to have been aware the female manager was likely to 'crack up' not only because the employer had placed disproportionate burdens on her but *because she was a woman*.[56]

---

54 Regina Graycar, 'The Gender of Judgments: An Introduction' in Margaret Thornton (ed), *Public and Private – Feminist Legal Debates*, Oxford: Oxford University Press, 1995, p. 262; Regina Graycar, 'The Gender of Judgments: Some Reflections on "Bias"', *University of British Columbia Law Review*, 32, 1998, 1; Jennifer Nedelsky, 'Judgment, Diversity and Relational Autonomy' in Ronald Beiner and Jennifer Nedelsky (eds), *Judgment, Imagination and Politics*, Maryland: Rowman and Littlefield, 2001, 103 pp. 114–115; Rosemary Hunter, 'Can *Feminist* Judges Make a Difference?', *International Journal of the Legal Profession*, 15(1–2), 2008, 7.

55 Mike McIntyre, 'No jail for rapist because victim "wanted to party"', *National Post*, 24 February 2011.

56 *Bonser v UK Coal Mining Ltd* [2003] EWCA Civ 1296 [27] discussed in Jesse Elvin, 'The continuing use of problematic sexual stereotypes in judicial decision-making', *Feminist Legal Studies*, 18(3), 2010, 275.

Or the remarks of a New York judge that domestic abuse cases are a 'waste of the court's time' and that most women asked to get 'smacked around'.[57] It is tempting, as when Regina Graycar compiled a similar list back in 1995,[58] to assume that these comments are anachronistic, relics of a time when such attitudes were commonplace and uncontroversial. In fact, all of these comments were made within the last 10 years.

However, while it is clear that 'crude and problematic [sexual] stereotypes' continue to find their way into judgment,[59] these examples may prove to be something of a red herring. After all, most, if not all, would agree that these comments are inappropriate. There is a perhaps greater danger of more subtle distortions, found in a judicial 'common sense', informed and shaped by the same narrow range of experiences and perspectives, which have become so familiar that we fail to see them as partial.[60] The problem here lies not simply in the partiality of these views, but that they are then able to assume a superior status and legitimacy by virtue of their speaker, which in turn works to exclude or marginalise alternative viewpoints:

> There is no place in their judgments for multiple and perhaps contradictory 'experiences' of the same event; and no awareness of the manner in which their own experience is inescapably perspectival in nature.[61]

It has been suggested that a woman judge, by adding to the judiciary's common or general knowledge by incorporating women's stories into their 'common sense' understanding of the world, is able to go some way to readdressing this disparity. Rosemary Hunter, in her study of Justice Marcia Neave, a judge on the Victorian Court of Appeal, argues (albeit when focusing on Neave's difference as a *feminist* judge) that 'the most obvious and common way' she 'made a difference', was by

> making generalised statements which brought previously excluded social experiences into legal discourse, and in some instances challenged gender bias, to expand and transform law's 'common knowledge' of the world.[62]

---

57 Kenneth Lovett, 'Judge resigns over "wife beat" talk', *New York Post*, 7 January 2004 discussed in Joan D Klein, 'Remarks', *University of Toledo Law Review*, 36, 2004–2005, 911, p. 918.

58 Graycar, 'The Gender of Judgments', pp. 269–271.

59 Elvin, 'Problematic sexual stereotypes', p. 277.

60 Hunter, 'Can *Feminist* Judges Make a Difference?', p. 11; Graycar, 'Some Reflections on "Bias"', p. 10.

61 Moira Gatens, *Imaginary Bodies – Ethics, Power and Corporeality*, London: Routledge, 1996, p. 138.

62 Rosemary Hunter, 'An Account of Feminist Judging' in Rosemary Hunter, Clare McGlynn and Erika Rackley, *Feminist Judgments: From Theory to Practice*, Oxford: Hart Publishing, 2010), 30, p. 38. Although Hunter focuses on *feminist* judges the same point can be made here in relation to women judges (Hunter, 'Can *Feminist* Judges Make a Difference?', pp. 8–10). This is not to suggest that women judges and feminist judges are one and the same. Clearly, just as there can be male feminist judges, not all women judges will identify with or display feminist politics. The point here is that

Of course, the woman (and indeed feminist) judge needs to be careful how she does this, not least because the doctrine of judicial notice does not always pre-empt or defeat suspicions of bias.[63] Nonetheless as the number of women judges increases, particularly in the higher courts, the insights and perspectives of women will become part of – and change – the broader body of legal knowledge to which all judges and counsel (whatever their predisposition) are exposed and with which they must engage. And over time, these values and insights will benefit not only the litigants who appear before them but, as these arguments become part of the jurisprudence of a particular jurisdiction, *all* litigants. In this way, women judges may enrich the judicial decision-making process and begin to redress the 'disad-vantage'[64] of their colleagues, *even when they are not sitting next to them on the Bench*. One example of women judges adding to this pool of common judicial knowledge and of this knowledge then being tapped into by other (male) judges is *Parkinson v St James and Seacroft Hospital NHS Trust*.[65]

Parkinson v St James and Seacroft Hospital NHS Trust

Described by Lady Hale in 2005 as one obvious exception to the view that 'the great majority of her judgments could have been written or spoken by a man',[66] *Parkinson v St James and Seacroft Hospital NHS Trust* is the second in a trilogy of so-called 'wrongful birth' cases decided over a four-year period at the turn of this century. At issue was the extent of a doctor's liability in cases where a child is conceived following a negligently performed vasectomy or sterilisation procedure: should the doctor be responsible for the full costs of the child's upkeep or should the parents be expected to bear the financial burden of bringing up a child they had taken positive steps to ensure they would not have?[67]

---

the presence of women on the Bench provides for the opportunity for men to draw on women's viewpoints, while accepting that our expectation of a woman judge who does not identify as femi-nist will be different from one who does and that a woman judge who does not identify as a feminist may be more likely to reach the same conclusion as her male colleagues.

63 Judicial notice enables judges to make use of 'their general information' and 'knowledge of common affairs which men of ordinary intelligence possess' (Hunter, 'An Account of Feminist Judging', p. 39). See further, Rosemary Hunter, 'Justice Marcia Neave: Case Study of a Feminist Judge' in Ulrike Schultz and Gisela Shaw (eds), *Gender and Judging*, Oxford: Hart Publishing, forthcoming.

64 Brenda Hale, 'Equality in the Judiciary: A Tale of Two Continents', 10th Pilgrim Fathers' Lecture, 24 October 2003.

65 [2001] EWCA Civ 560. This section draws on arguments I made in Erika Rackley, 'Difference in the House of Lords', *Social and Legal Studies*, 15(2), 2006, p. 163.

66 Lady Hale, 'Making a Difference? Why We Need a More Diverse Judiciary', *Northern Ireland Legal Quarterly*, 56(3), 2005, 281, p. 289.

67 The cases deserve fuller treatment than is possible here. For an excellent and insightful discussion of this problematic area of case law see further Nicolette Priaulx, *The Harm Paradox: Tort Law and the Unwanted Child in an Era of Choice*, Abingdon: Routledge-Cavendish, 2007.

In the first of these cases, *McFarlane v Tayside Health Authority*,[68] the majority of the House of Lords, overruling around 15 years of settled law, limited the doctor's liability to the mother's claim for pain and suffering involved with the pregnancy and childbirth and the immediate costs related to this. The doctor's duty of care, they concluded, only extended so far as was 'fair, just and reasonable', and it would be a step too far to compensate the parents for the full costs of raising the child. One reason for this was that the claim fell foul of the courts' usual exclusionary rule for recovery of pure economic losses. Moreover, as Lord Millett argued,

> [t]he law must take the birth of a normal, healthy baby to be a blessing, not a detriment . . . It would be repugnant to [society's] own sense of value to do otherwise. It would be morally offensive to regard a normal, healthy baby as more trouble and expense than it is worth.[69]

Just two years later, *Parkinson* came before a Court of Appeal panel which included Lady Justice Hale. Here the facts were slightly different: the child born after the negligently performed procedure was not healthy but disabled. This allowed the court to distinguish *McFarlane* and to hold that the mother could recover for the *additional* costs involved in bringing up a disabled child. Lady Justice Hale argued: '[t]his analysis treats a disabled child as having exactly the same worth as a non-disabled child. It affords him the same dignity and status. It simply acknowledges that he costs more'.[70] However, while the Court of Appeal's decision was grounded, in the first instance, on the simple economic reality that disabled children cost more to raise than healthy children, Lady Justice Hale used her judgment to offer a vivid account of the experience of pregnancy, childbirth and childcare:

> Not surprisingly, their Lordships did not go into detail about what is entailed in the invasion of bodily integrity caused by conception, pregnancy and child birth. But it is worthwhile spelling out the more obvious features . . . From the moment a woman conceives, profound physical changes take place in her body and continue to take place not only for the duration of the pregnancy but for some time thereafter . . . along with these physical and psychological consequences goes a severe curtailment of personal autonomy. Literally, one's life is no longer just one's own but also someone else's . . . The responsible pregnant woman forgoes or moderates the pleasure of alcohol and tobacco. She changes her diet. She submits to regular and intrusive medical examinations. She takes certain sorts of exercise and forgoes others. She can

68 [2000] 2 AC 59.
69 ibid., pp. 113–114.
70 [2001] EWCA Civ 560 [90].

no longer wear her favourite clothes. She is unlikely to be able to continue in paid employment throughout the pregnancy or to return to it immediately thereafter. The process of giving birth is rightly termed 'labour'. It is hard work, often painful and sometime dangerous.[71]

She continues,

The labour does not stop when the child is born. Bringing up children is hard work. The obligation to provide or make acceptable and safe arrangements for the child's care and supervision lasts for 24 hours a day, 7 days a week, all year round, until the child becomes old enough to take care of himself.[72]

Here Lady Justice Hale offers a judicial account of pregnancy and motherhood informed (one can only assume) by her own experiences as a mother.[73] For while this account is intelligible to those who have not given birth, in the first instance it is more likely to be made by a mother[74] – someone who has in fact had these experiences – who can relate the full reality and magnitude of pregnancy and childbirth. For this reason, and as Lady Justice Hale notes at the outset, it is not surprising that we do not see the all male panel in *McFarlane* addressing the physical, emotional and social impact of pregnancy, nor that they prefer instead to deal in the more familiar currency of the monetary costs of bringing up a child.[75] Indeed, the real significance of this distinctive perspective motherhood provides, and which Lady Justice Hale brings to the case, is that it shows that the focus on the economic implications of the defendant's negligence is too narrow. For, notwithstanding the (substantial) economic costs of bringing up a child, the real, immediate effect of the claimant's (unwanted) pregnancy are deeply personal, involving far-reaching changes to her body, lifestyle and opportunities; that is, 'the invasion of the mother's right to bodily integrity and autonomy' combined with the imposition of considerable and lengthy caring responsibilities for a child she never intended to have.[76] So, while the authority of *McFarlane* meant that the Court of Appeal in *Parkinson* could do no more than allow recovery for the increased monetary costs entailed by the child's disability, here Lady Justice Hale showed why to see these claims as concerned primarily with the *financial*

---

71   ibid., [64–68].

72   ibid., [70–71]

73   JK Mason, 'Wrongful Pregnancy, Wrongful Birth and Wrongful Terminology', *Edinburgh Law Review*, 6, 2002, 46, p. 64.

74   This is not to suggest that it is not possible for a man (particularly an engaged father) to relate to the reality and magnitude of pregnancy and childbirth. It is, however, to suggest that this is less likely and that men are less likely to put this into judgment.

75   A point that she had made much earlier as an academic in her path-breaking text on women and law (Susan Atkins and Brenda Hoggett, *Women and the Law*, Oxford: Blackwell, 1984, p. 90).

76   [2001] EWCA Civ 560 [73] (Lady Justice Hale).

implications of parenthood was to set off on the wrong foot and to miss what was, in many ways, the principal 'harm' the defendants caused.

The decision in *Parkinson* was subsequently extended by the majority of the Court of Appeal, again including Lady Justice Hale, in *Rees v Darlington Memorial Hospital*[77] to allow a severely visually impaired mother to recover the additional costs of raising a child attributable to her disability. On appeal, however, a majority of the House of Lords rejected the Court of Appeal's decision.[78] Yet, for present purposes, what is significant is that the majority nonetheless awarded the claimant a conventional sum of £15,000 on the basis that the defendant's action amounted to an invasion of Ms Rees's bodily autonomy. The award was intended, in Lord Bingham's words, to 'afford some measure of recognition of the wrong done. And afford a more ample measure of justice than the pure *McFarlane* rule':

> I question the fairness of a rule which denies the victim of a legal wrong any recompense at all beyond an award immediately related to the unwanted pregnancy and birth. The spectre of well-to-do parents plundering the National Health Service should not blind one to other realities: that of the single mother with young children, struggling to make ends meet and counting the days until her children are of an age to enable her to work more hours and so enable the family to live a less straitened existence; the mother whose burning ambition is to put domestic chores so far as possible behind her and embark on a new career or resume an old one. Examples can be multiplied. To speak of losing the freedom to limit the size of one's family is to mask the real loss suffered in a situation of this kind. This is that a parent, particularly (even today) the mother, has been denied, through the negligence of another, the opportunity to live her life in the way that she wished and planned.[79]

Although the possibility of a fixed sum being awarded on the basis of the claimant's lost autonomy was first mooted by Lord Millett in *McFarlane*, his concern was only with the parents' autonomy in determining the size of their family.[80] As Lord Bingham notes in the passage above, however, the autonomy implications of unwanted pregnancy and parenthood reach far beyond this. And, in so doing, we see the majority of the House of Lords accepting the strength of the broader arguments first raised by Lady Justice Hale in *Parkinson*. For, although the law lords in *Rees* differed as to whether justice was better served through the imposition of a conventional award or creating an exception to *McFarlane*, it is clear that all are motivated by a deeper understanding of extent and impact of the legal wrong or

---

77 [2003] UKHL 52.
78 Interestingly, the minority in *Rees* included Lord Steyn and Lord Hope who, although in the majority in *McFarlane*, were now of the view that justice required an exception to the *McFarlane* rule against recovery (itself an exception to the usual tortious principles allowing recovery).
79 [2003] UKHL 52 [8].
80 [2000] 2 AC 59 p. 114; [2003] UKHL 52 [122].

harm inflicted by the doctor's negligence. Between *McFarlane* and *Rees*, we see then an important shift in the House of Lords' characterisation of the real injury involved in wrongful birth claims, a shift anticipated and, we might surmise, precipitated (at least in part) by Lady Justice Hale's judgment in *Parkinson*.

In fact, there is little doubt that, in Lady Hale's words, despite 'losing the battle', she 'won the war'.[81] Her judgment in *Parkinson* deliberately and dramatically altered the adjudicative landscape, exposing the limitations of a judiciary comprised entirely of men considering an issue which men and women experience and look at 'rather differently'.[82] However, the point here is not simply that Lady Justice Hale took a different starting point from and revealed a different under-standing of the gist of these claims to the male judges, but that this understanding, once expressed and heard, was then taken up by her male colleagues, although not perhaps in quite the same way Lady Justice Hale herself might have envis-aged. So, notwithstanding the fact that the status of *Parkinson* and the exception to *McFarlane* it introduced remain in doubt, it is clear that Lady Justice Hale's judgment has had and shall continue to have an effect on the development of the law and on the reasoning of judges charged with deciding these cases. Her pres-ence and insights not only revealed the limitations of the approach taken in *McFarlane*, but also the benefit the introduction of a different perspective can have on the decision-making process. The significance of Hale LJ's judgment in *Parkinson* lies not simply in the fact that it was written by a woman but in the extent to which it highlighted her (male) colleagues' 'blindness' to the real issue and enabled them to reach a different, *better* conclusion. Her broader perspective, in Nicky Priaulx's words

> offered a different perspective for the judicial forum to take into account, a dialogue that embraces a diversity of experiential perspectives – an opportu-nity [for the other judges] to start to 'get it'. And consequently, for those who

81 Hale, 'Making a Difference?', p. 290. And, of course, as Lady Hale has recent suggested, had the cases been conceptualised on the basis of personal autonomy rather than pure economic loss 'from the beginning we wouldn't have had some of the anomalies we now have in compensating' claims for wrongful birth (Lady Hale, Panel Discussion on 'Women, Feminism and the Law', Law Society Junior Lawyers Division Webinar, November 2011).

82 Brenda Hale, 'The Value of Life and the Cost of Living: Damages for Wrongful Birth', *British Actuarial Journal*, 7, 2001, 747. This view is supported by the dissenting judgment of Lord Millett in *McFarlane* and Christian Witting's suggestion that Mrs McFarlane's pregnancy did not amount to orthodox physical damage but rather was 'socially constructed' as such: 'the mother's conception was an entirely natural event that her physiological constitution was designed to induce and accommodate' ('Physical Damage in Negligence', *Cambridge Law Journal*, 6(1), 2002, 189, p. 192). This argument has encountered strong criticism from women and men (see, eg, Joanne Conaghan, 'Tort Law and Feminist Critique', *Current Legal Problems*, 56, 2003, 175; Priaulx, *The Harm Paradox*, pp. 33–38; Donal Nolan, 'New Forms of Damage in Negligence', *Modern Law Review*, 70(1), 2007, 59, pp. 71–77; Janice Richardson, 'The Concept of Harm for Actions in Wrongful Birth: Nature and Pre-Modern Views of Women', *Australian Feminist Law Journal*, 35, 2011, 127.

lack firsthand knowledge of the experiences of conception, pregnancy and childbirth, such an experiential deficit may not matter, *if* met by a willingness to integrate the voices of women.[83]

A diverse judiciary is a better judiciary

So, where does this leave us? What is clear is that the judiciary is weaker and its ability to do justice is hampered, the *less* judges are exposed to perspectives and experiences that are different to their own, and hence the more limited the range of viewpoints and insights they have access to. Women judges benefit the judiciary not just in the insights and experiences they can bring to their own decision-making but in the contribution they make to judging, and hence to the law, more generally. As Jennifer Nedelsky notes:

> What makes it possible for us to genuinely judge, to move beyond our idiosyncrasies and preferences, is our capacity to achieve an 'enlargement of mind'. We do this by taking different perspectives into account. This is the path out of the blindness of our subjective private conditions. The more views we are able to take into account, the less likely we are to be locked into one perspective, whether through fear, anger or ignorance. It is the capacity for 'enlargement of mind' that makes autonomous, impartial judgment possible.[84]

Women judges can through their interaction with their colleagues make a difference to the quality and substance of judicial decision-making across the board. As Lord Justice Etherton notes, 'a well reasoned and well presented minority view may be effective in shifting the position of the majority to a more qualified and compromising position than it otherwise would have taken'.[85] And so it is likely that women judges will play an educative role, informing and improving judicial knowledge and ensuring that 'relevant arguments are not overlooked or brushed aside and that insupportable preconceptions are challenged'.[86] As Lady Hale notes,

> [i]t becomes harder to give voice to sexist or racist views if there is a woman or minority ethnic judge around the lunch table, no longer a servant but an equal. Better still, perhaps, if they are voiced and can then be challenged.[87]

83 Priaulx, *The Harm Paradox*, p. 47.
84 Jennifer Nedelsky, 'Embodied Diversity and the Challenges to Law', *McGill Law Journal*, 42, 1997, 91, p. 107.
85 Etherton, 'Liberty, the Archetype and Diversity', p. 745.
86 ibid., p. 746.
87 Hale, 'A Minority Opinion?', p. 334.

Of course, this is not to suggest that an increase in the number of women in the judiciary will automatically mean that *all* (male) judges will immediately become more enlightened or open to certain views, any more than 30 years of increasing numbers of women among barristers has impacted on entrenched views of, for example rape and rape complainants, in certain areas of the Bar.[88] Nor is it to suggest that *every* woman judge will (be able to or willing to) challenge problematic sexual stereotypes deployed by (some) male judges.[89] However, what we can expect, and indeed can see happening, is not only that the presence of women judges will have an impact on the reasoning of their male colleagues in the appellate courts, but that an increase in the number of women judges across the judiciary will inform and improve its processes and reasoning generally.

Decision-making is better when better-informed, and judges with a broader knowledge are better placed to decide well than those whose knowledge is more limited. Insofar as this knowledge comes from, or is reinforced by, their colleagues in the judiciary then the more diverse this group is, the more varied and helpful the body of knowledge and collective wisdom they will have to draw on when making their decisions. None of this is contentious. As Richard Posner has argued, '[t]he heterogeneity of the judiciary encourages a proliferation of varied insights and retards group polarisation, and at the same time anchors law more firmly in durable public opinion'.[90] A more diverse Bench expands the judiciary's common knowledge, and so the result of judicial diversity is not, in the end, greater variation and divergence in judicial decision-making, but rather *better* decisions; the contributions of women judges become part of the law and legal argument through cross-fertilisation with the viewpoints and perspectives already expressed through the law. Nor is it the first time this has been suggested. In 1921, former US Supreme Court Justice Benjamin Cardozo suggested that '[t]he eccentricities of judges balance one another . . . out of the attrition of diverse minds there is beaten something which has a constancy and uniformity and average value greater than its component elements'.[91] More recently, Lady Hale made a similar point in the course of making what she termed 'a positive case for judicial diversity' in her Maccabaean Lecture in Jurisprudence at the British Academy:

> I do believe that a more diverse judiciary will be a better judiciary. Diversity of background and experience enriches the law. Women lead different lives

---

88 Jennifer Temkin, 'Prosecuting and Defending Rape: Perspectives from the Bar', *Journal of Law and Society*, 27, 2000, 219, p. 225.

89 See, eg, the Court of Appeal's decision in *R v Clinton* [2012] EWCA Crim 2 in which the Lord Chief Justice, giving the only judgment, effectively rewrote the loss of control defence (established in the Coroners and Justice Act 2009) despite the presence of two women judges in the case (one at trial and one in the Court of Appeal).

90 Posner, *How Judges Think*, p. 255.

91 Benjamin N Cardozo, *The Nature of the Judicial Process*, New Haven: Yale University Press, 1921, p. 177.

from men, largely because we have visibly different bodies from men. This is not to say that all women are the same, any more than that all men are the same . . . But by and large, the interaction between our own internal sense of being a woman and the outside world's perception of us as women leads to a different set of everyday and lifetime experiences . . . It is just as important that these different experiences should play their part in shaping and administering the law as the experiences of a certain class of men have played for centuries. They will not always make a difference but sometimes they will and should.[92]

The argument should by now be clear: the judiciary is enriched in sum, through the diversity of its parts. The judiciary is stronger, and the justice dispensed better, the more varied the perspectives and experiences that are involved in its decision-making: 'a more diverse judiciary is a better judiciary. And a better judiciary means better justice'.[93]

Here then we have an argument for the real value of a diverse judiciary. And, unlike arguments for diversity grounded in legitimacy and equity, this is an argument which turns on its head the traditional rejoinder to moves to increase judicial diversity: that, notwithstanding the good of a diverse judiciary, appointments must always be made on merit and hence irrespective of a candidate's gender, race, ethnicity, sexuality and so on. If a diverse judiciary is a better judiciary, a judiciary which is better placed to make better decisions, diversity and merit go hand in hand, anyone who has an interest in ensuring that our judiciary is the best it can be also has a reason for seeing that it is as diverse as it can be. Appointment on merit, far from impeding the pursuit of diversity, provides an argument for it.

Maximising diversity, maximising merit

Merit is the 'bedrock' of the Judicial Appointment Commission's (JAC) selection criteria,[94] the one non-negotiable criterion for choosing judges.[95] And why not? After all, when it comes to appointing judges, it seems obvious that the best appointments are those who will do the job the best. As Christopher Stephens,

---

92 Hale, 'A Minority Opinion?', p. 331.
93 Lord Falconer, 'Increasing Judicial Diversity', Women Lawyers' Forum, London, 5 March 2005. See also, Sherrilyn A Ifill, 'Judicial Diversity', *Green Bag*, 13, 2D, 2009, 45; Jennifer Nedelsky, 'Judgment, Diversity and Relational Autonomy', p. 118; Hale, 'A Minority Opinion?', p. 331; Terence Etherton, 'Liberty, the Archetype and Diversity: A Philosophy of Judging', *Public Law*, 2010, 727, p. 728; Cheryl Thomas, *Judicial Diversity in the United Kingdom and Other Jurisdictions: A Review of Research, Policies and Practices*, London: The Commission for Judicial Appointments, 2005 [1.7].
94 Baroness Prashar, 'Speech by Baroness Prashar', London School of Economics Student Law Society, 22 February 2007.
95 Constitutional Reform Act 2005, s 63.

Chair of the JAC, explained to the House of Lords Constitution Committee: 'if merit is the cornerstone of what we do, it is our statutory duty to find the very best person. The very best person is not the second-best or third-best person'.[96] But this seems to put the appointment of merit on a collision course with attempts to secure greater judicial diversity. For whatever the legitimacy and equality gains of having more women on the Bench, appointment on merit requires that, in all cases, we ask which candidate will make the best judge, whatever his or her sex. Appointment on merit requires an assessment of 'the relative ability of the candidate to perform the functions that will be required of them if they are appointed', it is not, and cannot be, concerned with 'the make-up of the judiciary as a whole'.[97] Merit seems to have not only the first, but also the last word on judicial appointment and diversity is its hostage: we will get more women only if and when they are good enough.[98] But any increase in diversity is then just a welcome side-effect of appointment on merit, or the lack of diversity a necessary evil. At most, diversity is left as a relevant consideration in judicial appointment only where merit runs out, where two or more candidates are seen to be equally meritorious, in which case the diversity 'gains' one might bring may provide a tie-breaker. And, even here, the extent to which diversity really has a role to play in practice may be doubted. While there is no reason to think that appointment on merit *never* leads to occasions where the merits of candidates are equally balanced and factors *other than merit* have to be taken into account in order to decide between them, there is similarly no reason to think that this is, and even less to rely on it being, a common occurrence.[99] Those seeking to argue for the importance of diversity in the judiciary and judicial appointments appear to have little room for manoeuvre: either they grasp the nettle and argue for appointments on some basis *other than* merit or they are reduced simply to claiming that the way we have gone about identifying merit has been distorted by misconceptions about what merit is and where it might be found, hoping that, when those misconceptions are addressed, a more diverse judiciary will emerge.

96 Christopher Stephens, Oral evidence, Constitution Committee Inquiry, 7 December 2011, Q347.
97 Jonathan Sumption, 'The Constitutional Reform Act 2005' in *Judicial Appointments: Balancing Independence, Accountability and Legitimacy*, London: Judicial Appointments Commission, 2010, p. 31, 36.
98 See, eg, Jonathan Sumption, Justice Committee, 'The work of the Judicial Appointments Commission', Minutes of Evidence, 7 September 2010, Q24.
99 Indeed, the JAC in response to the Advisory Panel on Judicial Diversity's Recommendation 21 that they make use of the positive action provisions included in the Equality Act 2010 suggested that these would never be 'relevant in practice': 'The JAC will always select on merit and has to date been able to distinguish between the relevant merits of different candidates based on a careful assessment of an applicant's entire profile and background' (Judicial Diversity Taskforce, *Improving Judicial Diversity Progress Towards Delivery of the 'Report of the Advisory Panel on Judicial Diversity 2010'*, London: Ministry of Justice, May 2011 (McNally Report), p. 33). It is clear, however, that the Lord Chancellor and others believe there is a benefit in the greater deployment of sections 158 and 159 of the Equalities Act 2010 (see discussion in Chapter 3, fn 138–139 and accompanying text).

Merit, dislodged

Those questioning the primacy of merit in judicial appointments are, in essence, questioning whether the best appointment is always the one who will make the best judge. On this view, we might say that while having a strong judiciary, full of the best judges we can get, is clearly important, it is not the only value we might want to promote in judicial appointments. So here, we might say, there is also a value in the public having confidence in the judiciary and this is threatened if the judiciary is not, at least broadly, representative of the society it serves. This then allows us to argue that it might be better, on occasion, to appoint candidates who, although good, are not the strongest – are not 'the best' – for the broader benefit this brings in terms of public confidence.[100] In other words, the good of having the strongest judiciary we can get and the good of having a judiciary which in fact has the public's confidence may sometimes point in different directions, and we might question whether it should always be the former which prevails. Advancing diversity, rather than simply being a welcome side effect of appointment on merit, might be placed at the heart of the appointments process allowing for the introduction of strong forms of positive action, quotas, targets and such like – the potential temporary cost to the quality of the judiciary is outweighed by the political objectives of, say, equality of opportunity, judicial legitimacy or democracy. To this extent, being a woman may be a quality which – given the current make-up of the judiciary – works to a candidate's advantage not because she deserves to be prioritised *as a woman* (for example, to remedy historical injustices), but rather because her inclusion will, through balancing the gender profile of the judiciary as a whole, make for a judiciary which has, say, greater public confidence or which promotes the message of gender parity. Although, of course, once the gender-imbalance is redressed, this potential 'advantage' is lost.

There are a number of problems with this approach. We might reasonably think that whatever public confidence gains a more diverse judiciary might bring would soon be lost if it was known that these judges were not there on their own merits. Few would agree that the gains of a more diverse judiciary should come at the cost of not appointing those best up to the job. It is not enough for a judge to 'pass muster'.[101] We might think that the application of the law and the pursuit of justice are so important that they can have no qualification, no conditions; that nothing ever justifies appointing candidates we think to be (even slightly) weaker, whatever other benefits this might bring. It is unlikely to find favour with those, like Lord Irvine, who believe that the concerns about the judiciary *as a whole* ought to have nothing whatsoever to do with individual appointments:

100 Kate Malleson, 'Justifying Gender Equality on the Bench: Why Difference Won't Do', *Feminist Legal Studies*, 11, 2003, 1, p. 17.
101 Lord Irvine, Oral evidence, Constitution Committee Inquiry, 6 July 2011, Q30.

[T]o assert that diversity is a component of merit is sleight of hand, and not a very skilful one at that. A more diverse judiciary is a desirable social objective, but . . . the merit principle should be paramount.[102]

On this view judicial appointments should adhere to the principle of what Thomas Legg describes as 'maximal' merit, that is the view that only the best candidate should be appointed and the purpose of the appointments process is to identify that candidate.[103]

Similarly, attempts to present this approach as somehow 'redefining' or 'rethinking' merit,[104] face the objection that there are not in fact arguments for appointment on merit at all. The tension between merit and diversity 'cannot be finessed away by redefining merit as somehow including reflectiveness of the community'.[105] The argument that appointment must be made on merit is the argument that the only basis on which judicial appointments should be made is who will do the best job, who will make the best judge. No doubt there are other gains that our judiciary might secure and so other bases upon which judicial appointments could be made. But to argue that considerations other than who would be the best judge are or should be relevant to judicial appointment is, in truth, not to redefine merit but to reject it as the sole basis for judicial appointment. Either judicial appointments are made on merit, that is on the basis of who will do the job the best, or on the basis of some other consideration, such as democratic legitimacy or promoting public confidence in the judiciary. It may be that there are good reasons for choosing the latter; say, for adopting a principle of so-called 'minimal' merit, allowing those making judicial appointments to look to some other policy objective once candidates have passed a minimum threshold.[106] But the upshot of this approach is that, to this extent, appointments will no longer be made simply on merit. Thus, while it may be possible to carve out some middle ground, some form of 'merit + . . . diversity, equality and so on' test which determines who to appoint, we should see this as an argument for what it is: appointment on *something in addition to* merit. As such those making these arguments would do better to bite the bullet and to make the case *against* appointment on merit, to present the argument for why the gains of diversity should trump appointing the person best able to do the job. For the real question here is substantive not semantic: on what basis should appointments be made? What considerations ought to be seen as

---

102 ibid., Q28.
103 Thomas Legg, 'Brave New World: The New Supreme Court and Judicial Appointments', *Legal Studies*, 2004, 45, p. 50.
104 See, eg, Malleson, 'Justifying Gender Equality on the Bench', pp. 16–17; Kate Malleson, 'Rethinking the Merit Principle in Judicial Selection', *Journal of Law and Society*, 33(1), 2006, 126; Alan Paterson, *Lawyers and the Public Good: Democracy in Action?*, Cambridge: Cambridge University Press, 2012, pp. 144–145; Paterson and Paterson, *Guarding the Guardians?* pp. 44–51.
105 Legg, 'Brave New World', p. 50.
106 ibid., p. 51.

relevant to judicial appointments? To suggest that all that is at stake here is the definition of merit is to misrepresent what are genuine and fundamental differences of opinion as to the basis upon which judicial appointment should be made, a misrepresentation which serves only as a distraction from discussion of these substantive issues.

Merit, distorted

Another response is to say that while the aim to appoint on merit is correct, we have been doing this badly and that our pursuit of the best judges has been skewed by misguided assumptions and biases about where merit is to be found and how it is to be identified: that understandings of what makes a good judge remain 'linked to more deep-rooted British – especially English – unconscious assumptions about who is "the best": well bred, well spoken, well educated, white males'.[107] And that this both disadvantages those who fall outside these categories and benefits those who do, enabling, in former Court of Appeal judge Stephen Sedley's words, '. . . the average – sometimes very average – white, male practitioner . . . [to] reach the upper tranche of the legal profession',[108] and to believe that they have done so 'on merit'.[109] In other words,

> We are all caught up in the discourse of the 'best' person and want to believe in merit based objective criteria, rather than extraneous factors, as the basis of appointment, but are at a loss to know how best to conduct the process of identification and evaluation.[110]

One place to start thinking about what we mean by merit is with the JAC's list of the qualities and abilities of a good judge. These include: intellectual capability; personal attributes, such as integrity, sound judgement, decisiveness; ability to understand and deal with people fairly, which includes an awareness of diversity;[111] authority and communication skills; and

---

107 Lady Hale, 'Making a Difference?', p. 282.
108 Stephen Sedley, 'On the Move', *The London Review of Books*, 8 October 2009, p. 5.
109 Brenda Hale, 'Equality and the Judiciary: Why Should We Want More Women Judges?', *Public Law*, 2001, 489, p. 493; Shami Chakrabarti, 'The Judiciary: Why Diversity and Merit Matter' in *Judicial Appointments: Balancing Independence, Accountability and Legitimacy*, London: Judicial Appointments Commission, 2010, 67 pp. 68–69.
110 Margaret Thornton, '"Otherness" on the Bench: How Merit is Gendered', *Sydney Law Review*, 29, 2007, 391, p. 402.
111 This reference to diversity was added to the merit criteria in September 2011 in light of Recommendation 20 of the Advisory Panel on Judicial Diversity (Advisory Panel on Judicial Diversity, *The Report of the Advisory Panel on Judicial Diversity 2010*, London: Ministry of Justice, 2010). Although the JAC was keen to stress that considerations of diversity informed the assessment of all the merit criteria, in fact the formulation adopted is somewhat weaker than that suggested by the advisory panel. In particular the requirement that a candidate's awareness and

efficiency.[112] However, this only takes us so far. In order for it to be put into practice, to form the basis of selection, there are three further steps: interpretation – fleshing out what we mean by, for example, sound judgement or decisiveness; identification – how we, in practice, go about identifying these qualities and, finally, assessment – weighing and balancing the various considerations which are seen to go to candidates' merit, which then allows us to say who, all things considered, is the strongest candidate.

It is likely that gender imbalance creeps, to a greater or lesser extent, in at each stage. So, the abstract criteria might be fleshed out in a way that means that men are more likely to display a particular characteristic than women, for example, by assuming a correlation between a physical 'presence' or tone of voice and authority.[113] In other cases, while our fuller conception of, say, intelligence or integrity remains gender neutral – we might, for example, see this as encompassing logical thinking, critical reasoning ability, lack of bias and so on – the problem comes in at the point at which we begin to identify those who possess these characteristics. Here it may be, as Lady Hale suggests, that people who have certain social backgrounds and who speak and dress in a particular way are *more likely to be seen as* intelligent and able. To be clear, this is not to suggest that anyone thinks that intelligence does in fact equate to a certain style of presentation. It is simply to suggest that when we go looking for certain qualities, we often end up (perhaps unintentionally) prioritising people who display these characteristics because of historical or conventional assumptions and shorthand as to how these attributes tend to be displayed.[114] We may also find this in the final stage of the process, when balancing the qualities and characteristics of a good judge, where the weight given to some attributes over others may mean that those typically associated with women (and reinforced by a distinctly gendered career path) count for less.

What this suggests, rather unfashionably, is that there is nothing intrinsically wrong with the notion of appointment on merit as a strategy for choosing judges. Rather, the problem is how we have gone about interpreting, identifying and assessing merit. That is to say, even in relation to, for example, notions of authority,

---

understanding of diversity be 'acquired by relevant experience' is missing. This is an important omission. It is difficult to see how a candidate can make a credible claim of awareness and understanding of diversity without reference to personal experience (Equal Justices Initiative, 'Response to the Judicial Appointments Commission to the consultation exercise on amending the JAC's merit criterion: an ability to understand and deal fairly', on file with author).

112 JAC website, 'Qualities and Abilities'. Online. Available: http://jac.judiciary.gov.uk/application-process/112.htm.

113 Margaret Thornton, *Dissonance and Distrust: Women in the Legal Profession*, Oxford: Oxford University Press, 1996, p. 109; Kamlesh Bahl, Evidence to the Home Affairs Committee, Minutes of Evidence and Appendices (Third Report of Session 1995–6, Volume II), p. 211; Commission for Judicial Appointments, *Annual Report 2002*, London: Lord Chancellor's Department, 2002, [6.22–6.25].

114 Malleson, 'Rethinking the Merit Principle', pp. 138–139.

where difficulties may plausibly arise at the interpretation stage (distorting the potentially gender-neutral identification that follows), the problem is not inherent in the concept of authority itself or its place in the merit criteria. There are good reasons for wanting judges to be authoritative, for wanting them, to use the JAC's formulation, to 'inspire confidence and respect' and 'maintain authority when challenged'. Rather the point is that this does not mean that we ought to prefer those whose manifestation of authority lies in their physicality and/or status over candidates who inspire respect and maintain authority in other ways, such as through their membership of a non-traditional group. Indeed, if we think properly about why it is important for a judge to be authoritative, it seems implausible to suggest that the need to ensure judicial proceedings are conducted in an orderly way and that members of the public defer to their outcome, supports a preference for those with greater physical bearing rather than, for example, those who inspire respect through the extent to which they reflect and empathise with their community. So, it is important that in pinning down what we mean by intelligence, good judgment or authority and so on in the judicial context, we think carefully about why we want judges to display certain qualities and attributes. What then becomes crucial is how we identify these criteria or attributes: where we go to find them and how we know them when we see them.

It seems likely that such mis-identifications of merit can go a long way to explaining the lack of diversity in the judiciary. As Lord Neuberger MR in his oral evidence to the House of Lords Select Committee on the Constitution notes:

> The idea that women are less good judges than men is fanciful . . . But if that is right . . . why are 80 per cent or 90 per cent of judges male? It suggests, purely on a statistical basis, that we do not have the best people because there must be some women out there who are better than the less good men who are judges.[115]

There is no need, therefore, to abandon appointment on merit, or to seek its redefinition. Rather, we need to tackle the distorting effects of its (mis)interpretation and (mis)identification head on, to ensure that we make efforts to look for merit wherever and however it is to be found. And, in so doing, unless we really think that women are less capable of being authoritative or having good judgment then this will not only increase diversity, but will also improve the quality of the judges chosen. As Kate Malleson notes, 'unless we believe that white, male barristers from elite chambers are inherently better suited to be judges than any other lawyers, the inclusion of other groups of lawyers in the recruitment will increase competition and so raise standards'.[116]

---

115 Oral evidence, Constitution Committee Inquiry, 16 November 2011, Q251.
116 Kate Malleson, 'The New Judicial Appointments Commission: New Wine in New Bottles?' in Kate Malleson and Peter H Russell (eds), *Appointing Judges in an Age of Judicial Power: Critical Perspectives from Around the World*, Toronto: University of Toronto, 2006, p. 39, 44.

It may be (and has been) argued that this asks too much of merit. Attempts to deploy merit as a 'pre-existing standard defined solely with reference to the functions of the position and without reference to the candidate pool'[117] are typically derided as perversely naïve or the effective servant of the status quo.[118] Not only are conceptions of merit likely to be distorted by prejudice and bias, but merit and the concept of 'good' judging are inherently subjective so that all understandings of merit are not just threatened by *but are in fact derived from* our own, individual priorities, preferences and prejudices. But can this be right? When we argue about examples of good and bad judgment do we really think we are doing no more than offering our own personal preferences for comparison (and which others may take or leave as they please)? No doubt, what constitutes good judging will always be open to argument and is a question on which reasonable people may reasonably differ. But it does not follow from this that there is no such thing as good judging, no such thing as good or bad judges, no such thing as merit. If we really thought this, then debates about judging the quality of judicial decision-making would make no sense. For, although we may disagree over what is good judging, nobody sensibly thinks that all judgments and all judges are just as good as each other. Indeed, if this were true, we should be just as happy appointing our judges by lottery, safe in the knowledge that no judge is any better or worse than any other. We do not do this because we know that it matters who our judges are, and we know this because we know not all judges are equal: some are better than others.

Merit in diversity

What appears to have been missed so far is the possibility that diversity might have a bearing on merit. It is assumed that appointment on merit, in the last resort, admits that diversity has no meaningful role to play in our selection of judges, except as merit's servant or foot-soldier. Each is confined to its own distinct spheres: '[d]iversity in the field; merit in the selection'.[119] However, if we accept, with Lord Justice Etherton, Lady Hale, Justice Sotomayor and others, that the judiciary and the justice it dispenses are *better* for the variety of experiences, skills and insights of its members, then we are able to say that diversity is an important factor in making judicial appointments while *at the same time* accepting the orthodoxy that appointments must be made on merit. We are no longer faced with having to choose between advancing diversity and appointment on merit. Arguments for judicial diversity grounded in its contribution to the quality of

117 Malleson, 'Rethinking the Merit Principle', p. 140.
118 ibid.; Thornton, '"Otherness" on the Bench'; Regina Graycar, 'Gender, Race, Bias and Perspective: OR, How Otherness Colours Your Judgment', *International Journal of the Legal Profession*, 15(1–2), 2008, 73.
119 Baroness Prashar, 'Judicial Appointments: A New System for a New Century', Centre for Crime and Justice Studies, King's College London, March 2007, [65].

judicial decision-making and arguments for appointment on merit point in the same direction.

As such, there is no need to rethink or redefine 'merit', nor are we limited to educating those appointing judges in how to recognise merit in all its guises. Rather, we can accept merit on its own terms – as simply ensuring the candidate who will do the best job is appointed – while arguing that diversity is essential to this pursuit. Once we accept that a judiciary is stronger, and the justice dispensed better for its breadth of experience, anyone concerned with ensuring that our judiciary is as good as it can be has a reason to seek diversity. A commitment to appointment on merit, to ensuring that we have a set of judges who will do the job of judging as well as possible, requires that one also be committed to (amongst other things) a diverse judiciary. Just as 'diversity means the search for merit wherever it can be found',[120] appointment on merit requires the same search for diversity.

When judicial diversity is valued and promoted simply on the basis of equity and legitimacy, we have no good answer to those who object that efforts to increase diversity will lead to a 'diluting of standards' or a 'dumbing down' of the judiciary.[121] However, once we see that diversity is essential to the *quality* of judicial decision-making, we can meet this objection head on. This ties diversity to the ability of judges to do their job. It goes to the heart of arguments for the supremacy of appointment on merit and meets them on their own terms. If we want the best possible judiciary, if we want a judiciary that is comprised of individuals who are (on any view) the best, then we must also be committed to ensuring (amongst other things) that they are drawn from as varied and diverse backgrounds as possible. Insofar as a judiciary is enriched and the *quality* of its decision-making is improved by the diversity of its membership, then the more varied the people making the decision, the *better* the decision is likely to be. In this way, merit and diversity stand and fall together. Judicial diversity is not simply desirable, but essential. A diverse judiciary is a stronger judiciary, a judiciary better positioned to do justice, to develop and apply the law reasonably and fairly. And, were we to achieve this, were the judges *really* to be diverse, then it would go a long way to justifying the familiar claim that we have one of the best judiciaries in the world.

Letting go of the default judge, welcoming diversity

Aside from these *substantive* benefits a diverse judiciary brings to the quality of judicial decisions, there is a further reason for embracing the argument that diversity of experience enriches the processes and practice of judging. For, whatever

---

120 Prashar, 'Speech to London School of Economics'.
121 Chakrabarti, 'Why Diversity and Merit Matter', p. 69; Jonathan Karas, 'Dumbing down for diversity', *Legal Week*, 5 April 2007.

one's views on how often women judges are likely make a difference *as women*, and whatever this difference is, whatever one's views on where and when gender does or should have an impact on judicial decision-making, progress toward a more diverse judiciary will be harder and slower – as we are seeing – unless and until differences in the way women judge, and the different perspectives and insights they can offer, are acknowledged and welcomed. Accordingly, *whatever* our reasons for wanting a diverse judiciary – whether we see the real value of judicial diversity in increased public confidence, in shoring up the democratic legitimacy of the institution, or in the substantive difference such a judiciary will make – *true* diversity will be possible only once we make space for the idea that women really do belong as judges.

For, as we have seen, one of the greatest obstacles to a diverse judiciary has been and remains the image of the default judge and our unwillingness to embrace fully the reality that *who* the judge is matters. Our association of good judging with the physical and attitudinal characteristics we are used to seeing in our (non-diverse) judges, an association which encourages the perception that judging can and should be both uniform and neutral – and that who the judge is *should not matter*, and that deviations from this norm are not to be welcomed, but rather challenged and criticised – retains a tight grip on our understandings of the judge and judging. It underpins Lord Judge's view that it is 'perfectly obvious that background, ethnicity, religion, sexuality and gender are utterly irrelevant to the ability of an individual to be a good judge',[122] and reappears again in the challenges to the authority of women and other non-traditional judges discussed in Chapter 4. It is this image of the judge which makes the experience of women judges (and those of other non-traditional groups) often one of hostility, antagonism and isolation, that allows *the mere possibility* that they might bring the diversity of their life experiences to their judging to work *against* them, to transform their identity into a source of potential bias.[123]

Recognising that judges' bringing their own perspectives to bear on their decision-making is not only legitimate but valuable matters because it challenges this uniform or default image of the judge, this (mis)understanding of judicial impartiality and neutrality. The argument that diversity of experience enriches the processes and practice of judging, that diversity in judging is a good thing, acknowledges the reality that there is no single approach to judging, that the appearance of neutrality which women judges are seen to threaten is an illusion. Male judges, just as much as women, resort to their own perspectives, experiences and values when deciding cases and insofar as this has gone unnoticed this is largely because the *absence* of judicial diversity has meant that we have not been exposed to a wider array of arguments. This, then, is the grain of truth in the 'bias' accusations – women judges will on occasion judge differently to their male colleagues because

122   Lord Judge, 'Equality in Justice Day', Royal Courts of Justice, London, 24 October 2008.
123   Berns, *To Speak as a Judge*, p. 18, fn 20.

there will be times when they will and are required to draw on their own (different) perspectives. The mistake is to think that male judges have not been doing this all along *and* to think – in either case – that this is problematic.[124] Indeed, far from being a cause for complaint or criticism, once we accept that *all* judges will sometimes fall back on their own values and experiences, their own sense of justice, not only is there is no longer a uniform image for women to fall outside of and to threaten but, as we have seen, this provides one of the strongest arguments in favour of judicial diversity.

In exploding the myth of the default judge and embracing the idea of differences in judicial approach, this argument for judicial diversity not only provides a truer, better informed understanding of what judges do and the extent to which they are able to bring their distinct perspectives and values to bear on their decision-making, but also, insofar as this makes the Bench a more comfortable place for women to be, provides a catalyst towards achieving a more diverse Bench. Put bluntly, women are more likely to consider a judicial career if judicial appointment comes not with the threat of marginalisation or open hostility, but rather with the promise that their differences will be welcomed and their contributions valued. And so, whether we think that the real value of a diverse judiciary lies in the substance of its decision-making or in the increased public confidence and legitimacy it offers, there is reason to think that we will get there only once we acknowledge the real difference women judges can make: once we see how a more diverse judiciary really is a better judiciary.

124 Patricia Cain, 'Good and Bad Bias: A Comment on Feminist Theory and Judging', *Southern California Law Review*, 61, 1988, 1945, p. 1946; Judith Resnik, 'On the Bias: Feminist Reconsiderations of the Aspirations for our Judges', *Southern California Law Review*, 61, 1988, 1877.

Concluding remarks

Despite significant policy development and initiatives in recent years concerning the diversity of our judiciary, progress has been slow; the number of women judges, especially at senior levels, remains small. Securing a judiciary that reflects the diversity of the population it serves is proving harder than we thought. At the same time debates about judicial diversity are becoming increasingly stale – stymied through a combination of over-familiarity, a lack of urgency and a dogged infatuation with the views and interests of the legal profession, particularly the Bar. A proliferation of diversity-focused panels, taskforces, consultations and reports focused on both the judiciary and legal profession has largely failed to move the debate forward. Their lack of historical perspective and context, and their failure to identify and make explicit, common themes across these various surveys and reports, enables their findings to be presented as if each cohort of women lawyers and judges is facing a 'new' set of problems, as if they are the first to encounter obstacles to their progression. So, too, the problems are diagnosed and solutions offered without any clear sense that all this has been said and done before. As a result, the clock is continually reset. Whatever starting point one uses – just short of a century since women first entered the legal profession, 47 years since the first woman was appointed to the High Court bench, two decades since women reached a critical mass in the legal profession, eight years since Lady Hale's appointment to the House of Lords, and six years since fundamental changes to the appointments process – we are little closer to addressing the structural and cultural barriers to a more diverse judiciary. Or, indeed, to answering Baroness Neuberger's, chair of one of the more recent advisory panels on judicial diversity, own question – *whatever's happening to women?*[1]

The argument of this book is that a diverse judiciary will remain out of reach unless and until we get clearer on what difference women judges can and should make to the judiciary. It is only by appreciating the substantive contribution women judges can make to judging that we will see what we really do have to gain

---

1 Julia Neuberger, *Whatever's Happening to Women? Promises, practices and pay offs*, London: Kyle Cathie, 1991. I thank Clare McGlynn for this reference.

from a diverse judiciary. And it is only by treating the distinctive perspectives and insights women judges can offer as a cause for celebration, and not suspicion, that we will make the judiciary a place where more good women lawyers want to be.

This focus on the difference women judges make brings into sharp relief the extent to which prevailing images of the judge and judging are enmeshed in notions of sameness and uniformity. It highlights the extent to which these images, and in particular that which I have termed our 'default judge', are so familiar that they are routinely overlooked. Yet, failing to confront these instinctive images of the judge and of judging comes at a price, excluding those who do not fit this mould and setting them up as threats to the judicial norm. Such has been the fate of the woman judge. The default judge operates to prevent women from becoming and allowing them to make a difference as judges. In the absence of any suitable alternatives, the 'default judge' becomes the popular, intuitive image of the judge. And although we may – when pushed – view him as an ideological construct, or fairytale even, his status as fiction does not prevent him from having operative effects. This attractive yet ultimately limiting image of the judge continues to exercise enormous power – promulgating and perpetuating a particular worldview under a cloak of apparent objectivity, neutrality and detachment. The woman judge is then seen as a threat not just to the physical and social homogeneity of the judiciary but also to these very characteristics and values – her divergence from the default judge is an almost automatic confirmation of bias. Her authority and distance collapse the legitimacy of her judgment is always open to question. Little wonder that many highly qualified women still think that the judiciary is not for people like them. And while for some this sense of exclusion manifests itself in the decision to not join the Bench, for others it takes a more sinister turn. There is a sense in which the woman judge is *so* deviant she is subject to an irrepressible desire to conform, she is induced to deny herself and sell her voice – just like Andersen's mermaid.

But while this goes some way to explaining why, despite repeated efforts, our attempts to secure greater diversity in our judiciary have fallen short, it also points a way forward. For, by getting a clearer sense of what our judges really do and how they do it, we can see that women judges and judicial diversity more broadly do not threaten but rather enrich the judiciary and judicial decision-making. We can see that the criticism of women judges relying on their own view as women is mistaken, not because they do not do this – they do – but because this is what *all* judges do. The default image of the judge is not, and cannot be, true; who the judge is matters. *All* judges judge differently. *All* judges have different and particular views of what justice requires, what the judge's function is and so on. And *all* judges at times, when the rules run out, have to fall back on their own sense of justice or fairness to inform their decision-making and inevitably, on these occasions and to this extent, outcomes will differ from judge to judge. The most we might say is that insofar as a woman's perspectives will (sometimes) differ from a man's, women judges will introduce *different* views into their judicial decisions and into the law. But this, far from being a cause for complaint and criticism, provides one of the strongest arguments in favour of judicial diversity.

For, while difference-based arguments have fallen out of favour in recent years, their rejection has been grounded in misplaced assumptions about where women's difference might be located and expressed. But rejecting, as we should, the claim that there is a distinctive woman's perspective – a 'different voice' – does not require us also to reject the suggestion that women judges *are* different and that they will, on occasion, judge differently to their male colleagues. Judging is informed by the judge's background, personal experiences and the perspectives these provide, and there is no reason to doubt that gender is one feature – indeed a central and ever-present feature – of a judge's identity, which will contribute to the outlook and attitudes upon which good judging often depends. And the insights these experiences provide are insights which we should welcome, for they enrich our judiciary and inform and enhance the quality of judicial decision-making.

There is then no need to move on from difference, for women judges to adopt the guise of the little mermaid or to distance themselves from their right to be different. In fact, from difference comes diversity. Insofar as the judiciary is stronger and the justice dispensed better the more diverse its decision-makers, we have reason to seek out and embrace judicial difference. Not only that, but we also have an argument for judicial diversity in which the standard opponent to measures to increase diversity – appointment on merit – is in fact its greatest ally. For if a diverse judiciary really is a better judiciary, a judiciary better placed to apply and to develop the law fairly and reasonably, then merit and diversity go hand in hand. Diversity is not only a legitimate part of, but is essential to, appointment on merit. A judiciary lacking in diversity is one lacking in an essential resource for good decision-making. A diverse judiciary is a better judiciary. It is better not (just) because it is more representative and democratically legitimate, but because it is better positioned to do its job – to deliver justice.

Bibliography

Abbas, Tahir, *Diversity in the Senior Judiciary: A Literature Review of Research on Ethnic Inequalities*, London: The Commission for Judicial Appointments, 2005.

Abel-Smith, Brian and Robert Stevens, *Lawyers and the Courts: A Sociological Study of the English Legal System 1750–1965*, London: Heinemann, 1967.

Abrahamson, Shirley S., 'The Woman Has Robes: Four Questions', *Golden Gate University Law Review*, 14, 1984, 489.

Addley, Esther, 'The women of the year', *The Guardian*, 19 December 2003.

Advisory Panel on Judicial Diversity, *The Report of the Advisory Panel on Judicial Diversity 2010*, London: Ministry of Justice, 2010.

Aliotta, Jilda M., 'Justice O'Connor and the Equal Protection Clause: A Feminine Voice?', *Judicature*, 78, 1995.

Allen, Anthony, *Barriers to Application for Judicial Appointment Research*, London: BMRB Social, 2009.

Alridge, Alex, 'Are law firms finally addressing the need for a better work-life balance?', *The Guardian*, 1 July 2011.

Alridge, Alex, 'The case of the sleepless lawyers', *The Guardian*, 4 August 2011.

Anderson, Ellen, *Judging Bertha Wilson – Law as Large as Life*, Toronto: University of Toronto Press, 2002.

Anon, 'Tongue Meat', in Angela Carter (ed), *The Virago Book of Fairy Tales*, London: Virago Press, 1990.

Anon, 'Women and the Bar', *Law Society Gazette*, 27 June 1990.

Anon, 'Lord Mackay hits out on judicial appointments', *Law Society Gazette*, 30 July 1991.

Anon, 'Butler-Sloss is content to be a unisex judge', *The Times*, 21 November 2000.

Anon, 'What reduced a top woman judge to tears?', *The Daily Mail*, 22 June 2004.

Anon, 'What planet ARE judges living on?', *The Daily Mail*, 31 May 2006.

Anon, 'Hannah Wright: Obituary', *The Times*, 25 February 2008.

Anon, 'Focus: Magic Circle work-life balance – work, rest and fair play', *The Lawyer*, 26 July 2010.

Anon, 'Everything to do with justice: former Qld Chief Magistrate Diane Fingleton', *Lawyers Weekly*, 29 September 2010.

Anon, 'Shout at your spouse and risk losing your home: It's just the same as domestic violence, warns woman judge', *The Daily Mail*, 27 January 2011.

Anon, 'It still pays to be a man – annual traineeship stats published', *Solicitors Journal*, 5 April 2011.

Anon, 'The law of motherhood', *The Guardian*, 28 April 2011.

Arden, Lady Justice, 'Diversity in the appointment of Queen's Counsel and judges: what does the future hold?', Address to the Chancery Bar Association, London, 12 January 2007.

Arden, Lady Justice, 'Magna Carta and the Judges – Realising the Vision', Royal Holloway, University of London, June 2011.

Askin, Kelly, 'Sexual Violence in Decisions and Indictments of the Yugoslav and Rwandan Tribunals: Current Status', *American Journal of International Law*, 93(1), 1999, 97.

Atkins, Susan and Brenda Hoggett, *Women and the Law*, Oxford: Blackwell, 1984.

Auchmuty, Rosemary, 'Whatever happened to Miss Bebb? *Bebb v The Law Society* and women's legal history', *Legal Studies*, 31(2), 2011, 199.

Auerbach, Judy, Linda Blum, Vicki Smith and Christine Williams, '*On Gilligan's "In a Different Voice"*', *Feminist Studies*, 11(1), 1985, 149.

Bacik, Ivana and Eileen Drew, 'Struggling with juggling: Gender and work/life balance in the legal professions', *Women's Studies International Forum*, 29, 2006, 136.

Backhouse, Constance, 'The Chilly Climate for Women Judges: Reflections on the Backlash from the *Ewanchuk* Case', *Canadian Journal of Women and Law*, 15, 2003, 167.

Barmes, Lizzie and Kate Malleson, 'The Legal Profession as Gatekeeper to the Judiciary: Design Faults in Measures to Enhance Diversity', *Modern Law Review*, 74(2), 2011, 245.

Bartlett, Katharine T., 'Gender Law', *Duke Journal of Gender Law and Policy*, 1, 1994, 1.

Barwick, H., J. Burns and A. Gray, *Gender Equality in the New Zealand Judicial System: Judges' Perceptions of Gender Issues*, Wellington: Joint Working Group on Gender Equality, 1996.

Bazelon, Emily, 'The place of women on the court', *New York Times Magazine*, 12 July 2009.

BBC News Online, 'High Court gets first black judge', 2 September 2004.

Beiner, Theresa, 'Female Judging', *University of Toledo Law Review*, 36, 2005, 821.

Belleau, Marie-Clarie and Rebecca Johnson, 'Judging Gender: Difference and Dissent at the Supreme Court of Canada', *International Journal of the Legal Profession*, 15(1–2), 2008, 57.

Beloff, Michael, 'Sisters-in-Law: The Irresistible Rise of Women in Wigs', The Gray's Inn Reading 2009.

Berns, Sandra, *To Speak as a Judge – Difference, Voice and Power*, Dartmouth: Ashgate, 1999.

Berns, Sandra and Paula Baron, 'Bloody Bones: A Legal Ghost Story and Entertainment in Two Voices to Speak as a Judge', *Australian Feminist Law Journal*, 2, 1994, 125.

de Bertodano, Sylvia, 'Women used to talk about how little time they had taken off to have children', *The Times*, 4 June 2009.

Bindman, Geoffrey, 'Is the system of judicial appointments illegal?', *Law Society Gazette*, 27 February 1991, 24.

Bingham, Lord, 'The Judges: Active or Passive', 139, 2006, *Proceedings of the British Academy* 55.

Bingham, Lord, 'The Law Lords: who has served' in Louis Blom-Cooper, Brice Dickson and Gavin Drewry (eds), *The Judicial House of Lords 1876–2009*, Oxford: Oxford University Press, 2009.

Biskupiz, Joan, 'Ginsburg: Court needs another woman', *USA Today*, 10 May 2009.

Blom-Cooper, Louis, Brice Dickson and Gavin Drewry (eds), *The Judicial House of Lords 1876–2009*, Oxford: Oxford University Press, 2009.

Boigeol, Anne, 'Male Strategies in the Face of the Feminisation of a Profession: The Case of the French Judiciary', in Ulrike Schultz and Gisela Shaw (eds), *Women in the World's Legal Professions*, Oxford: Hart Publishing, 2003, p. 401.

Bowcott, Owen, 'UK Supreme Court's only female judge calls for more diversity in appointments', *The Guardian*, 25 October 2011.

Boyd, Christina L., Lee Epstein and Andrew D. Martin, 'Untangling the Causal Effects of Sex on Judging', *American Journal of Political Science*, 54(2), 2010, 389.

Braithwaite, Jo, 'The strategic use of demand side diversity pressure on the solicitors' profession', *Journal of Law and Society*, 37(3), 2010, 442.

Brennann William J. Jr, 'Reason, Passion, and "The Progress of the Law"', *Cardozo Law Review*, 10, 1998, 3.

Bright, 'David, 'The Other Woman: Lizzie Cyr and the Origins of the "Persons Case"', *Canadian Journal of Law & Society*, 13, 1998, 99.

Brooks, Dianne L., 'A Commentary on the Essence of Anti-Essentialism in Feminist Legal Theory', *Feminist Legal Studies*, 2(2), 1994, 115.

Bryant, Diana, 'Creating Justice', Australian Women Lawyers Second National Conference, Melbourne, 13 June 2008.

Butler, Judith, *Gender Trouble: Feminism and the Subversion of Identity*, New York: Routledge, 1990.

Byrne, Matt, 'UK's top firms fail to increase female equity partner figures', *The Lawyer*, 14 September 2011.

Cahn, Naomi, 'Styles of Lawyering', *Hastings Law Journal*, 43, 1992, 1039.

Cain, Patricia, 'Good and Bad Bias: A Comment on Feminist Theory and Judging', *Southern California Law Review*, 61, 1988, 1945.

Canadian Judicial Council News Release, 'Judicial Council closes file in complaint against BC Madam Justice Southin', 21 March 2003.

Cardinal, Monique C., 'Why aren't Women Sharia Court Judges? The Case of Syria', *Islamic Law and Society*, 17, 2010, 185.

Cardozo, Benjamin N., *The Nature of the Judicial Process*, New Haven: Yale University Press, 1921.

Carter, Angela, 'Introduction', in Angela Carter (ed), *Angela Carter's Book of Fairy Tales*, London: Virago Press, 2005.

Cashman, Greer Fay, 'Beinisch attends her final swearing-in ceremony', *The Jerusalem Post*, 3 January 2012.

Cavendish, Richard (ed), *Mythology: An Illustrated Encyclopedia of the Principal Myths and Religions of the World*, London: Little, Brown & Company, 1992.

CBC News, 'Canada Alberta judge apologizes for part of his letter', 10 November 2000.

Chakrabarti, Shami, 'The Judiciary: Why Diversity and Merit Matter', in *Judicial Appointments: Balancing Independence, Accountability and Legitimacy*, London: Judicial Appointments Commission, 2010, 67.

Chamallas, Martha, *Introduction to Feminist Legal Theory*, 2nd edn, New York: Aspen Publishing, 2003.

Chaudhry, Mehvish, 'Particular Social Groups Post *Fornah*', *Journal of Immigration, Asylum and Nationality Law*, 2008, 21(2), 137.

Chellel Kit, 'Female partners defy glass ceiling in record numbers', *The Lawyer*, 8 September 2008.

Childs, Sarah, Joni Lovenduski and Rosie Campbell, *Women at the Top 2005: Changing Numbers, Changing Politics?*, London: Hansard Society, 2005.

Chittenden, Tara, *Career Experiences of Gay and Lesbian Solicitors* (Research Study 53), London: Law Society, 2006.

Choi, Stephen J., Mitu Gulati, Mirya Holman and Eric A. Posner, 'Judging Women', *Journal of Empirical Studies*, 8(3), 2011, 504.

Clark, Mary L., 'Introducing a parliamentary confirmation process for new Supreme Court justices: its pros and cons, and the lessons learned from the US experience', *Public Law*, 2010, 464.

Clarke, Anthony, 'Open Societies and the Rule of Law', Atkin Lecture 2008, The Reform Club, London, 13 November 2008.

Clarke, Lord, 'Selecting Judges: Merit, Moral Courage, Judgment and Diversity', Speech, 22 September 2009.

Cole, Bill, Nina Fletcher, Tara Chittenden and Joanne Cox, *Trends in the Solicitors' Profession: Annual Statistical Report 2009*, London: Law Society, 2010.

Collier, Richard, 'Work-life balance: ladies only?', *The Lawyer*, 23 May 2005.

Collier, Richard, ' "Nutty Professors", "Men in Suits" and "New Entrepreneurs": Corporality, Subjectivity and Change in the Law School and Legal Practice', *Social & Legal Studies*, 7, 2008, 27.

Collier, Richard, *Men, Law and Gender: Essays on the 'Men' of Law*, London: Routledge, 2010.

Commission for Judicial Appointments, *Annual Report 2002*, London: Lord Chancellor's Department, 2002.

Commission for Judicial Appointments, *Annual Report 2003*, London: Commission for Judicial Appointments, 2003.

Commission for Judicial Appointments, *Annual Report 2004*, London: Commission for Judicial Appointments, 2004.

Commission for Judicial Appointments, *Annual Report 2005*, London: Commission for Judicial Appointments, 2005.

Conaghan, Joanne, 'Reassessing the Feminist Theoretical Project in Law', *Journal of Law and Society*, 27(3), 2000, 351.

Conaghan, Joanne, 'Tort Law and Feminist Critique', *Current Legal Problems*, 56, 2003, 175.

Cooper, Davina, *Challenging Diversity: Rethinking Equality and the Value of Difference*, Cambridge: Cambridge University Press, 2004.

Cornes, Richard, 'Gains (and Dangers of Losses) in Translation – the Leadership Function of the United Kingdom's Supreme Court, Parameters and Prospects', *Public Law*, 2011, 509.

Cragg, Stephen, 'Legislation update', *The Times*, 24 October 2006.

Crenshaw, Kimberlé, 'Mapping the Margins: Intersectionality, Identity Politics, and Violence Against Women of Color', *Stanford Law Review*, 43, 1991, 1241.

Cruickshank, Elizabeth (ed), *Women in the Law: Strategic Career Management*, London: Law Society, 2003.

Darbyshire, Penny, *Sitting in Judgment: The Working Lives of Judges*, Oxford: Hart Publishing, 2011.

Davis, Rowenna, 'Why children must be called to the Bar', *The Guardian*, 15 June 2010.

Davis, Sue, Susan Haire and Donald R. Songer, 'Voting Behaviour and Gender on the US Court of Appeals', *Judicature*, 77(3), 1993, 129.

Department for Constitutional Affairs, *Constitutional Reform: A New Way of Appointing Judges*, CP 10/03, London: Department for Constitutional Affairs, 2003.

Department for Constitutional Affairs, *Constitutional Reform: A Supreme Court for the United Kingdom*, CP 11/03, London: Department for Constitutional Affairs, 2003.

Department for Constitutional Affairs, 'Summary of Responses to the Consultation Paper' (January 2004).

Department for Constitutional Affairs, *Increasing Diversity in the Judiciary*, CP25/04, London: Department for Constitutional Affairs, 2004.

Department of Economic and Social Affairs, *The World's Women 2010: Constitutional Reform: A New Way of Appointing Judges. Trends and Statistics*, New York: United Nations, 2010.

Devlin, Richard, 'We Can't Go On Together with Suspicious Minds: Judicial Bias and Racialized Perspective in *R* v *RDS*', *Dalhousie Law Journal*, 18, 1995, 408.

Dickson, Brice, 'A Hard Act to Follow: The Bingham Court, 2000–8', in Louis Blom-Cooper, Brice Dickson and Gavin Drewry (eds), *The Judicial House of Lords 1876–2009*, Oxford: Oxford University Press, 2009, p. 255.

Dixon, Rosalind, 'Female Justices, Feminism and the Politics of Judicial Appointment: A Re-Examination', *Yale Journal of Law and Feminism*, 21(2), 2010, 297.

Dobbs, Mrs Justice, 'Diversity in the Judiciary – Lecture', Queen Mary University of London, London, 17 October 2007.

Doughty, Steve, 'The first lady of the Law Lords (and she wants to abolish marriage)', *The Daily Mail* 24 October 2003.

Drakopoulou, Maria, 'The Ethic of Care, Female Subjectivity and Feminist Legal Scholarship', *Feminist Legal Studies*, 8(2), 2000, 199.

Duff, Liz and Lisa Webley, *Equality and Diversity: Women Solicitors*, Research Study 48(2) (Qualitative Findings and Literature Review), London: Law Society, 2004.

Duvillard, Laureline, 'Women find no justice in law profession', *swissinfo.ch*, 13 May 2011.

Dworkin, Ronald, *Taking Rights Seriously*, London: Duckworth, 1977.

Dworkin, Ronald, *Law's Empire*, Oxford: Hart Publishing, 1986.

Dworkin, Ronald, 'Justice Sotomayor: The Unjust Hearings', *The New York Review of Books*, 24 September 2009.

Dyer, Clare, 'Solicitors boycott "old-boys' network"', *The Guardian*, 28 September 1999.

Dyer, Clare, 'First 10 high court judges under new diversity rules', *The Guardian*, 28 January 2008.

Editorial, 'Judging Sonia Sotomayor', *New York Times*, 30 May 2009.

Electoral Reform Research, *Survey of Barristers Changing Practice Status 2001–9*, London: Electoral Reform Services, March 2011.

Elliot, John, 'Justice father talked of "suicide in front of Blair"', *The Sunday Times*, 22 January 2006.

Elvin, Jesse, 'The continuing use of problematic sexual stereotypes in judicial decision-making', *Feminist Legal Studies*, 18(3), 2010, 275.

Entry to the Bar Working Party, *Final Report*, London: Bar Council, 2007.

Epstein, Cynthia Fuchs, *Deceptive Distinctions*, New Haven: Yale University Press, 1988.

Equality and Human Rights Commission, *Sex and Power: 2011*, London: Equality and Human Rights Commission, 2011.

Equality and Human Rights Commission, *Sex and Power 2008*, London: Equality and Human Rights Commission, 2008.

Equal Opportunities Commission, *Sex and Power: Who Runs Britain? 2007*, London: Equal Opportunities Commission, 2007.

Etherton, Terence, 'Liberty, the Archetype and Diversity: A Philosophy of Judging', *Public Law*, 2010, 727.

European Commission, *More Women in Senior Positions: Key to Economic Stability and Growth*, Directorate-General for Employment, Social Affairs and Equal Opportunities Unit G1, January 2010.

Evans, Catherine, '"Pale, male" courts in Wales "need more women judges"', *BBC News Online*, 27 May 2011.

Falconer, Charlie, 'Opening up our Institutions for the Future', Speech to the Labour Party Conference, 29 September 2004.

Falconer, Lord, 'Increasing Judicial Diversity' Women Lawyers' Forum, London, 5 March 2005.

Falconer, Lord, 'Increasing Judicial Diversity: The Next Steps', Commission for Judicial Appointments, Institute of Mechanical Engineers, London, 2 November 2005.

Fineman, Martha, 'Feminist Theory and Law', *Harvard Journal of Law and Public Policy*, 18, 1995, 349.

Finnis, John, 'Natural Law: The Classical Tradition', in Jules Coleman and Scott Shapiro (eds), *The Oxford Handbook of Jurisprudence and Philosophy of Law*, Oxford: Oxford University Press, 2002, p. 1.

Fletcher, Nina, and Yulia Muratova, *Trends in the Solicitors' Profession: Annual Statistical Report 2010*, London: Law Society, 2011.

Fogarty, Chris, 'Trainees who bluffed their way in, want out', *The Lawyer*, 19 May 1998.

Francis, Andrew, 'Legal executives and the phantom of legal professionalism: The rise and rise of the third branch of the legal profession?', *International Journal of the Legal Profession*, 9(1), 2002, 5.

Fulford, Adrian, 'Diversity Speech', Middle Temple Hall, London, 20 January 2009.

Fuss, Diana, *Essentially Speaking: Feminism, Nature and Difference*, New York: Routledge, 1989.

Fuszara, Małgorzarta, 'Women Lawyers in Poland under the Impact of Post-1989 Transformation', in Ulrike Schultz and Gisela Shaw (eds), *Women in the World's Legal Professions*, Oxford: Hart Publishing, 2003, p. 371.

Gardner, John, 'Legal Positivism: 5½ Myths', *American Journal of Jurisprudence*, 46, 2001, 199.

Gatens, Moira, *Imaginary Bodies – Ethics, Power and Corporeality*, London: Routledge, 1996.

Genn, Hazel, *Paths to Justice: What People Do and Think About Going to Law*, Oxford: Hart Publishing, 1999.

Genn, Hazel, *The Attractiveness of Senior Judicial Appointment to Highly Qualified Practitioners – Report to the Judicial Executive Board*, London: Directorate of Judicial Office for England and Wales, 2008.

George, Robert, 'In Defence of Dissent: *R (McDonald) v Royal Borough of Kensington and Chelsea*', *Family Law*, October 2011, 1097.

Gerry, Felicity, 'Bar v Family: how to win both', *The Guardian*, 4 May 2011.

Gibb, Frances, 'More women join the judiciary', *The Times*, 1 February 2006.

Gibb, Frances, 'Men in grey suits asked if I had some kind of unspeakable sexual interest', *The Times*, 21 January 2009.

Gibb, Frances, 'How can ethnic minorities reach the top of the profession?', *The Times*, 23 April 2009.

Gibb, Frances, 'Brain "size of a planet" is not big enough for top court, say judges', *The Times*, 15 October 2009.

Gibb, Frances, 'Supreme ambition, jealousy and outrage', *The Times*, 4 February 2010.

Gibb, Frances, 'Supremely judicial choice – shame about the backbiting', *The Times*, 25 March 2010.

Gibb, Frances, 'Citizens need to be confident that judges reflect the full diversity of modern Britain', *The Times*, 7 July 2011.

Gibb, Frances, 'Men-only mentality puts the Garrick in contempt of a Supreme Court judge', *The Times*, 15 October 2011.

Gibb, Frances, 'Judges call for rethink on top appointments: Is it in the interests of democracy for the Lord Chancellor to have more say over who gets judicial posts?', *The Times*, 20 October 2011.

Gibb, Frances, 'Give women priority for top posts, judge urges', *The Times*, 14 November 2011.

Gibb, Frances, '"Leapfrog" lawyer who raised the Bar', *The Times*, 18 January 2012.

Gilligan, Carol, *In a Different Voice: Psychological Theory and Women's Development*, Cambridge, Mass.: Harvard University Press, 1982; repr 1993.

Glover, Stephen, 'Judges are unelected, out of touch and shockingly arrogant', *The Daily Mail*, 21 May 2011.

Graycar, Regina, 'The Gender of Judgments: An Introduction', in Margaret Thornton (ed), *Public and Private – Feminist Legal Debates*, Oxford: Oxford University Press, 1995, p. 262.

Graycar, Regina, 'The Gender of Judgments: Some Reflections on "Bias"', *University of British Columbia Law Review*, 32, 1998, 1.

Graycar, Regina, 'Gender, Race, Bias and Perspective: OR, How Otherness Colours Your Judgment', *International Journal of the Legal Profession*, 15(1–2), 2008, 73.

Lord Greene, 'Law and Progress', *Law Journal*, 94, 1944, 349.

Griffith, John, 'That Man Griffith', *London Review of Books*, 12(20), 25 October 1990.

Griffith, J.A.G., *The Politics of the Judiciary*, London: Fontana Press, 1977.

Griffith, J.A.G., *The Politics of the Judiciary*, 5th edn, London: Fontana Press, 1997.

Griffiths, Catrin, 'The gender agenda', in *Diversity Report 2010*, London: The Lawyer, 2010.

Griffiths, Catrin, 'Focus: Flexible working – now you see me . . .', *The Lawyer*, 1 February 2010.

Hale, Baroness, 'Making a Difference? Why We Need a More Diverse Judiciary', *Northern Ireland Legal Quarterly*, 56(3), 2005, 281.

Hale, Baroness, 'A Minority Opinion?', *Proceedings of the British Academy*, 154, 2008, 319.

Hale, Baroness, 'Dignity', Ethel Benjamin Commemorative Address, Dunedin Art Gallery, New Zealand, 7 May 2010.

Hale, Brenda, 'Equality and the Judiciary: Why Should We Want More Women Judges?', *Public Law*, 2001, 489.

Hale, Brenda, 'The Value of Life and the Cost of Living: Damages for Wrongful Birth', *British Actuarial Journal*, 7, 2001, 747.

Hale, Brenda, 'Judging Women and Women Judging', *Counsel*, 10–12 August 2002, 10.

Hale, Brenda, 'Equality in the Judiciary: A Tale of Two Continents', 10th Pilgrim Fathers' Lecture, 24 October 2003.

Hale, Brenda, 'Equality and autonomy in family law', *Journal of Social Welfare & Family Law*, 33(1), 2011, 3.

Hale, Lady, 'It's a Man's World: Redressing the Balance', Norfolk Law Lecture 2012, University of East Anglia, 16 February 2012.

Hale, Brenda and Rosemary Hunter, 'A Conversation with Baroness Hale', *Feminist Legal Studies*, 16(2), 2008, 237.

Hallett, Lady Justice, 'How the Judiciary is Changing', in *Judicial Appointments: Balancing Independence, Accountability and Legitimacy*, London: Judicial Appointments Commission, 2010, 89.

Harris, Angela P., 'Race and Essentialism in Feminist Legal Theory', *Stanford Law Review*, 42, 1990, 581.

Harris, Peter G., Robert H. George and Jonathan Herring, 'With this ring I thee wed (terms and conditions apply)', *Family Law*, April 2011, 367.

Hart, H.L.A., *The Concept of Law*, Oxford: Oxford University Press, 1961.

Harwood, Stephen, *Annual Statistical Report 1989*, London: Law Society, 1989.

Hawkes, C.P., *Chambers in the Temple: Comments and Conceits 'in Camera'*, London: Methuen & Co, 1930.

Herring, Jonathan, Peter G. Harris and Robert H. George, 'Ante-nuptial agreements: fairness, equality and presumptions', *Law Quarterly Review*, 127, 2011, 335.

Hirsch, Afua, 'Judicial culture still deters gay and lesbian lawyers, says researchers', *The Guardian*, 4 July 2010.

Hitchings, Emma, 'From Pre-Nups to Post-Nups: Dealing with Marital Property Agreements', *Family Law*, November 2009, 1056.

Holland, Lesley and Lynne Spender, *Without Prejudice? Sex Equality at the Bar and in the Judiciary*, Bournemouth: TMS Management Consultants, 1992.

Home Affairs Select Committee, *Home Affairs Select Committee Report on Judicial Appointments Procedures*, London: HMSO, 1996.

Hood, R.G., Stephen Shute and Florence Seemungal, *Ethnic Minorities in the Criminal Courts: Perceptions of Fairness and Equality of Treatment*, 2/03, London: Lord Chancellor's Office, 2003.

Horne, Alexander, *The Changing Constitution: A Case for Judicial Hearings*, London: Study of Parliament Group, 2010.

House of Commons Constitutional Affairs Committee, *Judicial Appointments and a Supreme Court (Court of Final Appeal)*, (First Report of Session 2003–04, Volume 1) HC 48-1, 2004.

House of Lords, *Constitutional Reform Bill – First Report* (Volume I, HL Paper No 125-I), 2004.

House of Lords Select Committee on the Constitution, *Judicial Appointments* (HL Paper 272), 2012.

Hunt, Ruth and Sam Dick, *Serves you Right: Lesbian and Gay Expectations of Discrimination*, London: Stonewall, 2008.

Hunter, Rosemary, 'Fear and Loathing in the Sunshine State', *Australian Feminist Studies*, 19(44), 2004, 145.

Hunter, Rosemary, 'The High Price of Success: The Backlash Against Women Judges in Australia', in Elizabeth Sheehy and Shelia McIntyre (eds), *Calling for Change: Women, Law, and the Legal Profession*, Ottawa: Ottawa University Press, 2006, p. 281.

Hunter, Rosemary, 'Can *Feminist* Judges Make a Difference?', *International Journal of the Legal Profession*, 15(1–2), 2008, 7.

Hunter, Rosemary, 'Appointment of a New Supreme Court Justice – A Missed Opportunity', *The Barrister*, 8 June–30 July 2010, p. 32.

Hunter, Rosemary, 'An Account of Feminist Judging', in Rosemary Hunter, Clare McGlynn and Erika Rackley, *Feminist Judgments: From Theory to Practice*, Oxford: Hart Publishing, 2010, p. 30.

Hunter, Rosemary, 'Justice Marcia Neave: Case Study of a Feminist Judge', in Ulrike Schultz and Gisela Shaw (eds), *Gender and Judging*, Oxford: Hart Publishing, forthcoming.

Ifill, Sherrilyn A., 'Judicial Diversity', *Green Bag*, 13, 2D, 2009, 45.

Insight Oxford, *Obstacles and Barriers to the Career Development of Women Solicitors*, London: Law Society, London, 2010.

Irvine, Lord, 'Setting New Bench Marks', *The Guardian*, 4 March 1992.

Irvine, Lord, 'Speech to Minority Lawyers Conference', London, 29 November 1997.

Irvine, Lord, 'Speech to the Association of Women Barristers', The Barbican, London, 11 February 1998.

Irvine, Lord, 'Speech to 1998 Women Lawyer Conference', London, 25 April 1998.

Irvine, Lord, 'IBA World Women Lawyers Conference', Old Hall Lincoln's Inn, London, 1 March 2001.

Irvine, Lord, 'Speech to the Association of Women Solicitors', Painter Stainers Hall, London, 23 March 2001.

Jenkins, John, *Trends in the Solicitors' Profession – Annual Statistical Report 1994*, London: Law Society, 1994.

Jenkins, John and Danielle Walker, *Annual Statistical Report 1993*, London: Law Society, 1993.

Judge, Lord, 'Equality in Justice Day', Royal Courts of Justice, London, 24 October 2008.

Judge, Lord, 'Encouraging Diversity in the Judiciary', Minority Lawyers Conference, London, 25 April 2009.

Judge, Lord, 'Foreword', in Hazel Genn, *The Attractiveness of Senior Judicial Appointment to Highly Qualified Practitioners – Report to the Judicial Executive Board*, London: Directorate of Judicial Office for England and Wales, 2008, p. 4.

Judicial Appointments & Conduct Ombudsman, *Annual Report 2010–11*, London: Stationery Office, 2011.

Judicial Appointments Commission, *Annual Report 2007–2008: Selecting on Merit and Encouraging Diversity*, London: Judicial Appointments Commission, 2008.

Judicial Appointments Commission, *Annual Report 2010/11 Building the Best Judiciary for a Diverse Society*, London: Judicial Appointments Commission, 2011.

Judicial Appointments Commission, 'News Release: Women continue to succeed in judicial appointments', 1 December 2011.

Judicial Diversity Taskforce, *Improving Judicial Diversity Progress Towards Delivery of the 'Report of the Advisory Panel on Judicial Diversity 2010'*, London: Ministry of Justice, May 2011.

Junior Lawyers Division, *Work-life balance policy*, London: Law Society, 2008.

Junqueria, Eliane Botelho, 'Women in the Judiciary: A perspective from Brazil', in Ulrike Schultz and Gisela Shaw (eds), *Women in the World's Legal Professions*, Oxford: Hart Publishing, 2003, p. 437.

JUSTICE, *The Judiciary in England and Wales*, London: JUSTICE, 1992.

Justice Committee, *Second Report of Session 2010–2011: Appointment of the Chairman of the Judicial Appointments Commission*, HC 770, 31 January 2011.

Karas, Jonathan, 'Dumbing down for diversity', *Legal Week*, 5 April 2007.

Kennedy, Duncan, *A Critique of Adjudication {fin de siècle}*, Cambridge, Mass.: Harvard University Press, 1997.

Kennedy, Helena, 'Women at the Bar', in Robert Hazell (ed), *The Bar on Trial*, London: Quartet Books, 1978, p. 148.

Kennedy, Helena, *Eve was Framed – Women and British Justice*, London: Chatto & Windus, 1992.

Kenney, Sally, 'Moving Beyond Difference: A New Scholarly Agenda for Gender and Judging', paper presented at the Law and Society annual meeting, Baltimore, 6–9 July 2006.

Kenney, Sally J., 'Gender on the Agenda: How the Paucity of Women Judges Became an Issue', *The Journal of Politics*, 70(3), 2008, 717.

Kenney, Sally J., 'Thinking About Gender and Judging', *International Journal of the Legal Profession*, 1–2, 2008, 87.

Kerber, Linda K., Catherine G. Greeno, Eleanor E. Maccoby, Zella Luria, Carol B. Stack and Carol Gilligan, 'On "In a Different Voice": An Interdisciplinary Forum', *Signs*, 11(2), 1986, 304.

King, Kimi L. and Megan Greening, 'Gender Justice or Just Gender? The Role of Gender in Sexual Assault Decisions in the International Criminal Tribunal for the Former Yugoslavia', *Social Science Quarterly*, 88(5), 2007, 1049.

Kirby, Michael, 'Judicial Dissent: Common Law and Civil Law Traditions', *Law Quarterly Review*, 123, 2007, 379.

Kirby, Terry, 'Mark Saunders shoot-out: "It is a great life – but it is all acting"', *The Telegraph*, 20 August 2008.

Klein, Joan D., 'Remarks', *University of Toledo Law Review*, 36, 2004–2005, 911.

Lacey, Nicola, *Unspeakable Subjects: Feminist Essays in Legal and Social Theory*, Oxford: Hart Publishing, 1998.

Langdon-Down, Grania, 'More women equals more money', *The Independent*, 23 April 1997.

Law Commission, *Marital Property Agreements*, CP198, London: Law Commission, 2011.

Law Society, 'Judicial Appointments Commission: A Discussion Paper', January 2000.

Law Society, *Broadening the Bench: Law Society proposals for reforming the way judges are appointed*, London: Law Society, October 2000.

Law Society, *Number of Solicitors on the Roll and Practising Certificate holders since 1950 – Fact Sheet Information Series*, London: Law Society, 2007.

Law Society, *Earnings and Work of Private Practice Solicitors in 2007 – Executive Summary*, London: Law Society, 2008.

Law Society, *Gender and Earnings in Private Practice: Findings from the 2008 Salary Survey*, London: Law Society, 2009.

Law Society, *Ethnic Diversity in Law Firms – Understanding the Barriers*, London: Law Society, 2010.

Law Society, *Law Society Survey of LGB Solicitors 2009: The Career Experience of LGB Solicitors*, London: Law Society, 2010.

Law Society, *Women Solicitors – Fact sheet series 2009*, London: Law Society, 2010.

Law Society, *Categories of work undertaken by solicitors – Fact sheet series 2010*, London: Law Society, 2010.

Law Society, *Flexible working and solicitors' work-life balance – Fact sheet series 2010*, London: Law Society, 2010.

Law Society, *The Work of Solicitors: Law Society Individuals Omnibus Spring 2010*, London: Law Society, 2011.

Law Society, *Diversity Profile of the Profession: A Short Synopsis*, London: Law Society, 2011.

Leader, 'In Praise of . . . Lady Hale of Richmond', *The Guardian*, 20 October 2006.

Legg, Thomas, 'Judges for the New Century', *Public Law*, 2001, 62.

Legg, Thomas, 'Brave New World: The New Supreme Court and Judicial Appointments', *Legal Studies*, 2004, 45.

Leith, Philip, Marie Lynch, Lisa Glennon, Brice Dickson and Sally Wheeler, *Propensity to apply for Judicial Office under the Northern Ireland Judicial Appointments System: A Qualitative Study for the Northern Ireland Judicial Appointments Commission*, Belfast: Law School Queens University Belfast, 2008.

Letts, Quentin, 'She smiled disdainfully at some other poor wretch', *The Daily Mail*, 19 November 2003.

Levy, Geoffrey, 'Architect of a marriage wrecking measure', *The Daily Mail*, 26 April 1996.

Levy, Geoffrey, 'Nine days after her divorce, she wed husband Number Two', *The Daily Mail*, 13 November 2003

Lewis, Naomi (trans), *Hans Andersen's Fairy Tales*, London: Penguin, 1981, p. 41.

Ley, Rebecca, 'Judges so out of touch with victim's lives', *The Sun*, 27 June 2007.

L'Heureux-Dubé, Claire, 'Outsiders on the Bench: The Continuing Struggle for Equality', *Wisconsin Women's Law Journal*, 2001, 15.

Lind, Sofia, 'Bending over backwards – How City law firms are handling the flexible working question', *Legal Week*, 22 September 2010.

Lindsey, Robert, 'Women Lawyers to push Lord Irvine over judicial selection', *The Lawyer*, 7 January 1997.

Lisners, John, 'Cleveland Judge Sex Scandal', *The News of the World*, 17 July 1988.

Lloyd Platt, Vanessa, 'The stress of being a female lawyer', *The Times*, 30 July 2009.

Lorber, Judith, *Paradoxes of Gender*, New Haven: Yale University Press, 1994.

Lord Chancellor's Department, *Judicial Appointments Annual Report 2001–2002*, London: Lord Chancellor's Department, 2002.

Lord Chancellor's Department Press Release, Discrimination in Judicial Appointments – Irvine's Statement, 29 November 1997.

Lovett, Kenneth, 'Judge resigns over "wife beat" talk', *New York Post*, 7 January 2004.

Mackay, Lord, 'In the News', *New Law Journal*, 145, 14 April 1995, 514.

Mackay, Lord, 'Selection of Judges Prior to the Establishment of the Judicial Appointments Commission in 2006', in *Judicial Appointments: Balancing Independence, Accountability and Legitimacy*, London: Judicial Appointments Commission, 2010, p. 67.

Makin, Kirk, 'Appointments of female judges slump under Harper's Tories', *Globe and Mail*, 11 November 2011.

Malleson, Kate, *The New Judiciary: The Effects of Expansion and Activism*, Dartmouth: Ashgate, 1999.

Malleson, Kate, 'Justifying Gender Equality on the Bench: Why Difference Won't Do', *Feminist Legal Studies*, 11, 2003, 1.

Malleson, Kate, 'Prospects for Parity: the Position of Women in the Judiciary of England and Wales', in Ulrike Schultz and Gisela Shaw (eds), *Women in the World's Legal Professions*, Oxford: Hart Publishing, 2003, p. 175.

Malleson, Kate, 'Rethinking the Merit Principle in Judicial Selection', *Journal of Law and Society*, 33(1), 2006, 126.

Malleson, Kate, 'Introduction' in Kate Malleson and Peter H. Russell (eds), *Appointing Judges in an Age of Judicial Power: Critical Perspectives from Around the World*, Toronto: University of Toronto, 2006.

Malleson, Kate, 'The New Judicial Appointments Commission: New Wine in New Bottles?', in Kate Malleson and Peter H. Russell (eds), *Appointing Judges in an Age of Judicial Power: Critical Perspectives from Around the World*, Toronto: University of Toronto, 2006 p. 39.

Malleson, Kate, 'Parliamentary Scrutiny of Supreme Court Nominees: A View from the UK', *Osgoode Hall Law Journal*, 44(3), 2006, 557.

Malleson, Kate, 'Diversity in the Judiciary: the Case for Positive Action', *Journal of Law and Society*, 36(3), 2009, 376.

Malleson, Kate, 'Gender Quotas for the Judiciary in England and Wales', in Ulrike Schultz and Gisela Shaw (eds), *Gender and Judging*, Oxford: Hart Publishing, forthcoming.

Malleson, Kate and Fareda Banda, *Factors affecting the decision to apply for Silk and Judicial Office* (Lord Chancellor's Department Research Programme 2/00), London: Lord Chancellor's Department, 2000.

Manning, Laura, 'Ilex rebuts study saying legal execs get raw deal', *The Lawyer*, 28 February 2011.

Marcus, Isabel and Paul Spiegelman, 'The 1984 James McCormick Mitchell Lecture – Feminist Discourse, Moral Values, and the Law – A Conversation', *Buffalo Law Review*, 34, 1985, 11.

Marinucci, Mimi, *Feminism is Queer*, London: Zed Books, 2010.

Marks, Peter, *Annual Statistical Report 1987*, London: Law Society, 1987.

Marks, Peter, *Annual Statistical Report 1988*, London: Law Society, 1988.

Mason, J.K., 'Wrongful Pregnancy, Wrongful Birth and Wrongful Terminology', *Edinburgh Law Review*, 6, 2002, 46.

McEwan, Dale, 'Ethnic minorities find top jobs out of reach', *The Lawyer*, 21 November 2011.

McGarity, Margaret D., 'Diversity in the Judiciary', *Wisconsin Women's Law Journal*, 8, 1992–1993, 175.

McGlynn, Clare, *The Woman Lawyer – Making the Difference*, London: Butterworths, 1998.

McGlynn, Clare, 'The Business of Equality in the Solicitors' Profession', *Modern Law Review*, 63, 2000, 442.

McGlynn, Clare, 'The Status of Women Lawyers in the United Kingdom', in Ulrike Schultz and Gisela Shaw (eds), *Women in the World's Legal Professions*, Oxford: Hart Publishing, 2003, p. 139.

McGlynn, Clare, 'Strategies for Reforming the English Solicitors' Profession: An Analysis of the Business Case for Sex Equality', in Ulrike Schultz and Gisela Shaw (eds), *Women in the World's Legal Professions*, Oxford: Hart Publishing, 2003, p. 159.

McIntyre, Mike, 'No jail for rapist because victim "wanted to party"', *National Post*, 24 February 2011.

McLachlin, Beverley, 'Promoting Gender Equality in the Judiciary', Seminar to the Association of Women Barristers, House of Commons, 2 July 2003.

McLeod-Roberts, Luke, '20 years of The Lawyer: Diversity', *The Lawyer*, 5 December 2007.

McLeod-Roberts, Luke, 'Part-time schemes help firms keep female partners working', *The Lawyer*, 1 February 2010.

McLeod-Roberts, Luke, 'A&O set benchmark for part-time work', *The Lawyer*, 1 February 2010.

McLeod-Roberts, Luke, 'A fifth of female lawyers choose kids over career', *The Lawyer*, 8 February 2010.

McLeod-Roberts, Luke, 'Minorities Report', in *Diversity Report 2010*, London: The Lawyer, 2010, p. 6.

McPartland, Corinne, 'Aspiring lawyers expect to work longer hours, says survey', *The Lawyer*, 22 April 2010.

McRae, Susan, *The Report of the Hansard Society on Women at the Top*, London: The Hansard Society, 1990.

Mears, Bill, 'Justice Ginsburg ready to welcome Sotomayor', *USA Today*, 16 June 2009.

Menkel-Meadow, Carrie, 'Portia in a Different Voice: Speculations on a Women's Lawyering Process', *Berkeley Women's Law Journal*, 1(1), 1985, 39.

Menkel-Meadow, Carrie, 'The Comparative Sociology of Women Lawyers: The "Feminization" of the Legal Profession', *Osgoode Hall Law Journal*, 24(4), 1986, 897.

Menkel-Meadow, Carrie, 'Excluded Voices: New Voices in the Legal Profession Making New Voices in the Law', *University of Miami Law Review*, 42, 1987, 29.

Menkel-Meadow, Carrie, 'Feminisation of the Legal Profession: the Comparative Sociology of Women Lawyers', in Richard Abel and Philip Lewis (eds), *Lawyers in Society: Comparative Theories*, Berkeley: University of California Press, 1989, p. 239.

Menkel-Meadow, Carrie, 'Portia Redux: Another Look at Gender, Feminism, and Legal Ethics', *Virginia Journal of Social Policy and Law*, 2, 1994, 75.

Miles, Joanna, 'Marriage and Divorce in the Supreme Court and the Law Commission: for Love or Money?', *Modern Law Review*, 74(3), 2011, 430.

Miller, Susan L., and Shana L. Maier, 'Moving Beyond Numbers: What Female Judges Say About Different Judicial Voices', *Journal of Women, Politics and Policy*, 29(4), 2008, 527.

Minda, Gary, 'Denial: Not Just a River in Egypt', *Cardozo Law Review*, 22, 2001, 901.

Ministry of Justice, *The Governance of Britain – Judicial Appointments*, Cm 7210, London: Ministry of Justice, 2007.

Ministry of Justice, *Improving Judicial Diversity: Progress Towards Delivery of the 'Report of the Advisory Panel on Judicial Diversity 2010'*, London: Ministry of Justice, 2011.

Ministry of Justice, *Appointments and Diversity: 'A Judiciary for the 21st Century'*, CP19/2011, London: Ministry of Justice, 2011.

Minow, Martha, and Elizabeth Spelman, 'Passion for Justice', in J.T. Noonan Jr and K.I. Winston, *The Responsible Judge: Readings in Judicial Ethics*, Westport: Praeger, 1993, p. 257.

Monaghan, Karon, 'Neuberger and the "F" word', Paper presented at Durham University, 22 February 2008.

Moorhead, Richard, Mark Sefton and Lesley Scanlan, *Just Satisfaction? What Drives Public and Participation Satisfaction with Courts and Tribunals*, London: Ministry of Justice, 2008.

Moran, Leslie J., 'Judicial Diversity and the Challenge of Sexuality: Some Preliminary Findings', *Sydney Law Review*, 28, 2006, 565.

Moran, Leslie J., and Daniel K. Winterfeldt, *Barriers to Applications for Judicial Appointment Research: Lesbian, Gay, Bisexual, and Transgender Experiences*, London: InterLaw Diversity Forum, 2010.

Morris, Anne, 'Embodying the Law: *Coker and Osamor v The Lord Chancellor and the Lord Chancellor's Department* [2002] IRLR 80 (Court of Appeal)', *Feminist Legal Studies*, 11, 2003, 45.

Morton, Ted, 'When judges square off: judicial mud-wrestling could end if McClung's apology was accepted', *Calgary Herald*, 6 March 1999.

Mossman, Mary Jane, *The First Women Lawyers: A Comparative Study of Gender, Law and the Professions*, Oxford: Hart Publishing, 2006.

Munro, Vanessa, *Law and Politics at the Perimeter: Re-Evaluating Key Debates in Feminist Theory*, Oxford: Hart Publishing, 2007.

Nedelsky, Jennifer, 'Embodied Diversity and the Challenges to Law', *McGill Law Journal*, 42, 1997, 91.

Nedelsky, Jennifer, 'Judgment, Diversity and Relational Autonomy', in Ronald Beiner and Jennifer Nedelsky (eds), *Judgment, Imagination and Politics*, Maryland: Rowman and Littlefield, 2001, 103.

Neuberger, Julia, *Whatever's Happening to Women? promises, practices and pay offs*, London: Kyle Cathie, 1991.

New Zealand Human Rights Commission, *New Zealand Census of Women's Participation 2010*, New Zealand: Human Rights Commission, 2010.

Nolan, Donal, 'New Forms of Damage in Negligence', *Modern Law Review*, 70(1), 2007, 59.

Northern Ireland Judicial Appointments Commission, *A Guide to Judicial Careers in Northern Ireland*, Belfast: Northern Ireland Judicial Appointments Commission, 2011.

O'Connor, Sandra Day, 'Portia's Progress', *New York University Law Review*, 66, 1991, 1546.

O'Connor, Sandra Day, 'The Majesty of the Law', Interview for Online News Hour, 9 June 2003.

Odone, Christina, 'I'm always shouting at my husband but no, Lady Hale, I don't think I ought to lose my home because of it', *The Telegraph*, 24 November 2011.

O'Grady, Sean, 'A Government of straight, white, privately educated men', *The Independent*, 7 August 2010.

Opinion Leader Research, *Judicial Diversity: Findings of a Consultation with Barristers, Solicitors and Judges – Final Report*, London: Department for Constitutional Affairs, 2006.

Ormerod, David, 'Appeal: Change in law since conviction – Court of Appeal's approach to conviction under previous law', *Criminal Law Review*, 1, 2008, 50.

Orvetti, Peter, 'Won't Ask, Won't Tell', *The Moderate Voice*, 18 May 2010.

Panel on Fair Access to the Professions, *Unleashing Aspiration: The Final Report of the Panel on Fair Access to the Professions*, London: Cabinet Office, July 2009.

Parker, Jon, 'Lawyers warn kids off career in law', *The Lawyer*, 1 July 2008.

Parnell, S. and C. Mathewson, 'Beatie Sticks with Tatt's Despite No-Women Vote', *Courier Mail*, 27 March 2003.

Paterson, Alan, *The Law Lords*, London: Macmillan, 1982.

Paterson, Alan, *Lawyers and the Public Good: Democracy in Action?* Cambridge: Cambridge University Press, 2012.

Paterson, Alan and Chris Paterson, *Guarding the Guardians? Towards an independent, accountable and diverse senior judiciary* (London: CentreForum, 2012).

Peach, Leonard, *An Independent Scrutiny of the Appointment Processes of Judges and Queen's Counsel*, London: HMSO, 1999.

Pearson, Rose and Albie Sachs, 'Barristers and Gentlemen: A Critical Look at Sexism in the Legal Profession', *Modern Law Review*, 43, 1980, 400.

Peresie, Jennifer L., 'Female Judges Matter: Gender and Collegial Decision-making in the Federal Appellate Courts', *Yale Law Journal*, 114(7), 2005, 1759.

Phillips, Lord, 'Constitutional Reform – One Year On', Judicial Studies Board Annual Lecture, Inner Temple, London, 22 March 2007.

Phillips, Melanie, 'I deplore his actions but actually his cause is just', *The Daily Mail*, 5 November 2003.

Phillips, Melanie, 'The Marriage Wrecker', *The Daily Mail*, 13 November 2003.

Pickering, Sharon, *Women, Boarders and Violence: Current Issues in Asylum, Forced Migration, and Trafficking*, New York: Springer, 2010.

Pike, Geoff and Dilys Robinson, *Barristers' Working Lives: A Biennial Survey of the Bar 2011*, London: Bar Council and Bar Standards Board, 2012.

Polden, Patrick, 'The Lady of Tower Bridge: Sybil Campbell, England's first woman judge', *Women's History Review*, 8(3), 1999, 505.

Posner, Richard, *How Judges Think*, Cambridge, Mass.: Harvard University Press, 2010.

Prashar, Baroness, 'Speech by Baroness Prashar', London School of Economics Student Law Society, 22 February 2007.

Prashar, Baroness, 'Judicial Appointments: A New System for a New Century', Centre for Crime and Justice Studies, King's College London, March 2007.

Prashar, Baroness, 'Speech to Chartered Institute of Patent Attorneys Congress', 30 October 2008.

Prashar, Baroness, 'Sweet & Maxwell Judicial Review Conference', 21 November 2008.

Priaulx, Nicolette, *The Harm Paradox: Tort Law and the Unwanted Child in an Era of Choice*, Abingdon: Routledge-Cavendish, 2007.

Pugh, Andrew, 'Proportion of lawyers educated at public school far outstrips national average', *The Lawyer*, 15 November 2010.

Rabkin, Franny, 'Women need a foot in the judiciary door', *Business Day*, 28 April 2010.

Rackley, Erika, 'Representations of the (woman) judge: Hercules, the little mermaid, and the vain and naked Emperor', *Legal Studies*, 22(4), 2002, 602.

Rackley, Erika, 'Difference in the House of Lords', *Social and Legal Studies*, 15(2), 2006, 163.

Rackley, Erika, 'Judicial diversity, the woman judge and fairy tale endings', *Legal Studies*, 27(1), 2007, 74.

Rackley, Erika, 'From Arachne to Charlotte: An Imaginative Revisiting of Gilligan's *In a Different Voice*', *William & Mary Journal of Women and the Law*, 13(3), 2007, 751.

Rackley, Erika, 'What a difference difference makes: gendered harms and judicial diversity', *International Journal of the Legal Profession*, 15(1–2), 2008, 37.

Rackley, Erika, 'Detailing Judicial Difference', *Feminist Legal Studies*, 17(1), 2009, 11.

Rackley, Erika, 'Rethinking Judicial Diversity', in Ulrike Schultz, and Gisela Shaw (eds), *Gender and Judging*, Oxford: Hart Publishing, forthcoming.

Raitt, Fiona, Margaret Callaghan, Gerda Siann, 'Still a glass ceiling for women solicitors?', *Law Society for Scotland Journal Online*, 1 July 2000.

Ramsey, Alan, 'Swimming Upstream and Against Spite', *Sydney Morning Herald*, 2 February 2005.

Rayner, Jonathan, 'Women lawyers believe they are paid less than male peers', *Law Society Gazette*, 10 March 2011.

Rayner, Jonathan, 'Stress still high', *Law Society Gazette*, 19 May 2011.

Rayner, Jonathan, 'City judicial diversity forum has not met in two years', *Law Society Gazette*, 15 December 2011.

Raz, Joseph, *Practical Reason and Norms*, 1st edn 1975, Oxford: Oxford University Press, 1999.

REAL Women of Canada, 'The Feminist Canaries are Singing Again' *REALity*, XIX (3), 2000.

REAL Women of Canada, 'The Risks to Society Caused by Fatherless Children', *REALity*, XXIX (g), 2010.

Redfern, Catherine and Kristin Aune, *Reclaiming the F Word: The New Feminist Movement*, London: Zed Books, 2010.

Refugee Women's Resource Project @ AsylumAid, *Women's Asylum News*, Issue 52, July/August 2005.

Refugee Women's Resource Project @ AsylumAid, *Women's Asylum News*, Issue 64, October 2006.

Rehaag, Sean, 'Do Women Refugee Judges Really Make a Difference? An Empirical Analysis of Gender and Outcomes in Canadian Refugee Decisions', *Canadian Journal of Women and Law*, 23, 2011, 627.

Reid, Lord, 'The Judge as Law Maker', *Journal of the Society of Public Teachers of Law*, 12, 1972, 22.

Resnik, Judith, 'On the Bias: Feminist Reconsiderations of the Aspirations for our Judges', *Southern California Law Review*, 61, 1988, 1877.

Richardson, Janice, 'The Concept of Harm for Actions in Wrongful Birth: Nature and Pre-Modern Views of Women', *Australian Feminist Law Journal*, 35, 2011, 127.

Rights of Women, *Focus on Women*, Issue 6, 2007.

Robins, Jon, 'Women, ethnic minorities and solicitors; the courts need you', *The Lawyer*, 5 December 2005.

Rogers, Jonathan, 'Fundamentally Objectionable', *New Law Journal*, 157, 2007, 1252.

Rosenberg, Joshua, 'Lawyers who merit judicial appointment are not reaching the bench', *Law Society Gazette*, 2 February 2010.

Rosenberg, Joshua, 'Lady Justice Hallett could become the first woman Lord Chief Justice', *Law Society Gazette*, 12 May 2011.

Rothwell, Rachel, 'Gazette survey: work-based discrimination still rife, say women solicitors', *Law Society Gazette*, 13 April 2011.

Rothwell, Rachel, 'What do men and women solicitors really think about discrimination?', *Law Society Gazette*, 15 April 2011.

Rudolph, Dana, 'Elena Kagan Isn't Lesbian – But Is Her Hair?', *Change.Org*, 12 May 2010. Online. Available: http://gayrights.change.org/blog/view/elena_kagan_isnt_lesbian_but_is_her_hair.

Russell, Jonathan, 'Your skimpy skirt and high heels just won't do, trainee solicitors told', *The Telegraph*, 8 April 2011.

Russell, Peter H., 'Conclusion', in Kate Malleson and Peter H. Russell (eds), *Appointing Judges in an Age of Judicial Power: Critical Perspectives from Around the World*, Toronto: University of Toronto, 2006, p. 429.

Sachs, Albie and Joan Hoff Wilson, *Sexism and the Law: A Study of Male Beliefs and Judicial Bias*, Oxford: Martin Robertson, 1978.

Salokar, Rebecca M. and Michael Wilson, 'Sandra Day O'Connor', in Rebecca M. Salokar and Mary L. Volcansek (eds), *Women in Law: A Bio-Bibliographical Sourcebook*, Westport, Connecticut: Greenwood Press, 1996, p. 210.

Samuels, Harriet, 'Women, Culture and Human Rights: Feminist Interventions in Human Rights Law?', in Reza Banakar (ed), *Rights in Context: Law and Justice in Late Modern Society*, Dartmouth: Ashgate, 2010, 317.

Sapa, 'JSC wants more black female judges', *Times LIVE*, 20 April 2011.

Satherley, Jessica, 'I was propositioned by the judge who promoted me: Top female Appeal Court justice's battle against sexism', *Daily Mail*, 8 November 2011.

Sauboorah, Jennifer, *Bar Barometer Trends in the Profile of the Bar*, London: Bar Council, March 2011.

Sauboorah, Jennifer, *Bar Barometer Trends in the Profile of the Bar*, London: Bar Council, December 2011.

Schatz, Phil, 'Judicial Profile: Hon. Ruth Bader Ginsburg, Associate Justice, Supreme Court of the United States', *The Federal Lawyer*, May 2010, pp. 27–28.

Scherpe, Jens M., 'Fairness, freedom and foreign elements – marital agreements in England and Wales after *Radmacher v Granatino*', *Child and Family Law Quarterly*, December, 2011, 4.

Schultz, Ulrike and Gisela Shaw (eds), *Women in the World's Legal Professions*, Oxford: Hart Publishing, 2003.

Schultz, Ulrike and Gisela Shaw (eds), 'Introduction: Women in the World's Legal Profession: Overview and Synthesis', in Ulrike Schultz and Gisela Shaw (eds), *Women in the World's Legal Professions*, Oxford: Hart Publishing, 2003, p. xxv.

Schultz, Ulrike and Gisela Shaw (eds), *Gender and Judging*, Oxford: Hart Publishing, forthcoming.

Sedley, Stephen, 'On the Move', *The London Review of Books*, 8 October 2009, p. 5.

Sen, Purna, 'Difference is not all that counts', in Deborah Cameron and Joan Scanlan (eds), *The Trouble and Strife Reader*, London: Bloomsbury Academic, 1999, p. 78.

Shaw, Gisela, 'Women Lawyers in the New Federal States of Germany from Quantity to Quality', in Ulrike Schultz and Gisela Shaw (eds), *Women in the World's Legal Professions*, Oxford: Hart Publishing, 2003, p. 323.

Siems, Jo, *Equality and Diversity: Women Solicitors*, (Research Study 48(1) (Quantitative Findings)), London: Law Society, 2004.

Slack, James, 'The judiciary is out of touch with the public, says poll', *The Daily Mail*, 8 March 2007.

Sommerlad, Hilary, 'Women Solicitors in a Fractured Profession', *International Journal of the Legal Profession*, 9(3), 2002, 213.

Sommerlad, Hilary, 'Researching and Theorizing the Processes of Professional Identity Formation', *Journal of Law and Society*, 2008, 34(2), 190.

Sommerlad, Hilary and Peter Sanderson, *Gender, Choice and Commitment: Women Solicitors in England and Wales and the Struggle for Equal Status*, Aldershot: Ashgate, 1998.

Sommerlad, Hilary, Lisa Webley, Liz Duff, Daniel Muzio and Jennifer Tomlison, *Diversity in the Legal Profession in England and Wales: A Qualitative Study of Barriers and Individual Choice*, London: University of Westminster, 2010.

Spelman, Elizabeth V., *Inessential Woman: Problems of Exclusion in Feminist Thought*, Boston: Beacon Press, 1988.

Spivak, Gayatri, 'In a Word', *Differences*, 1989, 124.

Stephens, R., 'Reform in haste and repent at leisure: Iolanthe, Lord High executioner and Brave New World', Legal Studies, 24, 2004, 33.

Sullivan, Rosaline, *Barriers to the Legal Profession*, London: Legal Services Board, July 2010.

Sumption, Jonathan, 'The Constitutional Reform Act 2005', in *Judicial Appointments: Balancing Independence, Accountability and Legitimacy*, London: Judicial Appointments Commission, 2010, p. 31.

Sutton Trust, *Briefing Note: The Educational Backgrounds of the UK's Top Solicitors, Barristers and Judges*, London: Sutton Trust, June 2005.

Sutton Trust, *The Educational Backgrounds of Leading Lawyers, Journalists, Vice Chancellors, Politicians, Medics and Chief Executives: The Sutton Trust Submission to the Milburn Commission on Access to the Professions*, London: Sutton Trust, March 2009.

Swift, James, 'Latham under fire for holding cooking event for female network', *The Lawyer*, 20 April 2012.

Taylor, Lord, *The Judiciary in the Nineties*, The Richard Dimbleby Lecture, 1992.

Temkin, Jennifer, 'Prosecuting and Defending Rape: Perspectives from the Bar', *Journal of Law and Society*, 27, 2000, 219.

Thomas, Cheryl, *Judicial Diversity in the United Kingdom and Other Jurisdictions: A Review of Research, Policies and Practices*, London: The Commission for Judicial Appointments, 2005.

Thomas, Cheryl and Kate Malleson, *Judicial Appointment Commissions: The European and North American Experience and the Possible Implications for the United Kingdom* (Lord Chancellor's Department Research Series 6/97), London: Lord Chancellor's Department, December 1997.

Thomas, Cheryl and Hazel Genn, *Appointment of Deputy District Judges 2003–2005*, London: The Commission for Judicial Appointments, 2006.

Thornton, Margaret, *Dissonance and Distrust: Women in the Legal Profession*, Oxford: Oxford University Press, 1996.

Thornton, Margaret, '"Otherness" on the Bench: How Merit is Gendered', *Sydney Law Review*, 29, 2007, 391.

Tibbetts, Janice, 'Alberta judge's remarks shake legal community: suggests supreme court justice to blame for male suicide rate', *The Gazette*, 27 February 1999.

Tibbetts, Janice and Shawn Ohler, 'Judges clash over landmark sex-assault ruling', *National Post*, 26 February 1999.

Tilby, Hilary, 'Stress at the Bar', *Counsel*, January 2010, pp. 18–19.

Todd, Richard, 'The Inevitable Triumph of the Ante-Nuptial Contract', *Family Law*, July 2006, 539.

Trochev, Alexi, 'Judicial Selection in Russia: Towards Accountability and Centralisation', in Kate Malleson and Peter H. Russell (eds), *Appointing Judges in an Age of Judicial Power: Critical Perspectives from Around the World*, Toronto: University of Toronto, 2006, p. 375.

Tsang, Linda, 'Lawyer of the Week', *The Times*, 28 November 2006.

Veerle, Miranda, *Cooking, Caring and Volunteering: Unpaid Work Around the World* (OECD Social, Employment and Migration Working Papers, No. 116), Paris: OECD Publishing, 2011.

Wachman, Richard, 'Sex and the City: Spearmint Rhino pulls bankers bearing bonuses', *The Guardian*, 20 February 2011.

Wald, Patricia M., 'Women on International Courts: Some Lessons Learned', *International Criminal Law Review*, 11, 2011, 401.

Ward, Stephanie F., 'Female Judicial Candidates are Held to Different Standards, Sotomayor Tells Students', *American Bar Association Journal*, 8 March 2011.

Warner, Marina, *From the Beast to the Blonde: On Fairy Tales and their Tellers*, London: Vintage, 1995.

Webley, Lisa and Liz Duff, 'Women Solicitors as a Barometer for Problems within the Legal Profession – Time to Put Values before Profits', *Journal of Law and Society*, 34(3), 2007, 374.

West, Robin, *Narrative, Authority, and Law*, Ann Arbor: University of Michigan Press, 1993.

Whitehead, Tom, 'Quotas could be introduced for judges to increase ethnic minorities and women', *The Telegraph*, 28 April 2009.

Williams, Patricia, *Alchemy of Race and Rights: Diary of a Law Professor*, Cambridge, Mass.: Harvard University Press, 1991.

Wilson, Bertha, 'Will Women Judges Really Make a Difference?', *Osgoode Hall Law Journal*, 28(3), 1990, 507.

Witting, Christian, 'Physical Damage in Negligence', *Cambridge Law Journal*, 6(1), 2002, 189.

Zayan, Jailan, 'Egypt Wrangles Over Whether Women Should be Judges', *The Daily Telegraph*, 25 February, 2010.

Index

Page numbers in *Italics* represent tables.
Page numbers followed by n represent endnotes.